DOCTORAL EDUCATION AND THE FACULTY OF THE FUTURE

Doctoral Education and the Faculty of the Future

EDITED BY

Ronald G. Ehrenberg
and Charlotte V. Kuh

Cornell University Press
Ithaca and London

First published 2009 by Cornell University Press
Printed in the United States of America

Library of Congress Cataloging-in-Publication Data

Doctoral education and the faculty of the future / edited by Ronald
G. Ehrenberg and Charlotte V. Kuh.
    p. cm.
  Papers originally presented at a conference held in Oct. 2006 at
the Cornell Higher Education Research Institute.
  Includes bibliographical references and index.
  ISBN 978–0–8014–4543–9 (cloth : alk. paper)
  1. Doctor of philosophy degree—United States—Congresses.
2. Universities and colleges—United States—Graduate work—
Congresses. 3. Universities and colleges—United States—Faculty—
Congresses. I. Ehrenberg, Ronald G. II. Kuh, Charlotte V.
III. Cornell Higher Education Research Institute.

  LB2386.D62 2009
  378.2—dc22

                2008027723

To our spouses with love

Contents

Doctoral Education and the Faculty of the Future

Introduction

RONALD G. EHRENBERG AND CHARLOTTE V. KUH

American colleges and universities are simultaneously facing large numbers of faculty retirements and expanding enrollments. Budget constraints, especially those at public higher education institutions, have led colleges and universities to substitute part-time and full-time non-tenure-track faculty for tenure-track faculty. Although this substitution will reduce the demand for new full-time tenure-track faculty, the demand for faculty members will likely be high in the decade ahead.

This heightened demand is coming at a time when the share of American college graduates who go on for PhD study is far below its historic high. Moreover, groups that historically have been underrepresented in PhD study, women and people of color, are composing a growing share of the pool of college graduates. Although the female share of PhD holders has increased substantially in many fields, these increased shares have not translated into equal increases in female representation in tenure-track faculty positions at major research universities. The share of PhDs going to U.S. citizens of color has increased at a much slower rate than that going to women, and both the shares of new American PhDs and faculty positions at American colleges and universities that go to people of color are still way below what would be predicted based on the number of American college graduates who are women or people of color.

The declining interest of American students in going on to PhD study is undoubtedly due to a number of factors. These include better labor market opportunities associated with professional degree programs, such as those in law, medicine, and business; long completion times to degree and low completion rates in PhD programs; how doctoral education is financed; the lengthy apprenticeship needed for doctoral study, which makes it difficult for students to complete degrees in a timely fashion; the need for (often multiple) postdoctoral appointments before PhD holders in many science and engineering fields can even contemplate a permanent academic position; the decline in the share of faculty positions that are tenured or on tenure track; and the failure of many PhD programs to adequately prepare their students for nonacademic employment opportunities.

At the same time, the share of PhDs earned in the United States by foreign students has substantially increased over the last thirty-five years, especially in key science and engineering fields. Many of these foreign PhD holders have remained employed in the United States. Through their roles as research assistants during their graduate study, postdoctoral researchers, and doctoral degree holders in academic and nonacademic employment, they have contributed substantially to our nation's scientific progress and to our college and university teaching programs.

Concern has been expressed, however, that the growing enrollment of foreign students in American PhD programs "crowds out" potential American citizen PhD holders and discourages them from pursuing PhD study. On the other hand, the aftermath of 9/11, the growth of research infrastructure and research support in other nations, and the growth of other nations' higher education systems all cast doubt on the ability of the United States to continue to rely on foreign PhD holders to meet our nation's need for scientific researchers and to fill future faculty positions.

Given all of these issues, in October 2006 the Cornell Higher Education Research Institute brought together a group of researchers from a wide number of science and social science fields, academic administrators, and policymakers for the conference "Doctoral Education and the Faculty of the Future." The sessions at the conference focused on efforts to increase and improve the supply of future faculty, and covered topics ranging from increasing undergraduate interest in doctoral study to improving the doctoral experience and the representation of underrepresented groups in doctoral education. The chapters in this book are revisions of the papers presented at that conference.[1]

IMPROVING DOCTORAL EDUCATION

The first section of *Doctoral Education* consists of five chapters concerned with ways to better understand and improve the processes of doctoral education. Numerous private foundations, government agencies, individual researchers, and universities have worried over the last two decades about how to improve doctoral education, and the chapters in this section summarize some of the major efforts and their findings. Each paper reports conclusions based on substantive empirical research.

In 1991 the Andrew W. Mellon Foundation launched the Graduate Education Initiative (GEI), a major intervention toward improving the structure and organization of PhD programs in the humanities and related social sciences, with the dual goals of improving the general quality of doctoral education and reducing high rates of student attrition that accompany long completion times to degree completion. In contrast to earlier programs, which had provided grant aid to individual students or to graduate schools to distribute as they saw fit, the focus of the GEI was at the departmental level. The program ran for ten years and involved fifty-four departments at ten major universities, as well as a slightly smaller number of "comparison" departments. In all, the Mellon Foundation devoted almost $85 million toward supporting the GEI.

In chapter 1, Ronald G. Ehrenberg, Harriet Zuckerman, Jeffrey Groen, and Sharon M. Brucker describe the GEI and the data collection efforts undertaken to help analyze the effectiveness of the GEI. It provides preliminary evidence of the program's effect on a wide variety of outcomes, including attrition rates, times to degree, early-career job market success, and early-career publications. This is the first study of doctoral education that has traced the educational and job market experiences of students who dropped out of PhD programs, and it finds that a substantial proportion of the dropouts received PhDs from other PhD programs and/or received professional degrees. The chapter concludes with a discussion of the more general lessons that the authors believe the GEI provides for improving graduate education.

Although the focus of the GEI was on the department, recently the Council of Graduate Schools has undertaken the PhD Completion Project, which stresses the important role of graduate schools and their deans in improving doctoral education. Begun in 2004 with support from Pfizer Inc. and the Ford Foundation, the PhD Completion Project now involves twenty-nine major research universities that are creating intervention strategies to improve doctoral education in science, engineering, and mathematics, evaluating the impact of pilot projects designed to implement these strategies and then disseminating best practice findings to graduate deans around the nation. An additional fifteen universities are participating in various aspects of the project.

In chapter 2, Daniel Deneke, Helen S. Frasier, and Kenneth Redd provide a progress report on the PhD Completion Project as of late 2006. They discuss the background of the project and the institutional factors that are believed to influence completion and attrition, including selection and admissions, mentoring and advising, financial support and structure, program environment, students' research experiences, and curricular processes and procedures. After providing background data on the nature of PhD programs and student outcomes, they summarize the directions in which the project is going.

At the turn of the twenty-first century, the Carnegie Foundation for the Advancement of Teaching sponsored the Carnegie Initiative on the Doctorate (CID). The CID was an action and research program that involved eighty-four participating departments from six disciplines (chemistry, education, English, history, mathematics, and neuroscience) in forty-four universities. The CID was designed to support departmental efforts to examine their doctoral programs.

In chapter 3, Chris M. Golde, Andrea Conklin Busche, Laura Jones, and George E. Walker summarize the nature of the CID and the two major themes that have emerged from the project as central to the foundation's thinking. The first is the important role of apprenticeship in the pedagogy of doctoral education and what the key characteristics of successful apprenticeship systems are. The second is the importance of a healthy and vibrant intellectual community for effective doctoral education. The authors elaborate on these two themes and how they interact to create outstanding doctoral programs.

Michael T. Nettles and Catherine Millett published an important book, *Three Magic Letters: Getting to the PhD*, in 2006. Based on a stratified sample of doctoral students in eleven fields at twenty-one doctoral-granting universities who had completed at least their first year of doctoral study in 1996, Nettles and Millett focused on how students navigate their doctoral experience, including the progress they are making toward completing their degrees. In chapter 4, Millett and Nettles summarize their analyses and findings. Their discussion focuses on racial/ethnic and gender differences in doctoral students' rates of progress and on the personal and program characteristics that influence students' degree completion and the amount of time that takes.

In chapter 5, the final study in the section, Maresi Nerad, director of the Center for Research and Innovation in Graduate Education at the University of Washington, confronts five common assumptions that faculty members and higher-education policymakers often have in mind when they think about doctoral education: (1) all students studying for

PhDs want to become professors; (2) professorial positions are highly desirable, and only the best students succeed in becoming professors; (3) career paths are linear, and new PhD recipients move directly into tenure-track academic positions after short delays due to postdoctoral fellowships; (4) successful PhD holders choose the very best job offer, unconstrained by relationship and family concerns; and (5) professors are more highly satisfied with their jobs than those with PhDs in non-academic employment. Using data from three national longitudinal studies that she and her colleagues conducted of the early career experiences of new doctoral recipients, Nerad shows that each of these assumptions is false. With that as a background, Nerad provides prescriptions for how doctoral programs should change in the future to meet the needs of students as well as the needs of the employers of new doctoral degree recipients.

Attracting Undergraduates to PhD Study

Our nation's private liberal arts colleges educate only a small percentage of American college students. However, the likelihood that their graduates will go on to earn PhDs is much higher than the likelihood that graduates of major U.S. research universities (where PhD education takes place) will do so. People often attribute the better performance of the liberal arts colleges to faculty at research universities being preoccupied with their graduate students and having neither the time nor the incentive to mentor undergraduates in research and/or encourage them to undertake PhD study.

Even among the most selective private liberal arts colleges, the share of students going on to PhD programs varies widely. If one is concerned about increasing the number of students going on to pursue PhDs, it is important to understand which characteristics of liberal arts colleges are associated with large numbers of their graduates receiving PhDs. In chapter 6, Robert Lemke addresses this issue. He finds that characteristics of the faculty (such as their research performance) and of their students (such as test scores and gender) clearly matter. But these factors do not tell the whole story. Through interviews with deans at colleges with large proportions of graduates going on for PhDs, Lemke concludes that providing a serious curriculum, encouraging students to take on challenges, and developing a campus environment that respects intellectual curiosity all appear to be factors that facilitate student interest in pursuing PhDs.

One aspect of the undergraduate experience that Lemke is unable to examine is the role of providing undergraduate research experiences for students. A number of federal and foundation programs have supported such efforts in the hope that these experiences will encourage our best undergraduates to pursue careers in the science and engineering fields and to consider going on to PhD study.

In chapter 7, Myles Boylan critically reviews the evaluations that have been made of undergraduate research experience programs in the science, technology, engineering, and mathematics (STEM) fields. There are numerous methodological issues that one must face when trying to summarize the lessons of the evaluations. For example, some of these programs target for participation high-achieving undergraduates who already are oriented toward graduate school; most evaluations do not include control or comparison groups of students who did not go through the programs; many evaluations lack information on long-term outcomes; and results may be discipline specific. Nonetheless, Boylan finds that the empirical findings of the studies are broadly consistent and that research experience programs do appear to increase the likelihood that students who were not in the highest achieving cohorts at their undergraduate institutions will go on to graduate study. Paradoxically, however, he finds that the increased knowledge of career opportunities that these programs provide may also be associated with increased student uncertainty about career plans.

Increasing the Representation of People of Color in the PhD Pool

The chapters in this section discuss alternative approaches to achieving increased representation of people of color among PhD recipients. They are written by individuals who have all played important, active roles in seeking to achieve this objective.

In chapter 8, Richard Tapia, an applied mathematician at Rice University and mentor of a large number of underrepresented minority PhD holders in the STEM fields, and his colleague Cynthia Johnson discuss the factors that they believe are responsible for the underrepresentation of minority students in the STEM fields. They argue that there is a serious need for universities to make substantial changes in the ways they interact with minority populations and that focusing on the nature of PhD programs and the support minority students receive in these programs is too limited. Put simply, minority students cannot be successful in their undergraduate studies without a good elementary and secondary background; they cannot be successful in graduate school without good undergraduate preparation; and they cannot realistically be candidates for academic jobs in the STEM fields at major American universities unless their PhDs come from top-ranked graduate programs. Hence, serious interventions at all stages of the pipeline are important if we are to substantially increase the number of underrepresented minorities in academic positions in the STEM fields at major American universities.

Carlos Castillo-Chavez, another applied mathematician and mentor for numerous minority STEM PhD recipients, and his colleague Carlos Castillo-Garsow echo Tapia and Johnson's concerns. However, while concerned about the problems that occur at all stages of the pipeline, they argue in chapter 9 that shifting the "blame" for the small number of minority PhD holders to the K–12 educational system and claiming that no progress can be made until improvements are made there ignores a history of successful long-term partnerships between federal agencies and universities. These partnerships have led to an increase in minority students receiving undergraduate degrees in the STEM fields and to a growing pool of these students ready to undertake graduate education in these fields. They describe their own very successful efforts to mentor undergraduate students for entry into STEM PhD programs, to successful completion of those programs, and on to productive careers. In their view, models such as their own program exist to greatly expand the production of minority PhD holders; the real problem is the lack of institutional and federal funding that would permit a large-scale expansion of such programs.

The American Economic Association has sponsored the Summer Minority Program to encourage and prepare minority undergraduate students to embark on doctoral study, receive PhDs, and move on to careers in both the academic and nonacademic sectors. As Charles Becker and Gregory Price describe in chapter 10, the program has evolved over time, been hosted by a variety of academic institutions, and is chronically underfunded. As a result, there have only been limited attempts to evaluate its effectiveness. Becker and Price describe a recent change in program design that has led to a natural experiment that allowed them to analyze the aspects of the program that are most likely to increase the likelihood that participants will proceed on to graduate study. They emphasize the range of outcomes that the program may influence, including improved interest in graduate study, improved performance in undergraduate courses, increased likelihood of admission to a top-ranked graduate program, and improved performance while in graduate school. Although their data do not permit them to analyze all of these outcomes, their findings about the program's effects are generally positive and they present an evaluation framework that can be usefully employed by other discipline-based groups.

In chapter 11, Cheryl Leggon and Willie Pearson Jr. analyze evaluations that have been undertaken in programs designed to improve the participation of underrepresented racial/ethnic minorities in the STEM disciplines in the United States. They focus on evaluations of what appear to be the most effective and promising programs at the undergraduate, graduate, postdoctoral, and junior faculty levels. Their goal is to identify what is known and what needs to be known about programs that are effective in diversifying the STEM workforce, and how evaluations should be designed to assure that they provide information that is useful to decision makers.

INCREASING THE REPRESENTATION OF WOMEN IN ACADEMIA

M. R. C. Greenwood, chancellor emeritus of the University of California–Santa Cruz, provides an overview in chapter 12 of the status of women in the STEM fields in academia. Today, over half of all bachelor's degrees in the STEM fields are granted to women, and their share of PhDs in most STEM fields is increasing. Although progress is most apparent in the life sciences and psychology, where over 50 percent of new PhD recipients are now women, it is evident in all fields. Data suggest, however, that women PhD holders in the STEM fields are much less likely than their male counterparts to wind up in tenure-track positions in major research universities, and the number of women in high-ranking academic or science and engineering policy positions is still rather small and fluctuating. Greenwood is particularly concerned about what she calls the "glass cliff"—a pattern of women moving into leadership positions in academia and then abruptly departing from them. She stresses that much additional work needs to be undertaken to remedy all of these inequities.

Jong-on Hahm spent a number of years as executive director of the National Research Council's Committee on Women in Science and Engineering. Chapter 13 summarizes the work of the committee in its efforts to examine the challenges to the recruitment, retention, and advancement of women in faculty positions in the life sciences at major research universities. Unlike the physical sciences and engineering, there is a large pool of women PhD holders in the life sciences. The reason there are so few women doctorate holders in faculty positions in the life sciences at research universities must relate to the recruitment, retention, and promotion processes. Hahm's chapter summarizes the departmental and institutional polices that can be pursued in order to increase the number of women applicants and the likelihood that recruited applicants will accept offers of employment, and discusses the retention of young female faculty and the likelihood of their promotion. She provides examples of specific policies pursued by individual institutions and provides the addresses of websites at which the reader can learn more about these policies.

Unlike that of the life sciences, the new PhD pool in engineering fields tends to be heavily male. The School of Engineering at Tufts University has a significantly larger percentage of women among both its students and its faculty than is the national average. In chapter 14, Linda Abriola, the dean of the Tufts Engineering School, and Margery Davies, the director of the Office of Diversity Education and Development for several schools at Tufts, describe policies that have been pursued in order to help explain why Tufts has been so successful in recruiting and retaining women in engineering at all levels. These include positive efforts to integrate the engineering and liberal arts schools, administrative commitment and leadership on diversity efforts, targeted student recruitment and support programs, features of the curriculum and extracurricular programs, careful monitoring of faculty hiring, and structural support for faculty—particularly junior faculty.

THE INTERNATIONALIZATION OF DOCTORAL EDUCATION

The final section deals with the internationalization of doctoral education and the likely impact of current U.S. government policies on the flow of international students and faculty to the United States. In chapter 15, Liang Zhang addresses the concern that foreign doctoral students are "crowding out" doctoral students who are U.S. citizens. He sees no evidence that this is occurring in science and engineering but finds that outside these fields, increases in foreign doctoral student numbers are associated with decreases in the numbers of American doctoral students. Zhang also finds that male U.S. citizens who are potential PhD students exhibit strong female-avoidance behavior in a number of academic fields. Put simply, American men appear to opt out of PhD study as the share of new female entrants into these fields increases. Why this occurs is an open question, but the implication is that an increase in the number of women going on to PhD study in these fields does not lead to an equal increase in the number of students going on to PhD study in these fields.

In chapter 16, Emily Blanchard, John Bound, and Sarah Turner use detailed data on the countries of origin of foreign PhD students to understand the factors that have led to the dramatic growth of foreign enrollments in U.S. doctoral programs. Although some of this growth represents relatively continuous adjustments in the choices of students from countries with long-standing diplomatic and trade ties with the United States, another share represents responses associated with dramatic changes in the political environment in foreign countries, such as the large increases in the number of Chinese students in the early 1980s and the number of Eastern European and former Soviet Union students in the early 1990s.

Blanchard, Bound, and Turner also caution that the flow of foreign PhD students to the United State does not always imply that these students desire to remain in the United States for employment after receiving their PhDs. Such decisions depend on the states of the labor and education markets for new PhDs in both the United States and the country of origin. An increase in the production of new PhDs from a given country at any point in time may be associated with the educational development of people who can staff the country's improving and growing university and technology sectors in the future, thus swelling the ranks of that country's students in the present but curtailing enrollments in the long run. They also analyze where foreign students go for doctoral study. Not surprisingly, foreign students from countries with well-developed higher education systems that include their own high-quality PhD programs only come to the United States for graduate study if they are accepted at our nation's most prestigious doctoral programs. In contrast, doctoral students from countries with few high-quality doctoral programs of their own often will be found enrolled in lower-ranked U.S. doctoral programs.

The enrollment of foreign students at U.S. universities, both at the doctoral and undergraduate levels, also depends on our government's policies toward foreign students. In chapter 17, Michael Olivas, a law professor who studies both higher education and immigration issues, describes what the "war on terror" has meant for U.S. colleges and universities. More specifically, he addresses how the United States regulates entry into its colleges and universities for international students, how antiterrorism laws have affected these practices, and how the changed ground rules associated with the so-called war on terror have affected the place of U.S. higher education in the world. Olivas finds that at the same time that we are making it more difficult for foreign students to study in the United States, a number of other countries in different parts of the world are moving in exactly the opposite direction. He worries about the implications for our nation's well-being; if fewer foreign students attend U.S. institutions this will have profound implications for the United States both because of its impact on the supply of highly trained STEM workers in our economy and because fewer foreign students will have experiences with American culture to take back to their home countries.

Olivas is also deeply concerned about the number of U.S. universities that are setting up branch campuses around the world. For example, Cornell University recently established a branch of its medical college in Qatar, and Texas A&M University and three other major U.S. institutions also have branch campuses there. Although recognizing the importance of providing educational opportunities for citizens worldwide, Olivas worries about the implications of the expansion of American universities across the globe at the same time that there are underserved populations at home, especially in low-income and minority communities. He takes the position that public higher education institutions, in particular, need to have a very clear academic justification for operating overseas. This, at least implicitly, takes the reader back to chapter 8, and Tapia and Johnson's conclusion that American universities need to think much more seriously about how they relate, or don't relate, to underserved populations here in the United States.

Concluding Remarks

In the final essay we summarize the major lessons of the chapters of this book, talk briefly about some topics that were not discussed, and point out areas in which future research relating to doctoral education will be needed.

I

Improving Doctoral Education

1

Changing the Education of Scholars

An Introduction to the Andrew W. Mellon Foundation's Graduate Education Initiative

Ronald G. Ehrenberg, Harriet Zuckerman,
Jeffrey A. Groen, and Sharon M. Brucker

In 1991 the Andrew W. Mellon Foundation launched the Graduate Education Initiative (GEI) to improve the structure and organization of PhD programs in the humanities and social sciences and to combat the high rates of student attrition and long time to degree completion prevailing in these fields. While attrition and time to completion were deemed to be important in and of themselves, and of great significance to degree seekers, they were also seen more broadly as indicators of the effectiveness of graduate programs. An array of characteristics of doctoral programs was earmarked as likely contributors to high attrition and long degree-completion time. These included unclear or conflicting expectations of the academic performance of students, a proliferation of specialized courses, elaborate and sometimes conflicting requirements, intermittent supervision, epistemological disagreements on fundamentals, and—not least—inadequate funding.[1] In short, the intention was to improve doctoral education and make it more efficient.

This was far from the first such effort to reduce times to degree completion and rates of attrition. Earlier interventions, which provided grants in aid to individual students or to graduate schools to distribute as they saw fit, had conspicuously failed.[2] Based on data that showed marked differences among graduate departments in the time it took to earn degrees; data about attrition rates among and within the sciences, social sciences, and humanities; and a great deal of experience on the ground, the architects of the GEI concluded that graduate education could be improved only if departments would change their PhD programs. The Mellon Foundation then shifted much of the support it provided for doctoral education away from fellowships for individual students and moved to block grants that would be awarded to major universities and the departments they selected.

Ten institutions—the University of California, Berkeley, the University of Chicago, Columbia University, Cornell University, Harvard University, the University of Michigan, the University of Pennsylvania, Princeton University, Stanford University, and Yale University— were each invited to nominate four to six departments to participate in the GEI. These universities were chosen because as a group they had attracted the largest number of fellowship winners of the Mellon Foundation's portable doctoral dissertation awards.[3] To be eligible for participation and funding, each department had to develop a plan to improve its doctoral program that would be consistent with the objectives of the Foundation. Departments were encouraged to carefully review their curricula, examinations, advising, and official timetables with an eye toward facilitating timely degree completion and reducing attrition (especially late attrition), while maintaining or increasing the quality of doctoral training they provided.[4] There was no requirement that the departments named by the universities be in need of particular help—that is, the departments did not need to have low completion rates and long times to degree completion, nor were they necessarily well-organized, thus meriting additional support. Universities made their own selections with the result that participating departments had a variety of profiles with respect to completion rates and times to degree completion. They did, however, share one major characteristic: a general reputation for turning out high-quality PhD holders.

The designers of the GEI encouraged departments to establish incentive structures that would promote students' timely progress through requirements they had to complete to earn the PhD, such as meeting foreign language requirements, passing comprehensive examinations, and completing dissertation proposals. For example, rather than guaranteeing incoming students that they would receive multiyear financial aid if they met departmental standards, the GEI sought to make annual financial aid contingent on the timely completion of a series of requirements. Funding for dissertation-year fellowships was encouraged, but only for students who had completed all other requirements before their sixth year of doctoral study and who were judged to be within one year of completing their dissertations.

The Mellon Foundation understood at the outset that it would take time for proposed changes in programs to be agreed on and implemented, that program changes would evolve over time, and that the changes that occurred would differ across the departments. As such, the GEI began with the expectation that the program would run for ten years, but left open the possibility of providing support for only five years if the evidence indicated that the effort had been ineffective. The program did in fact run for ten years, from 1991–92 to 2000–2001.[5] Approximately $58 million was provided by the Foundation to the ten universities and fifty-four participating departments and programs, an average in the range of $113,000 per department per year.[6] Moreover, to help the participating universities sustain the progress that had been made with the help of GEI grant funds, endowment grants were made to each participating university as the GEI ended, and subsequently each university received an additional challenge grant; the Foundation spent $22.5 million on these two types of grants. The challenge grants were contingent on proposals submitted by the universities that indicated how they would use such funds to continue improving their PhD programs in the humanities throughout the university; there was no requirement that the funds be used in the participating GEI departments. In all, the Foundation devoted almost $85 million in support of the GEI.[7]

Because the programmatic changes that the GEI induced would likely differ across departments and within each department over time, the framers of the GEI understood that it was important to learn not only whether on average the GEI led to improvements but also to identify programmatic changes associated with general changes that occurred. Understanding the mechanisms of change was essential if the successful innovations the GEI introduced were to be emulated by other departments. This led to the decision to collect evidence on characteristics of each department's doctoral program along with detailed data on student outcomes and the financial support students received.

Initially, the impact of the GEI on attrition rates and times to degree completion was to be assessed by comparing outcomes for students who had enrolled in these departments eight years before the instigation of the GEI with outcomes for students who enrolled in these same departments during the time the GEI was in place.[8] However, after the program began, Mellon Foundation staff quickly realized that even highly satisfactory changes in, say, attrition rates or times to degree completion could be caused by factors other than the GEI (for example, changes in the labor market for humanities and related social-science PhDs) that could not adequately be gauged using the original "pre/post" design.

As a result, the Foundation decided that comparative data would be needed on departments that were in the same disciplines as those in the GEI but which had not benefited from it. These departments would serve as "controls" while "treatment" departments would be those participating in the GEI and receiving financial aid—following the conventional terms used in evaluation studies of all kinds. A first step was to ask the universities participating in the GEI to provide similar data on student outcomes for departments that were not receiving GEI funding. This would make it possible to estimate the impact of the GEI over time and to hold constant other variables that might be expected to influence the outcomes.

Five of the universities had on hand sufficiently detailed information about other departments, and they agreed to provide it; the other five were unable to do so.[9] To increase the number of departments in the comparison group, the Foundation turned to a set of other universities with highly rated graduate programs for data on their departments in the humanities and related social sciences. The University of California, Los Angeles, the University of California, San Diego, and the University of North Carolina at Chapel Hill generously agreed to do so.[10] None of the departments designated as controls received funding, a condition necessary to make the planned comparisons as valid as possible.[11]

The 54 treatment and 47 comparison programs that participated in the GEI are listed in table 1.1. Because the universities, rather than the Foundation, selected the treatment departments and the comparison departments were selected if data were available, the two groups do not contain the same number of departments in each discipline. For example, there are only three East Asian studies programs, one ethics program, and one medieval studies program among the 101 treatment and comparison programs. To improve the comparability of the treatment and comparison groups, these three fields were eliminated from the analyses that underlie many of the findings we summarize below, in part because the sample sizes for East Asian studies were too small to obtain meaningful results and in part because no data were available for comparison departments for the other two fields. Ultimately, our empirical analyses drew on data from 51 treatment and 46 comparison departments.[12]

It is essential to underscore the fact that the treatment and comparison departments were not randomly assigned and thus there are differences between them on a number of dimensions, including program size, selectivity (as measured by entering student test scores), and doctoral program rankings. These differences are controlled for to the extent possible in our empirical analyses.

TABLE 1.1
Treatment (T) and Comparison (C) Programs Participating in the Graduate Education Initiative

Field (number of treatment, comparison programs)	Berkeley	Chicago	Columbia	Cornell	Harvard	Michigan[f]	Penn	Princeton	Stanford[g]	Yale	UCLA	UCSD	UNC
Anthropology (6, 4)			T[a]	C	T	T[e]		T	T	T	C	C	C
Art History (6, 3)	T		T	C	T	T[ab]		T	C	T	C		
Classics (3, 5)	T			C		T	T	C		C	C		C
Comp. Lit. (2, 4)	T			T		C		C		C	C		
East Asian Studies (1, 2)				C				T[e]			C		
English (9, 3)	T	T	T	T	T	T	T	C	T	T	C	C	
Ethics (1, 0)								T					
History (8, 3)	T	T		T		T	T	T[c]	T	T	C	C	C
Medieval Studies (1, 0)				T									
Music (3, 6)			T	C		C	T	C	C	T	C	C	C
Philosophy (4, 5)		T	T	C		T[a]			T	C	C	C	C
Politics/Government (4, 5)		T		T	T			T	C	C	C	C	C
Religion (2, 3)			T		T			C	C	C			
Romance Languages (2, 4)				C		C	T	T[ad]	C		C		
Total (54, 47)[f]	5, 0	4, 0	6, 0	5, 7	5, 0	8, 3	5, 0	7, 5	4, 5	5, 5	0, 11	0, 6	0, 5

[a] Added as a treatment program in 1996.
[b] Includes classical art and archaeology.
[c] Includes history of science.
[d] Includes German and Slavic languages.
[e] Ended treatment department status in 1995–96.
[f] Two interdisciplinary Michigan programs—anthropology and history, and American culture—were also treatment programs starting in 1997–98. They, along with Cornell's medieval studies program (which began as a treatment department in 1993) and Princeton's ethics program, have been excluded from the evaluation of the GEI because of a lack of any control programs in these fields.
[g] Stanford departments started treatment status one year later.

Data Collection: Departmental Databases—Evidence on Students

One condition universities were required to meet in order to receive GEI support was the provision of both quantitative data on students and their progress and qualitative data on departmental educational practices. Such data were needed if lessons were to be drawn from the GEI. Thus, participating universities were required to collect extensive data that would be submitted to the Foundation annually. Data were collected about all entrants to the relevant PhD programs, their demographic characteristics at entry, their progress through the program, and the financial support they received until completion or attrition occurred. This information was to be reported for entry cohorts in both treatment and comparison departments, starting with entrants from 1980 onward (ten years prior to the start of the GEI) and continuing through 2006 (six years after the completion of the GEI).[13] This design allowed for comparisons of treatment departments before the GEI was instituted and during its tenure and the comparison of GEI treatment with non-GEI control departments in the same time periods. Qualitative information was also collected annually from the treatment departments about the characteristics of their PhD programs and how those programs were evolving over time. This section describes the student-level data collection; we will describe the departmental reports in the next section.

The Foundation established standardized formats for data collection to assure comparability among institutions. In order to avoid variations in reporting due to the use of different measurement procedures, institutions were not asked to calculate their own times to degree completion, attrition rates, and completion rates. The Foundation asked that only raw data for each student and each department be reported, and it transformed these data into consistently defined measures.[14] To preserve the confidentiality of the data, the universities assigned identification numbers to each student for the purpose of creating longitudinal records, but the records they provided to the Foundation were anonymous. Further, the Foundation promised that when analyses of the data were published, neither individual student records nor individual departments would be identified.[15]

Two classes of data were routinely collected on students. The first consisted of students' demographic and educational characteristics at the time they entered PhD programs, including gender, citizenship, race, and ethnicity; their educational backgrounds (where and when they received their undergraduate degrees and whether each student had a master's degree upon entry); and scores on the verbal and mathematical portions of the Graduate Record Examination (GRE), if these were available.

The second class of data was reported annually by the institutions and provided information on each student's progress through the doctoral program[16] and the types of financial support that each received that year—whether each held a fellowship, teaching assistantship, or research assistantship; received a tuition stipend; and/or received summer support—as well as the dollar amount of each allocation.[17] These dollar amounts were to include funds from all sources, internal and external, but in more than a few instances information on external fellowships was incomplete. In addition, treatment departments were asked to indicate which students received academic-year or summer fellowships from the Foundation under the GEI program and the dollar amount of each of these awards.[18]

Initially, Sarah Turner, then on the Mellon Foundation staff and now on the faculty at the University of Virginia, designed and coordinated the data collection. In 1991 Sharon Brucker (one of the coauthors of this chapter) took over these responsibilities and has worked as data manager and analyst since then. During this time she has been in continuous touch with data representatives at each university to make sure the data were submitted annually and in proper form.[19] Each year, as new data were uploaded into the database, checks were made to ensure that the new data squared with information submitted in earlier years.[20] Consistency checking vastly improved the accuracy of the database. This required continuing vigilance on the part of Mellon Foundation staff, and the fact that the same staff member was in charge of the database throughout the entire period was of great assistance in this vigilance. The exceptional cooperation of the institutional representatives also helped to improve accuracy.[21]

Data Collection: Departmental Databases — Evidence on Programs

One of the original goals of the GEI was to encourage departments to examine their programs and identify areas where change would improve both the quality of the education students received and the effectiveness of the programs. Once needs were identified, changes were to be designed and implemented. The request for departmental introspection and examination was intended to encourage departments to consider their degree programs as a whole (piecemeal periodic reviews, for example, of language requirements or qualifying exams were common) and to give them incentives to make changes they deemed necessary.

Tracking how these changes affected some key departmental outcomes was intended to promote accountability, while maintaining a record of the changes that were made and their subsequent effects would serve— the Foundation hoped—as a means of identifying those innovations that proved useful. For all of these reasons, the Foundation required treatment departments to submit annual reports on how their programs were evolving.

The reports were not free-form narratives but instead were responses to questions Mellon Foundation staff posed each year in an effort to learn more about what was going on in the departments, both right and wrong.[22] In the meantime, Foundation staff went to considerable effort to try to identify each innovation that was being tried and then to summarize how such innovations were distributed among departments.

Table 1.2 identifies ten classes of innovations or changes in five sample departments,[23] spanning English, history, and two other fields, and details specific innovations within each class.[24] These innovations include:

- clarification of deadlines to be met and expectations for time to degree completion
- improvements in advising, such as required schedules, matching the substantive interests of students and their advisers, and formal group advising
- increased monitoring, such as early review of students' performance, requirements of faculty to submit reports on students' dissertations
- introduction of workshops and colloquia on dissertation prospectuses and writing and on job seeking and placement; increased collective activity among graduate students
- curricular changes, such as changes in coursework requirements, advancement to doctoral candidacy, examination formats, incomplete policies
- focused use of Mellon Foundation funding for summer study, predissertation research, and field trips, and particularly for dissertation-year fellowships
- changes in financial aid policies and tuition charges, introduction of guaranteed multiyear financial aid; increases in tuition past the sixth year of enrollment
- enforcement of rules already in place, including limits on the number of years of funding; prohibition on registration if deadlines are missed; and limits on funding if doctoral defense not scheduled
- changes in the timing of teaching assistantships and training for them
- structural changes, including reductions in the size of entering cohorts; and establishing department placement officers.

Of course, what departments said that they planned to do did not square perfectly with what was actually done and what survived over time.[25] Some departments designed long lists of intended changes and discovered it was difficult to make them, whereas others made only a few changes but took great pride in maintaining them. Stating that an innovation was put in place does not necessarily mean that it remained there.

TABLE 1.2
Innovations Implemented as Part of the Graduate Education Initiative: Examples from
Five Sample Departments

Innovation	English A	History B	History C	Other D	Other E
Expectations					
Clarify timetable/orientation	y	y	y	n	y
Clarify TTD expectations	n	n	y	n	n
Clarify ATC and prospectus deadlines	y	n	y	y	y
Advising					
Required schedule	y	y	y	n	y
Formal group advising	y	n	n	n	y
Monitoring					
Earlier review	y	n	y	y	y
Faculty to submit progress reports on dissertations	y	n	y	y	n
Group Workshops or Colloquia					
To reduce isolation	y	y(plan)	n	y	n
To prepare prospectus	y	n	y	y	n
To get dissertation started	n	n	n	y	n
Dissertation writing/feedback	y	y(plan)	y	y	y
Early seminar/fieldwork	n	n	n	n	n
Collaborative work	n	y	n	n	n
Job/profession preparation	n	n	y	n	n
Curricular Changes					
Coursework requirements	y	n	y	n	y
Writing requirements	n	n	n	y	n
Timing for advance to candidacy	n	n	y	y	y
Nature of advance to candidacy	y	n	n	y	y
Prospectus required to advance	n	n	y	y	n
Reduce language requirements	n	n	n	n	n
Modify incomplete policy	y	y	y	y(97)	n
Limit length of prospectus	n	n	y(97)	y	y
Courses graded	y	n	n	n	n
Preliminary fields identified earlier	n	y	y	n	y
Deadlines for submitting dissertation chapters	y	n	y	y	y
Use of Mellon Funding					
Summer language	0%	0%	9%	5%	0%
Summer travel/fieldwork	9%	22%	25%	50%	0%
Preadvancement to candidacy	0%	0%	0%	0%	0%
Postadvancement/start-up	13%	26%	0%	20%	2%
Completion of dissertation	78%	52%	66%	25%	98%
Tuition Policy					
Tuition increases after six years	n	n	n	n	y
Guaranteed multiyear packages	y	y	y	y	n
Enforcement of Rules					
Funding conditional on timing	y	y	n	y	y
Limit years funded	y	n	y	n	n

(Table 1.2—cont.)

Innovation	English A	History B	History C	Other D	Other E
Final-year support conditional on completing specific chapters	y	n	n	n	y
Can't register if deadlines are missed	n	n	n	n	n
No further funding (including TA) if dissertation defense not scheduled by end of dissertation write-up year	n	n	y	n	n
No TA if prospectus not on time	n	n	y	n	n
Postdoctorate position available if defense is scheduled by end of write-up fellowship year	n	y	y	n	n
TA Changes					
Reduced time as a teaching assistant	y	y	y	n	n
Enhance TA experience/design personal course	n	y	n	n	n
Improve training for teaching	n	n	n	n	n
Structural Changes					
Define summer tasks	n	n	y	y	n
Add placement advisor	y	n	n	n	n
Reduce size of entering cohort	y	n	n	n	y
Better match with available mentors	n	n	n	y	n

y(plan): planned to implement but no report that the department did so in annual reports.
y(97): implemented in 1997.
TTD: time to degree.
ATC: advancement to candidacy.
TA: teaching assistantship.

Of the changes departments made, many evolved as they were implemented; sometimes we have data on what occurred, but surely we do not have complete data. This suggests that the PhD program that students encounter at a given institution may differ from cohort to cohort, and that departmental reports do not provide enough detail to allow us to capture all changes that occurred.

To be effective, many program changes required that students understand and respond to them. However, when departments introduced an innovation, students did not necessarily understand it, much less respond appropriately. It thus might take time for innovations to be fully implemented, and subsequently to have an effect. Finally, departments may have introduced the same innovations, but their implementation in different graduate school environments can readily make them incomparable.

Foundation staff realized that to understand the changes treatment departments made and their effects, it would be necessary to ask students directly about their doctoral programs, the curriculum, the expectations their professors had, and about the prevailing departmental culture. Collecting such information from students, in both the treatment and comparison departments, would be more useful for sorting out the distinctive effects of the GEI than would analyzing the more general changes occurring in many departments. In large part, the Graduate Education Survey (GES) grew out of a need to get students' perspectives on their PhD programs. But Foundation staff also thought that doing a survey would provide an opportunity to learn more about former and current students themselves. To be sure, elementary information was available on students' demographic profiles, but it was clear that learning more about why they chose the graduate school they did; the nature and extent of time commitments; students' own assessment of the advising they received; the extent of competition in their departments; the employment they took outside graduate school; the reasons for and the timing of their leaving doctoral programs, and, if they did so, their publication records and job histories after leaving; whether they married or not; and their route to tenure if they chose that goal would provide a far richer understanding of graduate education in the humanities than has heretofore been available.

THE GRADUATE EDUCATION SURVEY

The Graduate Education Survey was designed by Foundation staff and conducted by Mathematica Policy Research. Between November 2002 and October 2003, the 18,320 students who had matriculated at the treatment and comparison departments from 1982 to 1996 were surveyed. Of these, 13,552 responded, producing a response rate of 74 percent, which is remarkably high in this context, particularly for a retrospective survey. As might be expected, the response rate was higher for individuals who had completed their PhDs (81.3 percent) as compared to the rate for students still enrolled in their programs (75.8 percent), which in turn was higher than the rate for those who had left their programs (62.8 percent). The response rate for the last group was lower in part because 20 percent of those who left programs, many of whom had departed graduate study fifteen to twenty years earlier, could not be located. For the same reason, response rates differed by entry cohort, with the response rates declining the farther back in time the recipients had been graduate students. The response rates of the 1991–96, 1986–90, and 1982–85 entering cohorts were 77 percent, 74 percent, and 70 percent, respectively.[26] Thus, while some self-selection plainly occurred, these response rates are high enough to make us confident that the data do represent the graduate populations of the relevant universities in the time period under discussion.

The first section of the questionnaire asked students about entering their graduate programs (including why they chose the programs they did and the type of financial aid they were offered), their department's academic expectations and requirements, and the means by which these expectations and requirements were conveyed to them. The second section asked questions about their interactions with dissertation advisers and departments, the overall learning environment in the departments, the time it took them to complete different phases of their programs, and their publications—if any—while in graduate school and during the first three years after graduation. The third section asked questions about their experiences as research and teaching assistants, including the intensity, extent, and nature of those experiences. It also asked about the extent and nature of students' nonassistantship employment at various stages of their programs. The fourth section solicited information on degree completion (which, as we indicate below, allowed us to check the accuracy of the data on degree completion that the institutions provided) and information on the subsequent educational experiences of those who left doctoral programs. A fifth section sought demographic information, including the students' marital status and the number of children in their families during their graduate study years. The final section solicited information on the respondents' employment status six months after degree completion or departure from their programs, three years later, and again as of the survey date. Information on early career publications was also requested.

Just as the accuracy of the institutional database was consistently checked, so too were the data supplied in the GES. In particular, we were intent on reconciling respondents' GES replies about their enrollment status (whether they had received the PhD, were still enrolled, or had dropped out of the program) with the data the institutions supplied. These checks were critical in discovering which respondents had in fact earned PhDs when their institutions had no record of their having done so.

One more comment about accuracy is in order. As long as studies have sought data on the published productivity of scientists and scholars, investigators have been skeptical about the accuracy of self-reported survey data on publication counts. This led the Foundation staff members who had access to the names of survey respondents to compare the self-reported publications data for a sample of respondents to publications information obtained from websites and bibliographical indexes. We can report that in almost all cases the self-reported publications data were close enough to the objective measures that we felt confident in our ability to use the self-reported data for the entire sample. As far as we know, this is the first time a validity check has been made on self-reported publications data.

What We Learned from the GEI

Taken together, the institutional databases and the GES are rich sources of information about graduate education. These databases have been analyzed by researchers at the Cornell Higher Education Research Institute and by Mellon Foundation staff. Details of our technical analyses and findings are reported in a number of journal articles, working papers, and a forthcoming book.[27] Here we summarize briefly some of our major findings concerning the impact of the GEI on attrition rates, completion rates, and times to degree completion in the humanities and related social science PhD programs; what characteristics of PhD programs in the humanities and related social sciences influence these outcomes, and how the GEI influenced these characteristics; what happened to students who left PhD programs prior to receiving their degrees; the early career job-market outcomes of new PhD recipients; and their graduate school publications and early career outcomes.[28]

Student Outcomes, Graduate Program Characteristics, and Their Interrelations

Our analyses suggest that the GEI had modest effects on student outcomes in the expected directions: attrition rates and times to degree completion were reduced and completion rates were increased. These effects, we find, were driven in part by intentional reductions in the size of entering cohorts, which in turn permitted departments to become more selective in their admissions, as gauged by GRE scores. Reductions in cohort size also allowed improvements to be made in financial support over and above improvements that were attributable to infusions of Mellon Foundation funds.

Some improvements in financial aid also occurred as students became more likely to receive guaranteed packages of multiyear support upon admission. Universities undoubtedly moved in this direction in order to enlarge their chances of successful recruitment of students in response to increased competition in the market for new PhD students. The framers of the GEI did not anticipate intense competition; their hope had been to make financial aid conditional on satisfactory progress through the program. It is clear that market forces intervened and strict adherence to the GEI's conditional regime was replaced by the inclination to make attractive awards to applicants. Although multiyear packages reduced the probability of students' dropping out early in their graduate careers, the same packages appear to have been associated with an increase in the probability of dropping out later on, thus leading to an unintended substitution of later attrition for early attrition. This is a finding bearing further exploration and discussion.

Analyses of the data collected in the GES identified different routes through which the characteristics of graduate programs in our sample influenced student outcomes. We find that improving advising and clarifying program requirements are associated with reduced attrition. Departmental expectations about the nature of dissertations also have strong effects on attrition, even when students are in the early years of their doctoral programs. In particular, departments that encourage students to finish their dissertations as quickly as possible have lower rates of attrition, whereas departments that emphasize the importance of students polishing their dissertations and publishing their work prior to graduating have higher rates of attrition. Similarly, graduation probabilities are higher when advising is improved and when departments expect that the dissertations will be completed promptly.

The GES data also reveal that students and their faculty advisers confront a trade-off. Students who publish while in graduate school are more likely to obtain tenure-track appointments at four-year institutions upon graduation. Those who publish while in graduate school are also more likely to publish soon after receiving their degrees. To the extent that faculty members are concerned about their students' career success and are eager for them to publish, advising students to publish while in graduate school may be good advice, even if doing so increases the likelihood that some students will drop out and it also increases the time it takes for others to finish.[29] Put simply, although the GEI designers had the explicit goals of reducing times to degree completion and attrition rates, it is not self-evident that both could be pursued at once, nor that they are consistent with promoting students' later academic careers. There are also indications that some faculty members did not accept the legitimacy of reducing time to degree completion and did not encourage students to finish quickly.[30] Faculty members' inclination to do what they think best for their students should be recognized when future efforts are made to change doctoral programs.

Our analyses also helped identify the effects of the GEI on important characteristics of doctoral programs. On average, the GEI seems to have prompted increases in seminar requirements, higher expectations for summer work keyed to students' progress, and clarification of program expectations. In smaller departments the GEI was associated with students being encouraged to finish their dissertations promptly, whereas in larger departments (in which financial support prior to the GEI was especially scarce) it was accompanied by improved financial support. The effect these GEI-related program characteristics had on student outcomes was modest; there remains considerable variation among departments in the presence of these characteristics even now. Hence, it is possible that there is still room for changes to be made that will have beneficial effects on student outcomes in the future.

Finally, it is worth emphasizing that financial factors are not the primary reason that students drop out of PhD programs, as some suppose. To be sure—except in the case of the rare individual of independent means—financial support is necessary for graduate students. But it is not a sufficient guarantee of degree completion. Even the most generous financial aid packages—for instance, those that include fellowships in each of the first six years that students are enrolled in their PhD programs—are associated with substantial rates of attrition. Amply supporting graduate students but doing nothing else will not solve the attrition problem.

Those Who Leave PhD Programs

Stated simply, leaving a PhD program without a degree does not spell failure, at least as far as the reports our sample members provided. The unique nature of the GES allowed us to ascertain what actually happened to former students who dropped out. Indeed, over 10 percent of the "dropouts" in the GES sample ultimately received PhDs from different departments, with many of these people receiving their PhDs in fields other than the ones in which they were initially enrolled.[31] Individuals who drop out early in their graduate programs are much more likely to receive PhDs elsewhere than those who leave later on. In addition, almost 20 percent of those who dropped out went on to receive professional degrees, including, among others, law and MBA degrees.

We also find that the incidence of what appears to be downward occupational mobility among those leaving their PhD programs is large, but only temporarily so. Although 10 percent of dropouts were employed in clerical and administrative positions six months after departure from graduate school, by the time three years had elapsed this percentage had been reduced and the majority was employed in professional occupations. This is far from the popular imagery of the long-term results of attrition.

Job Outcomes after the PhD

Much more so in the humanities and related social sciences than in the science and engineering fields, obtaining an academic job is a near necessity if one is to work in one's field, and obtaining a tenure-track position at a four-year institution is the prime measure of early-career success for new PhDs. About 30 percent of the cohort that received degrees between 1998 and 2000 found employment in tenure-track positions at four-year institutions six months after receipt of their PhDs. Yet three years later, 52 percent of this same cohort had tenure-track positions at four-year institutions—a considerable increase. To be sure, the 30 percent holding tenure-track jobs right out of graduate school was slightly smaller than those who had graduated earlier in the decade, and so was the 52 percent who had such jobs three years later. These data suggest that there is considerable early-career mobility for new PhD holders; indeed, about 50 percent of new PhD holders who had full-time non-tenure-track positions six months after receipt of the degree had moved to full-time tenure-track positions three years later. The data also suggest that tenure-track jobs were increasingly going to those who had accumulated some post-doctorate experience and had assembled a stronger set of credentials than those of new PhD holders.

As time to degree completion increases, the probability of obtaining a tenure-track position within three years of receiving a PhD monotonically declines, but only for those who took eight years or more to complete their studies. This is an important finding, for it demonstrates that time to degree completion matters in getting coveted tenure-track posts, but only if it exceeds the seven-year threshold. As we have already noted, publishing while in graduate school enhances job candidates' chances of obtaining tenure-track positions and it also enhances their chances of attaining tenure within fifteen years of entering graduate school.

Graduate-School and Early-Career Publication

About 40 percent of respondents to the GES published while in graduate school or had at least one book or refereed article accepted for publication. Within three years of receiving the PhD, about 67 percent had published one or more papers or books. Publishing while in graduate school is an important predictor of publishing soon after earning the degree, and PhD holders who reported that their departments expected them to publish while in graduate school published more often early in their careers than did other PhD holders in our sample.

As we have noted, this may help explain why our estimates of the effects of the GEI on time to degree completion are so modest. Faculty members at these top programs appear to be more concerned about preparing the next generation of scholars than they are about the time it takes for their students to complete their degrees. It is only among those who took more than seven years to complete their degrees that long time to degree completion is inversely correlated with tenure-track job probabilities. Faculty advisers, in this one sense, are quite realistic about not pressing for shorter degree-completion times. However—and this is important—taking more than seven years to complete one's PhD is far from unusual; in fact, over 50 percent of the degree holders in our sample took more than seven years. Thus, while advisers appear to have little incentive to press students who are apt to complete the degree within seven years, pressing those who are still in course eight years after matriculating seems justified, though the positive effect of publishing on the quality of jobs that degree recipients get must be weighed against the adverse effect of longer degree-completion times on job opportunities for this group.

Having said this much, we find that students who completed their degrees in five years were more likely than others to publish while in graduate school. As times to degree completion increase, probabilities of publishing while in graduate school decline in the GES sample; this is likely to be the outcome of a selection effect. With other factors held constant, the more talented and motivated that students are, the greater the likelihood of their publishing, and the shorter the time it will take for them to finish their degrees. It thus follows that the students with the shortest times to degree completion are those who have published most often while in graduate school, and are those who are most apt to be employed in tenure-track positions after receiving their degrees.

Although the explicit goal of the GEI was to enhance the effectiveness of graduate programs, its framers did not explicitly make transforming students into scholars who would contribute to the extension of knowledge a prime objective or an important indicator of program effectiveness. Nonetheless, it is reassuring, as we have noted, that as many as 40 percent of the students in the GEI published while still in graduate school, and further reassuring that we estimate that the GEI increased the probability of students publishing while in graduate school by roughly 20 percent to 25 percent. This is no small accomplishment, and one not typically taken into account in assessing graduate education. For reasons we do not yet understand, the GEI had a somewhat smaller impact on the propensity of degree recipients to publish early in their careers.

General Lessons

The GEI has confirmed that the microenvironments of departments matter greatly in doctoral education in the humanities and related social sciences. Many of the departmental characteristics that influence graduate students' progress are controlled by departments, not by the graduate dean or other central administrators. Although there is a strong role for graduate deans to play in improving graduate education—and the study by Daniel Denecke, Helen S. Frasier, and Kenneth Redd in this volume takes up this matter (see chapter 2)—future efforts to improve graduate education should focus on departments' roles. And one should not underestimate the difficulty of persuading faculty members to "buy into" program changes and, ultimately, of transforming departmental cultures. Our analyses suggest that innovations that are initiated at the departmental level are much more likely to be supported by the faculty than those that are initiated top down.

It is also clear that after programmatic innovations are introduced they evolve over time. Sometimes this is due to faculty turnover—for example, the departure of a concerned faculty member and/or the arrival of another. Sometimes shifts occur in response to external competitive pressures, as in the instance of the spread of multiyear guaranteed financial-aid packages. This inclination for practices and procedures to evolve in departments makes it important for departments and graduate deans to keep regular track of indicators of departmental performance by collecting relevant data so that progress toward desired outcomes does not inadvertently erode.

One important benefit of the GEI was to encourage institutions and departments to collect such data, and a number now do so routinely. An important role of graduate deans is to monitor and standardize data collection and, where appropriate, to respond to the messages they carry. The National Research Council evaluation of doctoral programs that is scheduled to be released in late 2008 is similarly pressing departments to collect such information, and we view this effort as very important.

The GES has shown that retrospective surveys of current and former students can provide detailed information on multiple characteristics of graduate programs unavailable in institutional records. Our analyses have shown that these characteristics can be aggregated using factor analysis into a smaller number of underlying factors and, with data from multiple departments and multiple entering cohorts, analysis of factors that most strongly influence graduation and attrition probabilities can be undertaken.

We strongly believe that similar analyses may be profitably undertaken in other fields of graduate study (such as science and engineering) where entirely different characteristics of graduate programs may prove important.[32] Such analyses require that departments have collected data on student characteristics, their progress through their programs, and the types of financial support that they receive each year, as well as a GES-style retrospective study. However, they do not require that a major intervention, such as the GEI, has already taken place.

The GEI did not collect several types of data that in retrospect we now think would have been useful in evaluating graduate education. First and foremost, the GEI lacked basic data on the faculty. No usable information was available on the number of program faculty in each department and their stability over time. No information was available on the workloads faculty members shouldered in advising and dissertation sponsorship, nor were data available on the presence of incentives for faculty to mentor doctoral students (for example, workload credit for supervising dissertations). No information was collected on the match (or mismatch) of students and faculty advisers according to their research interests, or on their gender and ethnicity, and no information was sought on advisers' past success in placing their students. We know from experience how time-consuming it is to collect satisfactory information on the number of faculty members in residence in each department. Collecting more thorough information on the faculty would surely prove a formidable task, but nonetheless a useful one. It goes without saying that a survey of faculty members' views about graduate programs, parallel to the GES survey of graduate students, would have been highly desirable. The annual narrative reports the departments provided were highly instructive but clearly no substitute for more systematic data.

Finally, we believe it is important to have modest expectations about the likely effects of foundation-related efforts to improve doctoral education. If the GEI experience can be generalized, a host of factors can emerge and coalesce to make it difficult to achieve all of a foundation's objectives.[33] Not only do the objectives of individual faculty members sometimes differ from those held by foundations or graduate deans, but competitive pressures in the market for doctoral students may also press for the adoption of policies at odds with those advocated by foundations. An excellent example of such unanticipated consequences coming into play can be found in the case of the GEI, in which multiyear guaranteed support rather than incentive-based financial aid became the norm. Similarly, conditions prevailing in the academic market may affect the decisions graduate students make about the timing of dissertation completion and job searches. As the difficulty of finding tenure-track employment has increased and brought with it growing concerns about getting a desirable job and losing health insurance, housing, and library privileges, doctoral students probably correctly perceive that rushing to finish their degrees quickly might not be in their best interests. Put simply, the "law" of unanticipated consequences prevails in efforts to change graduate education, as it does in all other domains in which purposive change is sought. It is difficult to predict all of the consequences of programs and how these will interact with the changing world. To our minds this does not counsel inaction, but it does counsel the need for regular monitoring of the desired outcomes and the need for continuing alertness to potential second- and third-order effects. The GEI was unique in scale, investment, duration, and departmental focus among efforts to improve graduate education. It was also unique in its intensive concern with monitoring its effects, not simply after the fact but from the outset and while it was under way. All these attributions make it *exemplary*—in the precise meaning of this word.

2

The Council of Graduate Schools' PhD Completion Project

Daniel D. Denecke, Helen S. Frasier, and Kenneth E. Redd

John Houseman earned an Academy Award, a Golden Globe Award, and a National Board of Review award for best supporting actor as the uncompromising Professor Kingsfield in James Bridges's *The Paper Chase*, the 1973 movie based on John Jay Osborne's novel dramatizing his experiences at Harvard Law School. The movie provides what is still probably American culture's most famous reference to attrition in graduate programs when Kingsfield welcomes the incoming class by stating, "Look to your left. Look to your right. One of you will not be here on graduation day." The professor's orientation speech is intended not so much to discourage as to inspire students, to convey that the program they are entering is elite, and that those who complete that program will be the elite of the elite. Graduates will have demonstrated their skills in a cutthroat game of survival of the fittest. And they will be able to take pride in the fact that they have done so in a program whose quality is established not despite but because of the eventual attrition of approximately one-third of their classmates.

It has been observed that, despite the popularity of this depiction of Harvard Law School in the 1970s as one characterized by high attrition, Kingsfield's "look to your left, look to your right" statement more accurately depicts a pre–World War II law school culture. Postwar improvements in the selection and admissions process, with the introduction of the Law School Admission Test (LSAT), and other changes in the institutional culture resulted in significantly higher annual completion rates. Today, U.S. law schools rank among the graduate degree fields with the very highest completion rates, consistently at or above 90 percent (Wilder 2003). And Harvard Law School, in particular, boasts a completion rate of over 98 percent (Law School Admission Council, 2007).

Few would argue that U.S. law schools have earned their increases in degree completion at the expense of quality. To the contrary, the high completion rates of the very best law schools are evidence of their pervasive commitment to quality at every stage from selection and admissions onward.

Completion rates for PhD programs in the United States are another story. The national average PhD completion rate has long been estimated to be about 50 percent. Recent data from the PhD Completion Project, the large-scale initiative sponsored by the Council of Graduate Schools (CGS), as described in this chapter, suggest that while the national average may now in fact be somewhat higher, universities still exhibit high rates and patterns of attrition that should be a matter for concern.

This attrition should concern us nationally in the United States, for across all fields doctoral programs continue to lose a large portion of students who have been judged by faculty and admissions committees to be among the very brightest and most talented in the world. Such attrition arguably impinges on the capacity of the United States to produce the talented researchers necessary for long-term success in a global knowledge economy. If future competitiveness and prosperity depend on our ability to expand and diversify a creative class engaged in research, innovation, and the solving of complex problems that require interdisciplinary and collaborative solutions, there is a strong argument to be made that PhD holders will play a vital role. Moreover, many of the minority groups driving growth in the broader population and in U.S. master's degree education are both underrepresented in doctoral enrollment and have historically lower PhD completion rates than majority students. Better understanding the factors behind this attrition should be a priority issue for both employers and policymakers.

Increasing PhD completion rates should be a matter of concern to universities as well, for attrition carries financial as well as reputational costs. The cost to an institution that invests resources in students who leave is especially significant if this attrition occurs after several years in the program. And as new doctoral assessment ratings and consumer-ranking tools make information about program outcomes such as employment rates, placement statistics, completion rates, and average time to degree more accessible to prospective students, those students may begin weighing more traditional attractors such as reputation and faculty name recognition with the risks implicit in attending a program where a high percentage do not complete the PhD program.[1]

Indeed, students themselves should be more cognizant of program outcomes such as completion rates both when they are deciding among programs and once they are enrolled in a program of doctoral study. Students rarely make the decision to leave a PhD program lightly. And while some departing students embrace the transition from PhD to professional-degree student or to a new vocation, for others the PhD aspiration has become more than a professional pathway—it has become part of their social and personal identity. In addition to incurring financial debts and opportunity costs, students have invested a great amount of intellectual and emotional energy into a degree program, and those who leave may do so with psychological scars that can take years to heal.

Of course, a PhD differs from a JD in many respects. Over the six-to-eight-year period typically required to complete a PhD, many things can transpire that are much less likely to occur in a three-year window typical of a professional degree such as a JD. In those seven years, "life happens." Students may decide to get married; they may have children; their spouses may take jobs that require them to move; or caretaking responsibilities for parents and/or dependents may derail a student's initial plans to take the most direct path to the PhD, or even to finish at all. Students in doctoral programs are also on a process of self-discovery and may find that a research career in their first field of choice is not for them. Although much of their undergraduate (and possibly master's degree) experience has prepared them to succeed in coursework, students often have had little preparation for the later stages of doctoral study. In some fields, they typically find out only at the dissertation stage what a major portion of their lives as professional researchers will entail: significant time spent in isolation, long-term and sometimes uncertain rewards, and the painstaking revision of countless drafts. For some students these activities have their own rewards and contribute to the thrill of academic research; for others, however—whether in pursuit of an academic or a nonacademic career—these can be deal breakers.

The stakes for individual students, programs, and institutions are high, as are the costs for every student admitted who does not complete the program. Given these high stakes, we know surprisingly little about PhD completion rates and even less about the variety and causes of attrition.[2] Part of the reason for this gap in our collective knowledge has had to do with questions of their "knowability." Most universities have not tracked the completion rates of their own PhD programs, and departments or programs are even less likely to have done so. Even when universities have tracked these data, most researchers who have tried to study completion, persistence, or attrition in a multi-institutional context have grappled with the difficulty of obtaining comparable data across programs and institutions. Universities measure and define such things as "candidacy," "stop-out," and "cohort" differently, and differences may exist even within the same university among different programs. In part for these reasons, and because there has been no external requirement or mandate that institutions collect these data, information about the PhD completion rates of specific institutions are not publicly available, as they are for JDs and bachelor's degrees.

Another reason for the relative paucity of data on PhD completion nationally lies in the academic culture, and, more specifically, in the prevailing set of assumptions about both the levels and the causes of student attrition from doctoral programs. In contrast to American law schools— where a complete cultural transformation has resulted in the general perception that high-quality education and high completion rates can be mutually reinforcing—it is still not uncommon to encounter graduate faculty in doctoral programs across the country who take pride in a "paper chase" culture and who fear that potential gains in increased PhD completion could come only at the cost of program quality. Nationally led graduate reform efforts have taken root in a number of areas, including professional development, future faculty preparation, the responsible conduct of research, civic scholarship, and disciplinary stewardship. But because of widespread disagreement about how to collect completion data and about what increases in degree completion really mean with respect to quality, doctoral education reform initiatives have not explicitly targeted degree completion per se—or when they have included data on completion they have done so only among a relatively select and resource-intensive set of institutions.[3]

In 2004, the CGS engaged senior administrators, faculty, graduate students, and the graduate education research community from across the spectrum of research universities in an effort to enhance our national understanding of PhD completion rates, attrition patterns, and the institutional factors that contribute to increased degree completion as well as to empower universities with proven strategies for positive change. The PhD Completion Project is grounded in two assumptions. The first is that degree completion is a measure of program *quality* and not simply of efficiency. This assumption is based on prior research (and anecdotal evidence from CGS member deans) suggesting that programs that have been able to achieve significant increases in completion rates over time have done so not by lowering academic standards but by making strategic improvements in a number of areas. These areas range from front-end enhancements in recruiting, selection, and admissions processes to back-end innovations in dissertation support and professional development. The improvements are designed by program faculty and senior administrators to make it easier for programs to ensure that the right students apply and are admitted in the first place, and that those who do enroll have as much institutional support as possible to enable them to focus on their academic studies and career aspirations. As findings emerge from the PhD Completion Project and from the National Research Council's assessment of doctoral programs, which in 2007 includes completion data for the first time, we believe these improvements will be reflected over time in higher completion rates and in programs that are more attractive to students and hence more competitive.

The second assumption of this project is that graduate deans are the best agents for institutional change. Most of the interventions sponsored by the PhD Completion Project are designed and implemented at the program level and require buy-in, championing, and evaluation by program faculty. However, the project also builds on prior CGS best practice initiatives, such as the Preparing Future Faculty (PFF) program (1993–2003), that have demonstrated that for institutional changes to outlive the championing of one or two faculty members, and to be diffused across the university beyond several departments active in the pilot phase of any given graduate reforms, the leadership of senior administrators is also essential.

Because there is still strong disagreement within the graduate education community about whether a focus on completion rates is the best framework to adopt if we wish to improve U.S. graduate education, we first answer the question, Why focus on completion? Next, because most graduate reform initiatives have focused on program-level interventions and faculty-led reforms, we discuss why graduate deans in this project are seen as the crucial agents for bringing about long-term sustainable change. Finally, we present some of the early findings from the PhD Completion Project and outline a few of the ways in which, as a result of this project, this focus on completion is resulting in concrete strategies for change in research universities across the United States and Canada.

Why Completion Is the Right Lever for Change

The data collected for the PhD Completion Project reflects the experiences of students who entered doctoral programs in the early 1990s. During the time that these students pursued their degrees, a number of influential graduate reform initiatives contributed to the reshaping of the American doctorate. These initiatives were sponsored by federal agencies, such as the National Science Foundation and the Office of Research Integrity; by private foundations and other nongovernmental organizations, such as the Atlantic Philanthropies, the Ford Foundation, the Andrew W. Mellon Foundation, the Pew Charitable Trusts, the Alfred P. Sloan Foundation, the Carnegie Foundation for the Advancement of Teaching, and the Woodrow Wilson National Fellowship Foundation. Some of these were also led by universities, such as the University of Washington's Reenvisioning the PhD initiative, and by regional bodies, such as the Southern Regional Educational Board's Compact for Faculty Diversity. Each of these various initiatives carved out its own unique approach to enhancing doctoral education, though they often sought to achieve progress on common goals, including the incorporation of professional development opportunities for students aspiring to faculty and nonacademic careers, the fostering of interdisciplinary research and collaboration, the diversification of the professoriate, and the reduction of attrition and time to degree.

Many universities took part in multiple initiatives. A university might, for example, have participated in the Mellon Graduate Education Initiative and have an Integrative Graduate Education and Research Traineeship grant from the National Science Foundation, have a universitywide PFF program, and have recently participated in the Carnegie Initiative on the Doctorate. Different programs might have officially participated in each, but ideas and best practices generated out of these initiatives often bled over into other departments and programs. Indeed, under strong graduate school leadership, such "contamination" is optimized.

From a research perspective, though, it is often difficult to assess the impact of any one initiative, as if these initiatives could be isolated from each other and from the general exchange of ideas and constant improvement that takes place regularly in doctoral programs. The establishment of "control" departments or universities is difficult, because the academic community is constantly engaged in improving doctoral programs by imitating and replicating what works. What often begins with seed money from particular funding sources to a specific number of universities for pilot projects can result in a much broader national movement. PFF programs, for example, now extend far beyond the original forty-four universities that received external grant funding to develop them, and the PhD Completion Project involves many more universities than the initial pool of grant recipients in the collection of data and exchange of best practices. Faculty members share ideas with each other about how to improve recruitment, retention, and professional development opportunities for graduate students and often return from disciplinary society meetings motivated to exercise leadership within these departments with newly defined goals. And graduate schools and graduate deans engage program faculty in dialogue about benchmarking and the possible adoption of proven practices through program assessment and review.

There are many levers through which universities strive to meet their long-term goals of improving doctoral programs: financial support and the optimal structuring of that support; academic socialization and the quality of mentoring and advising that students receive; and assurance that program requirements and expectations are both philosophically grounded and clearly communicated to students. Others are close cousins of degree completion goals, such as persistence or retention and time to degree. Given that a focus on each of these areas is known to be worthwhile, it is reasonable to ask, Why focus on degree completion per se? Although interventions in each of the areas described above play a role in the PhD Completion Project, CGS decided to focus on the overarching umbrella issue of degree completion for several reasons. First, because completion rates may be one of the best outcome measures by which to assess the impact of all that we do in striving to improve graduate education. Increasing rates of PhD completion may be an end in itself, but rates of completion can also serve as a metric by which, over time, we can measure the tangible effects that increases in funding or improvements in mentoring and/or the selection and admissions process may have.

Second, if U.S. doctoral programs only focus on the successful completion of those students they admit each year, they could have a major impact on the leaky pipeline of underrepresented minorities and women who enter with the motivation and talent to become successful faculty and professional researchers but who for one reason or another do not finally realize those initial aspirations. Also, as federal agencies, accrediting bodies, and state boards of education are increasingly looking to establish metrics by which to measure the productivity of programs and the return on investment of fellowship funding and/or public tax dollars, they have begun to turn to time to degree averages and degree completion rates as the key metrics. Such efforts to use completion rates as benchmarking data will be contentious and problematic, however, if universities continue to collect these data and define crucial terms in different ways. Through its member graduate deans, CGS is in a unique position to accelerate a community consensus on the collection of data. The PhD Completion Project will enhance the abilities, on the one hand, of those member institutions with preexisting capacity to collect data to use those data more effectively and, on the other hand, of those just developing the capacity to collect completion and attrition data to do so in dialogue with more experienced institutions as each works to identify appropriate strategies for institutional as well as program-level change.

WHY GRADUATE DEANS ARE THE BEST AGENTS OF CHANGE

While the collection and use of completion and attrition data are essential parts of the PhD Completion Project, it is not simply a data study. The ultimate goal of the project is to increase rates of PhD completion in North American graduate programs through the identification and broad dissemination of proven interventions (activities, resources, and policies). The majority of the interventions sponsored by the project are designed and implemented at the program level. Faculty leadership is thus essential. Graduate deans at each participating university, however, are designated as principal investigators. The CGS requires graduate dean leadership in this project because we believe, based on past experience with PFF programs, that deans are the agents of change best positioned within the university to ensure that those practices that prove effective in selected programs are sustained and that information about these practices is shared across disciplines through structured interdepartmental dialogues.

The leadership of graduate deans in the PhD Completion Project is also instrumental in enabling universities to address the twin obstacles to national progress on doctoral completion rates: skepticism about the accuracy and comparability of numbers on the one hand, and lingering assumptions behind the commonly held belief that current rates of attrition are either intransigent characteristics of a discipline or staples of program quality on the other. Graduate deans are ultimately responsible for the quality of graduate education across disciplines, and play an active role in regular program review. They are also becoming increasingly engaged in enrollment management, which requires tighter integration between institutional research and selection and admissions decisions. Graduate deans are most effective in assisting departments or programs to achieve their completion targets when they integrate the results of institutional research and program review with policymaking and often funding allocation decisions. Those deans who also participate in national discussions about PhD completion are able to lead evidence-based discussions on their campus about completion rates within a discipline to dispel myths of intransigence (such as, "That's just the way it is in physics") and show what peer and aspirational peer institutions have been able to achieve.

THE PhD COMPLETION PROJECT

The project is a six-year, grant-funded initiative that addresses the issues surrounding PhD completion and attrition. During the first phase of this project (2004–07), the CGS, with generous support from Pfizer Inc. and the Ford Foundation, provided funding to twenty-one major U.S. and Canadian research universities to create intervention strategies and pilot projects and to evaluate the impact of these projects on doctoral completion rates and attrition patterns. An additional twenty-four partner universities participated in various aspects of this project. This pool of universities expands with the second phase (2007–10). The PhD Completion Project aims to produce a cadre of graduate deans who are leaders on their campuses and in the national community who can speak to the value of the completion lever to effect change in doctoral programs, and who can point to specific strategies for effecting positive change in doctoral completion.

The project does not presume that all attrition is preventable, or that all attrition is necessarily bad. The primary focus of the project is not on those students who may ultimately lack the academic ability or desire to complete, although research suggests that overall the proportion of such students is low, and enhancements in selection and admissions processes may help to identify these students before admission. Nor is the focus of the project on that portion of attrition that is due to unforeseen personal events, although through the development of "family-friendly" policies some universities have begun to address these factors that were once generally perceived as outside the purview of institutional intervention. Rather, the project focuses on that larger portion of students who leave because of factors that are under the control or purview of the university, the graduate school, or the program. Researchers have identified a number of such areas, including selection and admissions, mentoring and advising, financial support, research experiences, the program environment, and curricular and administrative processes and procedures. The interventions that institutions have designed as part of this project address these areas, among others, and their interactions with other factors such as students' demographic and personal characteristics.

One of the main goals of this project is to identify proven strategies to increase PhD completion rates of underrepresented minorities in all fields, and of women, especially in the fields of sciences, engineering, and math where their overall completion rates are lower than those of men. Some universities report that the interventions that have proven most effective for underrepresented minorities and women have also benefited majority students. Others have reported that general improvements in mentoring and advising or dissertation writing groups, for example, have disproportionately benefited underrepresented minorities. The CGS hopes that the project will produce documented evidence about interventions that have proven effective in both cases—overall and by field.

As the project develops, and as additional data are submitted and analyzed, one of the long-term goals will be to document the net impact of clusters of interventions. Some of these may be documented to be most effective within specific fields and programs, and other interventions may work better in some institutional contexts than in others. While we recognize that it is unlikely that the project will ever be able to isolate one strategy from all others as having a decisive effect on completion, correlations of such cluster effects should be demonstrable and case studies will supplement quantitative analysis. Finally, it is not possible to establish controls at the outset of the project, as CGS member universities are all encouraged to exchange ideas about those practices that appear to be having an early positive impact, and to make midcourse corrections where appropriate, though it may be possible to establish some rough controls in retrospect at the end of the project. Research on the efficacy of interventions over time will have to work with this limitation.

EARLY FINDINGS FROM THE PhD COMPLETION PROJECT

The seminal studies from which we have inherited estimates of a national average completion rate of 50 percent, such as Bowen and Rudenstine 1992, reflect students who entered doctoral programs over three decades ago in a small number of relatively homogeneous resource-intensive universities.[4] By contrast, the PhD Completion Project data set includes a wider range and larger number of universities comprising the doctoral enterprise in North America, and reflects the experiences of students who entered doctoral programs more recently (starting in 1992). In phase one, these students were in participating programs at the following institutions: Arizona State University, the University of California–Los Angeles, the University of Cincinnati, Cornell University, Duke University, the University of Florida, the University of Georgia, Howard University, the University of Illinois at Urbana-Champaign, the University of Louisville, the University of Maryland–Baltimore County, the University of Missouri–Columbia, the University of Michigan, the University of Montreal, the University of North Carolina–Chapel Hill, North Carolina State University, the University of Notre Dame, Princeton University, Purdue University, Washington University, and Yale University.[5] The overall, average ten-year completion rate for students who enrolled in participating programs in these universities between 1992 and 1995 was 56.8 percent. This may suggest that improvements in doctoral education over the past decades, including those made possible by the national graduate reform initiatives mentioned above, have resulted in increases in PhD completion rates. Clearly, there is more room for improvement, however, and we are confident that the project will demonstrate even more positive change as data on completion rates for more recent cohorts are available, and as students benefit from the program-level interventions supported by this project.

In addition to submitting completion data for participating programs, universities are also submitting data, separately, on attrition, where they are asked to distinguish—as best as they are able—between students who withdraw (leave their educational programs with no intention to return) either with a master's degree or without one, and before and after candidacy; those who transfer; and those who stop out (leave their educational programs temporarily with an intention to return). Universities are also asked to conduct self-assessments about the extent and duration of activities, resources, and policies as well as exit surveys to capture student perceptions of those same departmental and institutional resources and activities in the seven areas identified in the literature on doctoral attrition and completion[6]: (1) selection and admissions; (2) mentoring and advising; (3) financial support and structure; (4) program environment; (5) research experience; (6) curricular processes and procedures; and (7) professional development.

While we outline some of the interventions designed by participating universities at the end of this chapter, the findings discussed here come from the completion data set. The CGS is still at the very early stages of analyzing these data, but some basic findings are already emerging from degree completion data alone that may cast new light on trends identified by prior research. In *PhD Completion and Attrition* (Council of Graduate Schools 2004), the CGS has published results of a literature review comparing fifteen of the most influential studies on PhD completion, persistence, and attrition in North American research doctoral programs. These prior studies used different methods and reflected different definitions and widely varying sample sizes; nevertheless, they tell overlapping stories of common trends by field and by demographic group for students who entered doctoral programs in the United States and Canada between 1962 and 1988. First, while completion rates might vary over time and within any given field, prior research suggests that the comparative hierarchy among fields remains fairly consistent, with engineering exhibiting the highest degree completion rates, followed by the life sciences, the physical sciences, the social sciences, and the humanities. (Council of Graduate Schools 2004, 8). Those studies that also looked at demographic differences saw that men, majority (white) students, and international students consistently completed degrees at higher rates on average than did women, minority students, and domestic students, respectively.

Figure 2.1 shows that seven years after enrollment, completion rates are distributed in a manner consistent with this hierarchy of fields,

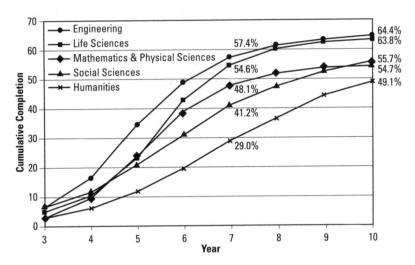

Figure 2.1. Average ten-year cumulative completion rates for students entering doctoral programs from 1992–93 through 1994–95, by year.

Source: Council of Graduate Schools Completion and Attrition Program data; baseline data as of October 9, 2006.

Note: Ten–year completion rates include all cohorts entering 1992–93 through 1994–95.

ranging from a high of approximately 57 percent in engineering to a low of 29 percent in the humanities.[7] After the seventh year, however, some clear changes in this hierarchical distribution have taken place. The life sciences have now caught up with engineering, with ten-year completion rates in both fields at approximately 64 percent. The average ten-year completion rate in the social sciences has surpassed that of the physical sciences and mathematics. And as neither the social sciences nor the humanities have even begun to plateau at the ten-year mark, extrapolating the trend lines in figure 2.1 suggests that eventually, given enough time, completion rates in the humanities may even surpass those of the physical sciences and mathematics. Percentages reflect cumulative average (mean) completion rates in years three through ten from enrollment for all doctoral students entering in academic years 1992–93 through 1994–95.

These early "broad brush" findings from the PhD Completion Project baseline data suggest that the time of completion may be a more important indicator of field differences than attrition. The differences in time to completion are clear when one looks across fields at the 50 percent mark—for example, to ask how long it takes half the students in any given field on average to complete their degrees: in engineering, this occurs around year 6; in the life sciences, at year 6.5; in the physical sciences and mathematics, at year 7.5; in the social sciences at year 8.5; and in the humanities, half of the students have not yet completed by year 10. The causes for these broad field differences in average time to degree numbers and degree completion rates (or percentages) are generally known, and include such things as different levels of financial support, differences between a collective lab environment and the solitary nature of much of the research in the humanities and social sciences, and different expectations of the dissertation in different fields. Many of these factors are relatively fixed characteristics of the field. Because time to completion varies so greatly by field, however, it is reasonable for universities whose policies and funding structures may reflect a seven-year norm and which are intended to encourage timely progress toward a degree to reflect upon both how these policies might impact overall completion rates and attrition patterns, as well as whether or not they might be having differential effects on students in different fields.

For institutions with such policies, their potentially differential effects on different demographic groups at that university should also be considered and analyzed. Some of the prior research on attrition and completion has focused on differences in completion rates between underrepresented minority and majority students, but the PhD Completion Project preliminary data suggests that differences in the timing of completion is an important factor here as well.[8] The numbers of underrepresented minorities in participating programs are small, so much so that the CGS requested that universities aggregate completion data for demographic groups by broad field rather than submit program-level completion data for those groups so as to protect the anonymity of individual students and comply with the requirements of institutional review boards. Although the numbers are small, the percentages are approximately proportionate to those enrolled in U.S. doctoral programs.[9] Overall, the PhD Completion Project data show, consistent with prior research, that underrepresented minorities are completing PhDs at lower rates than majority students in every field in both seven- and ten-year time horizons (see table 2.1). There is a notable difference, however, between seven- and ten-year completion rates for underrepresented minority groups: of approximately 20 percentage points in both the life sciences, which are generally known for shorter time to degree and high completion, and in the humanities (where the same is true for Asian Americans and majority white students). In every other field, the difference between seven- and ten-year rates for underrepresented minorities is between approximately 8 and 17 percentage points. In all fields, seven-year differences between underrepresented minority and majority (white) students are reduced by year ten, suggesting comparatively more late completion among minorities. This trend is most pronounced in the life sciences, where the largest

TABLE 2.1
Seven-Year vs. Ten-Year Completion Rates and Underrepresented Minority/
Majority Differences

	Underrepresented Minorities (URMs) (%)		Asian American (%)		Majority (White) (%)		Difference between URMs and Majority (White) (%)	
	7-Yr	10-Yr	7-Yr	10-Yr	7-Yr	10-Yr	7-Yr	10-Yr
Engineering	46.4	58.7	45.7	53.6	52.3	62.5	−5.9	−3.8
Life Sciences	43.4	63.2	45.2	55.9	54.3	63.8	−10.9	−0.6
Mathematics and Physical Sciences	40.1	47.6	41.8	52.3	47.9	54.3	−7.9	−6.7
Social Sciences	31.2	48.6	35.4	48.5	41.1	55.4	−9.9	−6.8
Humanities	32.4	52.7	33.1	55.4	35.9	55.3	−3.5	−2.6

Source: Council of Graduate Schools 2006b. Baseline data as of October 9, 2006.

difference between the average completion rates of underrepresented minorities and majority students at year seven (at 11 percentage points) has contracted to the smallest difference between the two groups by year ten (where it is less than 1 percentage point). While Asian American enrollment is much higher in science, technology, engineering, and mathematics (STEM) fields than that of underrepresented minorities, these data also show that in some fields, such as engineering, life sciences, and social sciences, Asian American students are completing at lower rates than majority students and may be experiencing some of the same obstacles to completion as underrepresented minorities or else may face unique challenges.

These overall data may be useful for understanding the extent to which doctoral programs, nationally, are meeting the goals of achieving equity in completion rates between minority and majority students, or for examining how a university's program might compare to these national trends. They are a crucial piece of the domestic talent puzzle. It is also important to look *within* the broad category of underrepresented minorities at specific trends among minority groups that may illuminate the need for different strategies for change. The PhD Completion Project data suggest, for example, that, overall, African American and Hispanic doctoral students exhibit contradictory completion trends by broad field.[10] Whereas there is almost no difference in completion rates between black students and majority white students in the humanities at either seven or ten years and a less than 5 percentage point difference in the social and life sciences at year ten, there are larger differences in both seven- and ten-year completion rates between the two groups in engineering and the physical sciences (between 9 and 13 percentage points).

By contrast, Hispanic students overall are completing at rates equal to or higher than majority white students in engineering, the life sciences, physical sciences, and mathematics, but are completing at rates lower than majority white students in the social sciences (by 7 percentage points) and the humanities (by 9 percentage points).[11] It would be easy to overinterpret these data given the small enrollment percentage of minority students in the programs represented in this study and the fact that these trends reflect students who entered doctoral programs in the early 1990s. As the project develops, more minority students will be represented in the data, however, and more recent data will hopefully reveal more progress in reducing differences. In the future, the project will also document those strategies that have enabled specific programs to make the greatest progress in closing such gaps.

NEXT STEPS

Some of the interventions that programs and institutions have implemented as a result of this project are based on recommendations of prior researchers. Others are innovations designed by the project participants to address specific issues, such as late attrition in the humanities or the academic climate in the sciences for women and minorities.[12] Examples of the kinds of interventions that universities are using completion and attrition data to evaluate include:

Selection and Admissions
- Preadmission and preenrollment campus visits, to ensure a good match between students and the department

Mentoring and Advising
- Online student progress tracking, with interactive capacities to encourage communication between students and faculty
- Regular faculty/student meetings to discuss dissertation completion for "stalled" students
- Faculty workshops and retreats focused on advising, mentoring, and conflict management
- Peer mentor dinners to review departmental policies and practices in, for example, STEM fields. At one university these dinner meetings have resulted in policy changes in two departments and have led to decreased students' feelings of isolation and lowered the rates of early student attrition.

Financial Support and Structure
- New family-leave policies for graduate students
- Restructured science fellowships, with multiple years of support for underrepresented minority students

Curricular and Administrative Processes and Procedures
- Reevaluation of currency of comprehensive exams
- Reexamination, revision, or implementation of time-limit and continuous registration policies

Program Environment
- Academic climate focus group for minorities and women in the physical sciences

Research Experiences
- Dissertation workshops and retreats
- Poster session presentations by coalition of students and faculty on PhD attrition and completion issues facing minorities and women at national conferences, with reports back to departments

Professional Development
- Career workshops to encourage students considering nonacademic careers to complete their studies, and to inform them that the PhD is highly valued outside as well as inside academia.
- Transitional professional development resources for students who "master out" into professional careers.

Future research plans include the generation of case studies and the quantitative and qualitative analysis of multiple datasets in the PhD Completion Project. These analyses will aim to measure the impact of the above interventions and to explore such questions as: What are the upper limits and feasible targets for change in completion rates and attrition patterns within any given discipline? Are there commonalities in institutional characteristics among those institutions that have achieved higher-than-average rates or more than average progress over time in increasing their completion rates that might suggest the limits of some departmental interventions? And given the variety of institutional missions and resources, which departmental and institutional practices (within fields, disciplines, and among demographic groups) have proven most effective, and in what combinations, and which of these have proven least effective, or even counterproductive? Different types of institutions will likely arrive at different strategies to address challenges that may be common across disciplines and/or across demographic groups. For example, restructuring financial support (e.g., to ensure more continuous funding, or funding for a longer period of time) may be more important in some disciplines than in others, but such restructuring may not be possible for every institution. In some disciplines, or for some demographic groups, even if strong correlations between financial support and degree completion might suggest otherwise, the most beneficial interventions may in fact be in the area of mentoring and advising. In other disciplines, the early introduction of students to research alongside coursework may be the most beneficial strategy.

Some factors may fall outside the realm of institution influence, such as employment conditions in a discipline or in the surrounding regional economy, as well as the screening out of students who enter doctoral programs with an undeclared master's degree objective. Institutional characteristics and departmental policies and practices may even, however, interact with these so-called external contingencies. Determining how universities might best innovate and respond in disciplines that are particularly susceptible to fluctuations in the job market over time or how they might retain students in a regional environment or discipline where master's students are highly attractive are some of the questions that participants have expressed an interest in using this project to explore. All such questions will require the joint efforts of the CGS, the graduate deans designated as principal investigators and faculty researchers at participating universities, and the broader graduate education research community to answer.

The PhD Completion Project has already had an important early impact on the two fronts described at the beginning of this chapter: encouraging greater campuswide confidence in completion data, and promoting cultural change through data- and information-based decision making. Many universities are reporting that their participation in the project has resulted in an entirely new or significantly enhanced central data infrastructure. The project is receiving the strong support of presidents and provosts, and is strengthening the capacity of universities to include time to completion and attrition in campus decision making. Strategies to address completion and attrition issues have been incorporated, for example, into strategic planning, program review and assessment, and funding decisions (e.g., through the allocation of block grants to reward departments that have made progress in addressing attrition); and at least one university has incorporated the degree progress of students under a graduate adviser's direction in tenure and promotion decision-making processes. Numerous workshops, retreats, and weekly "brown bag" lunches for students and/or faculty on PhD completion and success strategies have opened up discussions about completion issues that had not previously taken place. And universities have reported the inclusion of previously unobtainable information on such things as early attrition patterns in these discussions as key to obtaining faculty buy-in.

Completion data are enabling universities to evaluate the impact over time of strategies implemented in the past and those being tried as a result of the PhD Completion Project grants. Universities are also looking to the project to provide benchmarking tools for comparing their own programs to others in the discipline: overall, by institutional type, or by peer group. For these purposes, the CGS is currently giving to each research partner institution an individualized report that provides comparative data to facilitate such benchmarking. One of the next steps for the project in the area of benchmarking is to develop an online mechanism that would enable universities to tailor this tool to their own needs by selecting their own preferences for sorting these data and viewing average completion and attrition rates and patterns within these parameters, calculated from institutions whom they can identify as peers. We expect that this combination of using data internally, to evaluate the impact of a university's activities over time, and more comparatively, to measure the impact of one's own activities and completion and attrition patterns against those of others, will empower graduate deans and schools to work even more effectively with faculty to create an environment where PhD completion is a priority consideration in overall discussions of how to enhance doctoral programs.

LOOK TO THE FUTURE

Statistically speaking, an orientation to doctoral study in the United States with a national average completion rate of 50 percent could adapt *The Paper Chase*'s Professor Kingsfield's injunction to incoming students with the much shorter phrase, "Look to your left." Even if the average rates are somewhat higher now than they once were or were originally believed to be, however, Kingsfield's original "look to your left and look to your right" scenario still probably paints too optimistic a picture of the statistical likelihood that students who enroll in a PhD program in the United States will complete it. But the statistical thinking driving the PhD Completion Project is not intended to describe the limits of what is possible for individual students entering a closed lottery with fixed chances; rather, the data generated in this project are intended to provide senior administrators, faculty, and students with the information needed to work together to reshape the conditions and redraw the limits of what is possible. The hope is that all universities will benefit from the data and best practices that emerge from the project so as to be able to say, on orientation day, "Look to your left. Look to your right. We have done everything in our power to create the conditions for each of you to achieve a PhD in your chosen field. The rest is up to you."

3

ADVOCATING APPRENTICESHIP AND INTELLECTUAL COMMUNITY

Lessons from the Carnegie Initiative on the Doctorate

CHRIS M. GOLDE, ANDREA CONKLIN BUESCHEL,
LAURA JONES, AND GEORGE E. WALKER

Despite a well-established reputation for excellence internationally, doctoral education in the United States faces growing competition from emerging centers of educational innovation abroad. Recent reform efforts have addressed the ability of doctoral programs to serve the development of their students and their preparation for various professional positions, or to contribute to society more broadly. A growing chorus is calling for increased attention to disciplinary boundaries, collaboration within and across fields, and the ability to integrate knowledge in new ways (see, for example, Golde and Walker 2006). It is within this context that we redefine apprenticeship and ground it within intellectual community.

The Carnegie Initiative on the Doctorate (CID) was a research and action project created to support departments' efforts to reexamine their doctoral programs. In all, there were eighty-four participating departments representing forty-four universities. As the initiative unfolded, two ideas emerged as central to our thinking.[1] The first is a reappropriation of the signature pedagogy of doctoral education: apprenticeship. The second proposes that a healthy and vibrant intellectual community provides the best environment for effective graduate education, and argues that it is possible to create such a community deliberately. These two strategies should reinforce one another. Strong, healthy apprentice relationships help foster a vibrant intellectual community, and a robust intellectual community supports positive, learning-centered relationships between its members. Although they are independent ideas and can exist separately, we argue that doctoral programs are stronger when both are present.

APPRENTICESHIP PEDAGOGY

One distinctive feature of doctoral education is that much of the important teaching and learning takes place in a one-to-one relationship between a novice "apprentice" (student) and a "master" (adviser). We would go so far as to call apprenticeship the signature pedagogy of doctoral education.[2] The tradition of close work between a faculty master and student apprentice is not the only approach to graduate teaching and learning; there are lecture courses and independent study. But "elbow learning" in seminars and labs has been the prevailing pedagogy of graduate education since the founding of American universities.[3] When the relationship is good, it is very, very good. Outstanding advisers challenge their students, set high expectations and standards, generously share their expertise, and individually tailor their students' educational experiences to meet students' needs. Unfortunately, when the relationship is bad, it can be horrid.

Without belaboring horror stories, we must recognize that problems can emerge in these relationships. Conformity is one danger; another is the inability of apprentices to develop an independent voice and line of thought. More insidiously, the student may be dependent on one faculty adviser who neglects or exploits the student. Traditions of solo sponsorship are coupled with norms of faculty autonomy. Consequently, students usually believe they have few avenues of recourse when they are mistreated or when a relationship sours. Faculty members and administrators are reluctant to intervene. The culture of faculty autonomy inhibits discussion of advising strategies and philosophies among faculty members. Consequently, we usually hear those who have learned from excellent advisers referring to themselves as "lucky." This highlights the uneven and uncertain access students have to high-quality advising.

The apprenticeship model has strengths by comparison to other common cultures of graduate training. These include the osmosis approach (students learn by reading good research and being near faculty who are doing high-quality research); the sink-or-swim theory (students are thrown into their initial teaching experience or research assignment and thrash their way to completion of the assignment with little guidance); the talented-students-will-self-discover assumption ("good" students figure out what they need to know and go get it or abandon the process); and the high-pressure crucible strategy (a doctoral program proceeds as a set of high-stakes tests and hurdles). These models do little to actively promote learning or take a deliberate guiding hand in the formation of scholars. Indeed, the cognitive sciences have shown us that most people learn more and develop further in a more purposefully constructed environment (for a summary, see Bransford, Brown, and Cocking 2000).

We believe it is possible to imagine new forms of apprenticeship tailored to doctoral education in the twenty-first-century American university. We want to reappropriate the word *apprenticeship* and free it from its connotations of indentured servitude. We propose a shift of prepositions: from a system in which students are apprenticed *to* a faculty mentor to one in which they apprentice *with* several mentors. Simply put, apprenticeship relationships are reciprocal relationships in the service of learning. They need not be exclusively one-on-one or senior-junior in character. Apprenticeship comprises a set of skills, practices, and dispositions that can be developed deliberately to benefit all parties. Our reframed mode of apprenticeship—apprenticed *with*—has four features.

Intentional Pedagogy

Apprenticeship is a theory of teaching and learning. As Brown and his colleagues have noted, apprenticeship is probably most recognizable and widespread in graduate education.[4] It begins with the observation of expert practice, followed by many opportunities for the novice to practice the skill being developed. With repetition and success, students move from simple to complex tasks and to situations of increased ambiguity in which they must exert independent thinking and decision making.

The role of mentors should not be underestimated.[5] As expert practitioners (masters), they must understand and explain the constituent parts of expert practice and demonstrate how they fit together in a whole. Mentors are responsible for making expert practice—their own and that of others—visible and understandable. In teaching the elements of being an expert researcher and scholar, mentors devise assignments that allow students to practice key tasks in low stakes, carefully designed situations and move in step-by-step fashion toward more accomplished, independent practice. These might be simulations (defending a grant proposal to a mock panel review), problems with known solutions (identifying research questions in published articles), or well-designed small components of a larger work (a course on scholarly publication or dissertation proposal writing). The student engages in repetitive practice with coaching and feedback.

Mentors provide "scaffolding," structured support provided in decreasing amounts over time. "Scaffolding is the support the master gives apprentices in carrying out a task. This can range from doing almost the entire task for them to giving occasional hints as to what to do next" (Collins, Brown, and Holum 1991, 2). As support is removed, the mentor fades, and the student takes on increased responsibility. Students are encouraged to reflect on what they are learning and to compare their work with that of experts. By sequencing tasks and using scaffolding appropriately, students are guided to the expert performance, transferring their knowledge and understanding to increasingly diverse settings.

This approach expects a lot from the mentors. They themselves need to be expert, to understand their expertise well enough to be able to model the whole, and to break the whole apart into constituent components, develop strategies for teaching the pieces, and help students integrate them back into the whole (for other examples, see Grossman and Compton et al. 2005). They must know when to offer guidance, and when to let students try and fail. This assumes that mentors have an internal model of the typical apprentice's development over time, as well as experience with the kinds of scaffolding and coaching that will move students along the trajectory toward expertise, independence, and interdependence. Ideally, mentors should customize learning experiences for each student, whom they know well. We know that these skills are not ones every graduate faculty member possesses; however, we are confident that all faculty can not only learn but benefit from these practices.

Students also have to work on these relationships. For many students the informal, one-on-one style of apprenticeship may be a new way to learn, especially in the context of formal schooling. The experiential nature of apprenticeship learning expects students to reflect on what they have done in order to develop models and patterns to generalize in other contexts. Students must take active responsibility for their own learning, and to feel empowered to take risks and be willing to fail.

Multiple Relationships

Today's students are best served by having several mentors. "The rapid growth of fields and of interdisciplinary work...means that incoming students often do not have interests that map closely onto those of a single faculty member" (Damrosch 2006, 38). Even if a new student's interests converge with those of a faculty member, versatility and a broad intellectual curiosity are essential. The world of work, whether inside or outside of the academy (or both), is complex and changing rapidly. No one mentor can possibly teach all of the necessary skills equally well, nor should students expect him to. The complexity of contemporary questions demands that students be able to integrate multiple perspectives and work collaboratively.

For all of these reasons the solo mentorship model does not adequately serve. We believe in multiple apprenticeship relationships for every student. Students ought to have research mentors as well as teaching mentors, and a variety of less formal mentoring relationships with faculty and peers as well. Moving away from a single dissertation adviser as mentor is familiar to some but a frightening leap for many. The reality is that one or two faculty members will probably assume primary responsibility for each student's development. Even with only two mentors, we recognize that a shift from sole responsibility for the student to shared responsibility requires new arrangements in how students are funded and how they are expected to spend their time. For their part, students must take an active role in seeking out several faculty members with whom to learn and in reconciling conflicting advice and expectations from their multiple mentors. This is easier, of course, if the department fosters a culture in which students are encouraged to actively shape their own educations.

So far we have emphasized a one-on-one perspective on apprenticeship pedagogy. But groups—courses, research labs, writing groups, cohorts—are important minicommunities for learning. Participating in a multigenerational group provides access to many teachers. Science labs are one example of a multigenerational work group in which students are mentored and also learn to mentor. In a research lab there is usually a strong culture in a lab of "cascading mentoring," in which postdoctoral fellows mentor senior graduate students, senior graduate students mentor junior graduate students, and junior graduate students mentor undergraduates. In seminars, a faculty member can mentor a number of students concurrently, and peers can mentor one another; this requires a creative vision of the seminar as an occasion for apprenticeship.

Collective Responsibility

Although having multiple mentors can mean dividing responsibility for research and teaching apprenticeships, we believe that many mentors working collaboratively, from a shared vision of student development as stewards, is preferable.[6] Apprenticeship teaching of graduate students is one of the department's most important collective goals and responsibilities. Taking collective responsibility means setting clear expectations and holding one another accountable.

Once faculty members develop a shared vision of the knowledge, skills, and habits of mind that they expect of the program's graduates it is easy to communicate clear expectations for student achievement. This is a precursor to taking collective responsibility for ensuring student formation. By making norms and expectations explicit in apprenticeship relationships—regarding expected progress through the program, goals for student development, a timeline for formally and informally identifying mentors, customary speed of response to draft papers and chapters, and the scope of conversation and documentation from annual reviews—fear and the potential for misunderstandings are reduced and higher levels of achievement are possible.

Holding one another accountable for students' development does not need to be intrusive. Instead, we believe that faculty members need to have more of the kinds of conversations that many already do: "How is Mike progressing? He is working with you as a TA, isn't he? How well did his recent lecture go?" Making students' development everybody's business means integrating "checking up" into daily life. Formally, annual reviews are a minimum. Informally, it is about a culture of shared, rather than abdicated, responsibility. Nevertheless, setting shared expectations means that faculty members are responsible for calling each other on unacceptable behavior. Just as certain behaviors (not coming to class, yelling at students) are not tolerated in the classroom, they cannot be excused outside of it. Students must be held accountable as well. They cannot be passive recipients of education; instead, they must actively define their own near-term and career goals, and seek out the experiences that will help them learn. Setting clear expectations for progress and making the expectations for high quality work clear can aid in this (Lovitts 2007).

Relationships Characterized by Respect, Trust, and Reciprocity

Apprenticeship with (vs. apprenticeship to) requires wholehearted and generous engagement. Apprenticeship relationships are more likely to flourish when they cultivate the qualities of respect, trust, and reciprocity. These qualities are important not simply because it is more pleasant to be in such a relationship but because they set the conditions that facilitate learning. These are also characteristics of vibrant intellectual communities, which are environments that foster learning.

A stance of mutual respect is the hallmark of a good apprenticeship relationship. How are the mentor's ideas and feedback incorporated into the student's work in a way that recognizes the teacher's greater experience, but also respects the student's growing intellectual independence? How are the student's ideas given room to grow and develop? Personal respect (which does not presuppose affection or friendship) is also important, and can build from respect for ideas. Trust grows over time from interactions based on respect.

Reciprocity within the relationship is the third leg of the stool. It is generally understood what students get from a healthy mentoring relationship with a faculty member: training, advice, sponsorship, funding, support, encouragement, and feedback. Faculty members get something too: new ideas, infusions of energy and excitement, the satisfaction of seeing students succeed, an intellectual legacy. Approaching the relationship from a stance of reciprocity reduces the inhibiting effects of hierarchy and promotes the free exchange of knowledge in both directions.

INTELLECTUAL COMMUNITY

Doctoral education is much more than a set of one-on-one relationships between advisers and students. A healthy intellectual community is a second organizing principle that we believe is critical to the success of doctoral education. Intellectual community is a condition—indeed, the foundation—for the core work of doctoral education: building knowledge.

Although it is possible to create and amass a great deal of knowledge independently, much of what we learn comes from interaction with others, formally or informally. We achieve more as individual scholars when we interact with others. This happens when a casual conversation suggests a different approach, or when a colleague helps identify a weakness in an argument. Cognitive science reminds us that "learning is fundamentally social" (Wenger 1996, 3). The more opportunities we have to interact in an intellectual community—in class, in offices, in social spaces—the more likely we are to share ideas, collect input, and learn more.

A vibrant intellectual community that values debate and collaboration provides a supportive context for the work of research, teaching, and, of course, learning. The culture of the department—that is, the nature of the intellectual community—affects how people wrestle with ideas, how teaching is valued, how students learn to engage with senior colleagues, how failure is treated, how people work together, and how independence and risk taking are viewed. Taken together these patterns of social interaction shape how scholars are formed and how well they develop, carrying forward the traditions of the field into new areas of understanding. The intellectual community is, in this sense, not simply a matter of potlucks and hallway conversation; it is "the hidden curriculum," sending powerful messages about purpose, commitment, and roles (Bender 2006, 305).

Some would claim that doctoral programs, following the patterns of faculty rewards, are settings that value individual achievement. In fact, individual achievements may not be as individual as they seem: "The hothouse effect...asserts that such singular 'creatives' are more likely to emerge from within a group of skilled practitioners than from isolation" (Kunstler 2004, 3). The point is not simply being part of a group, but being part of the *right* group: engaging with others who are interested, passionate, thoughtful, and creative. These kinds of interactions and the ideas they generate are a hallmark of the intellectual community.

As with apprenticeship relationships, intellectual communities can be deliberately designed and shaped. It should not be an afterthought but an integral consideration in any aspect of departmental life. Knowledge building can happen in many settings. The most obvious is as part of the formal curriculum. Seminars that encourage respectful habits of debate create new ideas and perspectives; labs where all members are invited to critique a hypothesis: these are places where leadership and collaboration contribute to the intellectual life of the department. By debating the big ideas that shape our disciplines, we both solidify what we value and move beyond what is no longer relevant. These exchanges bring vitality and energy to a community.

We highlight four qualities of intellectual communities, several of which recall the earlier discussions of apprenticeship. These qualities help reinforce each other in the service of doctoral education.

Broadly Inclusive. For an intellectual community to thrive, there must be active participation by many; there must be an appreciation for the generative potential of multiple perspectives. Welcoming diversity of viewpoints includes making the community multigenerational, as graduate students, postdoctoral fellows, and faculty of all ranks have roles to play. A department with a healthy intellectual community is marked by the level to which its most junior members are invited into the activities of the department: serving on committees, hosting outside scholars, planning events.

Flexible and Forgiving. One of the most important parts of the learning process is trying something new, making mistakes, and learning from failure. Creating spaces—literally and metaphorically—in which to test out new thinking is an important activity for students *and* faculty. In an academic culture that increasingly values "productivity," the need for reflection and thought is profoundly undervalued. We recognize the challenges this presents in the very real demands of meeting deadlines and deliverables, but if a student is not offered an opportunity to learn from failure, she may never develop the courage to take risks and demonstrate creative, original thinking. Those skills are essential to becoming an excellent scholar and steward.

Respectful and Collegial. As one CID participant explains it, there must be "camaraderie built on engagement, if not agreement." Although many departments may be collegial in a nominal sense, departments that "emphasize consensus, shared power, consultation and collective responsibility" are more productive and vital places as a result of genuine connections and community (Massy, Wilger, and Colbeck 1994, 12).

While thriving communities will vary in the style of their collegiality, the atmosphere should support interaction rather than isolation. A vibrant intellectual community is a place where people enjoy spending time together and are generous with their time, ideas, and feedback. "The extent to which the department is seen as a social network of relationships as well as a professional, discipline-oriented, community of scholars" was identified in the mid-1970s an important dimension of the departmental environment that can positively or negatively affect the nature and quality of the graduate student experience (Hartnett 1976, 71).[7]

Purposeful and Deliberate. It is clear that the complex cultural construct "robust intellectual community" must be the product not of accident but of purposeful action. Like all highly functioning workplaces, this community must be created, nurtured, fostered, and tended. To be sustainable, however, collegial activities must become routine. We can create settings that allow people of all backgrounds to be experts: journal clubs that rotate leadership, creating time when each member is expected to present and facilitate discussion; a miniconference with a poster session gives students a chance to present their work and explain it to others. Not surprisingly, these moments correspond directly to opportunities to learn. Because no one is expected to have all the answers, an open and respectful community allows people to be comfortable with what they do not know.

Last, but not least, the social components need attention. Much of the research on organizational culture points to the value of informal interaction; Brown and Duguid (2000) call this "incidental learning." And although incidental learning is, by definition, not something that can be planned, it is possible to create settings that facilitate that possibility: coffee machines, kitchens, places where students (especially those who do not have on-campus offices) can connect with others and keep in touch with the activities of the department. Events can be planned to include unstructured time so that conversations develop naturally. There may be an agenda that includes specific topics to cover, but just as often there should be occasions—meals, games, walks—that allow people to connect at a more individual, one-on-one level.

Although often taken for granted, intellectual community frames and shapes the experiences of doctoral students and faculty in ways that are not often valued or even noticed. In fact, it is most often noticeable by its absence. By taking an active role in shaping intellectual community, it is possible to create new knowledge and develop the next generation of scholars. This process will not only strengthen the community but reinforce the many other activities that occur within it, including apprenticeship learning.

A REINFORCING PROCESS: APPRENTICESHIP
AND INTELLECTUAL COMMUNITY

Many of the activities and characteristics described above overlap and reinforce each other nicely. Leading a journal club meeting one week, a student might raise a question for which no one has an easy answer. That question might trigger a new idea for a journal article by a mentor who invites the student to collaborate. Each of these experiences strengthens the development of the student and the ongoing knowledge of the community. Although we do not want to conflate apprenticeship and intellectual community, we do think it's worth acknowledging the many overlapping features that make them stronger.

Humane Relationships. Whether in the more tightly coupled mentoring relationships that characterize apprenticeship, or in the casual relationships every departmental member has with many others, the same interpersonal qualities are desirable. Cultivating relationships based on trust, respect, and collegiality yields the kind of professional generosity that we all treasure in academic communities.

Collective Vision. Our vision of an intellectual community that supports effective graduate education is predicated on a shared sense of purpose. At the broadest level, we hold that an intellectual community puts knowledge development and learning at its center. More specifically, we argue that the department should have a vision of the skills, knowledge, and habits of mind of a prototypical graduate. Important, and in parallel, our vision of apprenticeship requires reciprocal commitments. This vision takes place in a community where every student has multiple mentors, and in which the department (and all its members) take collective responsibility for student success and learning.

Learning and Improving. Like conducting research or writing, mentoring is not an innate talent but a learnable skill. Applying the ideas of apprenticeship pedagogy to apprenticeship itself means that faculty members need opportunities to practice mentoring, and perhaps to be mentored as well. It is a highly individual, complex process that requires adaptation and change; it does not work all the time for all the people in all the same ways. The British have addressed this problem with recent reform efforts: "It is now normal for institutions to require new supervisors to be trained before supervising students; some institutions now require regular continuing professional development for existing supervisors" (Eley and Jennings 2005, ix). By the same token, intellectual communities must be deliberately nurtured and encouraged.

Despite these overlaps and synergies we want to be clear that apprenticeship and intellectual community are not the same thing. The latter is not simply an aggregation of apprenticeship relationships: intellectual community is the setting in which learning takes place. Apprenticeship, on the other hand, is a teaching and learning strategy, a form of pedagogy. They are reinforcing, but independent, ideas.

PREDICTABLE OBSTACLES

We have already hinted at some of the predictable challenges and obstacles to implementing our vision. Two deserve particular attention: traditions of faculty autonomy and a lack of time. Perhaps because of their individualized nature, and because the mentoring relationship has largely been a private one, faculty members rarely discuss their philosophies or strategies of teaching or mentoring with one another. This is a lost opportunity for learning. Moving to our new vision of apprenticeship means directly challenging the norms of privacy and autonomy that mark advising relationships today.

When faculty members invest in their relationships with students it can have many intrinsic rewards, and often has instrumental payoff in research as well. But it rarely comes with public accolades or rewards. Shifting the culture of advising will be easier if, as the Committee on Science, Engineering, and Public Policy suggests, advising programs are embedded "in institutional systems of rewards and promotions" (1997, 66).

It can also be a challenge to publicly debate and defend one's vision of the purpose and mission of a department. Engaging in these discussions forces members of the department to invest in the community, intellectually and personally. This process, and resulting new expectations, can also take more time and energy. It takes time to learn a new way of doing things, whether it is interacting differently with students, or co-constructing a curriculum. If things seem to be working reasonably well, it's hard to convince people to invest time in rethinking their approach. Usually a crisis or external pressure forces that change.

We do not advocate change for change's sake. "It is easy enough to increase the number of venues and opportunities for intellectual exchange," one CID program team has pointed out, "but how do we increase the intensity of the engagement with texts and ideas? It is easy enough to get people in a room to talk about their work to others, but how can we more deliberately foster intellectual identities and scholarly personae? Is doing more of the same going to produce a leap in quality?" (Walker, Golde, et al. 2008, 131). These questions put the focus where it should be: on intellectual community as a means. Simply proliferating activities and structures does not necessarily lead to greater intellectual engagement and development. Rather, these strategies must be linked to and evaluated in light of the outcomes they are intended to produce. This demands that the department members engage in the hard work of defining a shared commitment to those outcomes.

Why It Matters

Most doctoral students enter graduate school fired up with enthusiasm and idealism. Along the way, this passion often seems to disappear. The positive side of this is that romantic ideals of academic life are replaced by more realistic goals. The negative side is that the zeal with which many begin their studies is unnecessarily eroded. Faculty decry this shift as much as students do, deploring the loss of passion in the quest for knowledge and its replacement with technical competence. It is vital to figure out how to help students maintain a devotion to learning that drives discovery and accomplishment.

Writing this chapter affords us the opportunity to step back and critically examine the process and structures of doctoral education. We have done so in partnership with many dedicated faculty members and graduate students at CID-participating departments. We continue to be surprised by how little scholarly and research attention has been turned to this important, albeit small, sector of higher education. It is almost impossible to explain to those who do not spend their days in academia that most institutions do not know what proportion of their doctoral students complete their studies—never mind having a good theory about why. Our inability to document the normal practices of graduate education, wholly apart from a concerted effort to assess the effectiveness of conventional practice, is discomforting.

In this chapter we have outlined two ideas—a reclaimed vision of apprenticeship, and intellectual community—that we believe hold great promise for resolving some of the problems that face graduate education in the United States today. By recommitting our doctoral programs to learning, and formation of doctoral students as stewards of their discipline, we can achieve so much. We can develop interdisciplinary solutions to complex problems facing our world. We can tackle the conundrums of doctoral student attrition and diversity. We can create communities that will make departments more competitive for graduate students and new faculty. And we can create doctoral programs in which more students achieve their full potential.

4

THREE WAYS OF WINNING DOCTORAL EDUCATION

Rate of Progress, Degree Completion, and Time to Degree

CATHERINE M. MILLETT AND MICHAEL T. NETTLES

The timeliness with which students progress through and complete doctoral programs has been frequently studied and debated (Hartnett and Willingham 1979; Spurr 1970; Wright 1957). As doctoral degrees are the least prescriptive of higher education degrees, the amount of time that students are expected to take to complete them has never been established. Since doctoral education has the unique function of preparing scholars, researchers, and university faculty, some tolerance on time to degree may have more to do with universities placing more emphasis on ensuring that candidates are adequately prepared, at the expense of focusing on the speed at which they complete the requirements to earn the degree.

The doctoral education process is judged for its cost and efficiency in much the same way as other levels of higher education; therefore, there is tension among graduate faculty and administrators as they seek the appropriate balance between the emphasis on amount of time and assurance of full preparation. This explains why researchers have been paying attention to the amount of time students spend working on their

Much of this chapter was based on the analyses in Michael T. Nettles and Catherine M. Millett. *Three Magic Letters: Getting to Ph.D.* © 2006 The Johns Hopkins University Press. Reprinted with permission of The Johns Hopkins University Press.

doctoral degrees. Time to degree can be viewed as a measure of both student success and institutional efficiency. It is one way to assess the pace that students progress in doctoral education, and completing the degree is the sign that the ultimate degree objective has been reached. In Nettles and Millett 2006 we have invented yet another way to measure student progress toward the degree that captures the pace of progress in achieving milestones leading up to degree completion. The new measure is called "rate of progress" and is a measure of the relative speed with which students achieve eight milestones leading to doctoral degree completion.

Much of the reason for focusing on these three critical outcomes, and for creating a new measure, is our interest in finding clues that will increase the timeliness of students' degree completion. Our interest also lies in the equitable access to the critical experiences so that all students, regardless of race or ethnicity, gender, and personal background, have the opportunity to succeed in doctoral education on comparable schedules to completion. Given the estimate that only half of all doctoral students persist until graduation (Bowen and Rudenstine, 1992), students who start a doctoral program are taking a gamble. We need to figure out how to increase their odds of winning on their gamble. We are especially interested in the opportunities for doctoral students to make steady progress toward their degree, to complete their degree, and in the time that it takes them to complete their degree. Two questions guide our analyses of the doctoral experience: (1) What are the race/ethnicity and gender differences in doctoral student rate of progress in their degree programs, in doctoral degree completion, and in the elapsed time to their degrees? (2) What contributes to doctoral student rate of progress, degree completion, and elapsed time to degree?

Methodology and Data Analyses

The research presented in this chapter is based on our book *Three Magic Letters: Getting to PhD* (Nettles and Millett 2006). First, we will briefly describe the methodology and data analyses. (For a more detailed discussion, consult chapters 3 and 4 and appendixes A–D in *Three Magic Letters*).

The sampling plan is a three-stage design. The first stage involved selecting twenty-one doctoral-granting universities and inviting them to participate; the second stage involved selecting the eleven fields of study; and the third stage involved selecting a stratified sample of students from the participating universities and the relevant fields of study. Doctoral students who were beyond the first year of their doctoral coursework, and who were actively engaged in their programs in the fall of 1996, were selected from the following eleven fields: biological sciences, mathematics, economics, physical sciences, education, political science, engineering, psychology, English, sociology, and history. For analytic purposes, the fields were collapsed into education, engineering, the humanities, science and mathematics, and the social sciences.

The eighty-eight-item Survey of Doctoral Student Finances, Experiences, and Achievements was developed for this study. The survey consists of seven sections: (1) the application and enrollment process, (2) current doctoral program experience, (3) attendance patterns, (4) financing your doctoral education, (5) future plans, (6) undergraduate experiences, and (7) background. The sample has 9,036 doctoral students, representing a 70 percent response rate. Men and women are equally represented in the sample. The distribution of the sample by race/ethnicity and citizenship is U.S. African Americans (10 percent), U.S. Asian Americans (9 percent), U.S. Hispanics (7 percent), U.S. whites (58 percent), and international students (16 percent).

The conceptual framework for the study focused on how students navigate the doctoral experience, including the progress that they make toward completing their degrees. The background characteristics include a student's gender, race/ethnicity, marital or domestic partnership status, household income, age, whether the student has children under eighteen, and the student's parental socioeconomic status (a measure of education and occupation). Two admissions credentials, Graduate Record Examination (GRE) general test scores (verbal, quantitative, and analytical) and the selectivity of the undergraduate college are included in each of the analyses. The analysis of degree completion also included whether the student's current program was his first/only choice doctoral program. For predicting each outcome, we selected a variety of doctoral program experiences including whether the student was attending a public or private graduate school, had a master's degree upon entry, had ever had a fellowship, had ever been a research assistant, had ever been a teaching assistant, had incurred educational debt during the program, had a mentor, was always full-time, had some research productivity, had expected his first job to be a faculty or a postdoctoral position, and the amount of time the student was in his doctoral program.

The statistical analyses are both descriptive and relational. The descriptive analyses include analyses of variance for continuous outcomes and chi-squares (cross tabs) for dichotomous (binary) outcomes in order to reveal similarities and differences among the race and gender groups within fields of study on the various dependent measures. The relational analyses consist of regressions by field of study. At the graduate level, the norms and practices with respect to such issues as funding and scholarship vary considerably. Our goal is not to compare the experiences across the fields, but to observe if there is parity within a field for men and women and students of various race or ethnic population groups. We performed logistic (dichotomous outcomes) regressions for each of the five fields. The main goals of the analyses are to identify instances of significant race, gender, and disciplinary differences.

The Three Ways of Winning

Rate of Progress

We constructed our rate of progress measure by grouping individuals by their fields of study and reported stages of progress. We settled on the following eight stages of progress: (1) completed less than half of the courses required for a doctoral degree; (2) completed more than half, but not all, of the courses required for a doctoral degree; (3) completed all course work required for a doctoral degree; (4) completed preliminary or general examinations but not yet admitted to doctoral candidacy; (5) admitted to doctoral candidacy but not yet working on dissertation; (6) working on dissertation; (7) completed all degree requirements for a doctoral degree, but degree not yet been awarded; and (8) doctoral degree awarded. With five field groups (education, engineering, the humanities, science and mathematics, and the social sciences) and eight possible stages, there are forty possible field-stage pairs. Next, we calculated the median number of years for each of these forty pairs. We then calculated the number of years for each individual person in the sample, based on her field and stage. The rate of progress measure was constructed by dividing this field- and stage-specific median value by the time each individual reported being in her doctoral program at the time the survey was administered. Specifically, this rate of progress measure takes the form relative progress = (median years$_{fs}$/ years$_{ifs}$), where i = individual, f = field group, and s = stage of progress. Here, values strictly greater than 1 indicate a faster rate of progress relative to the median student in the same stage, values strictly less than 1 indicate slower progress, and values equal to 1 indicate that the student has taken the median number of years to reach her particular stage of progress.

In our sample we found that engineering students were making the fastest progress toward their doctoral degrees, followed by students in science and mathematics, education, the humanities, and the social sciences. Engineering and science and mathematics are the two fields where doctoral training is most like that of professional schools, with clearly defined curriculums and a priori expectations of time to completion.

We found that education students progressed at a faster pace than humanities and social science students, despite being older and more often in school only part-time. Doctoral students in the social sciences progressed at a slower pace than did students in each of the other fields. We found some major field differences between the sexes. In engineering, women progressed at a faster rate than men, and in the social sciences, men progressed more quickly than women.

Completion Rates

Our research, while mainly cross-sectional, has a longitudinal component. On the one hand, our survey represents a snapshot of doctoral students who had completed at least one year of study and were enrolled in the fall of 1996. On the other hand, we sought outcome measures of doctoral attainment by tracking our sample of individuals through degree completion. To accomplish this we relied on dissertation abstracts, the graduation records of the participating universities, and doctoral degree completion information obtained from the National Science Foundation's Survey of Earned Doctorates. This process allowed us to compile rates of completion. Doctoral students who transferred and completed their doctoral degree requirements at another university were not included in our group of degree completers. We collected three pieces of information on degree completion: whether a student had completed the degree, the type of doctoral degree attained, and the calendar year in which the degree was conferred.

Overall, nearly 62 percent of the sample completed their doctorates within four years of survey response, from 1997 to 2001, the latest year for which degree completion data are available. The remaining 38 percent may or may not complete their doctoral degrees; the only way their completion rates can be determined would be to continue the search for an indeterminate number of years, using the same three sources.

As we would expect from the foregoing discussion on rate of progress, among our sample the fields with the largest completion rates were engineering (75 percent) and science and mathematics (72 percent). The only difference in completion rates between men and women was in education, where 54 percent of the women completed their degrees, compared with 49 percent of the men. Among the race/ethnicity groups, the key differences were the lower completion rates of African Americans in contrast to white and international students in engineering, science and mathematics, and the social sciences. The only difference between Hispanics and whites was in engineering, with 56 percent of Hispanics completing their degrees compared with 79 percent of whites.

Elapsed Time to Degree

Rates of doctoral student progress have typically been measured in three ways: total time to degree (the length of time from completing the bachelor's degree to completing the doctorate); elapsed time to degree (the amount of time from entering a doctoral degree program to completion); and registered time to degree (the amount of time registered in the doctoral program, from starting the program to completion).

Our goal was to create a measure of elapsed time to degree. The attendance pattern section of the survey asked students when (by term and year) they had begun their doctoral programs. To calculate an individual's time to degree, we subtracted the year and term the student started his doctoral program from the year he received the degree. We have degree completion data to 2001. We assumed that all students received their doctoral degrees in the spring, and therefore we added half a year to each degree year. For example, a student who started a doctoral degree program in the fall term 1994 (1994.75) and received the doctoral degree in the early summer of 1999 (1999.50) had a time to degree of 4.75 years. Engineering students were the fastest, at 4.75 years, followed by students in education, science and mathematics, and the social sciences, each at 5.75 years; humanities students had the longest median time to degree, 6.75 years.

In addition to median elapsed time to degree, we looked at mean elapsed time to degree (5.97 years) and continued our analyses to identify differences among fields and by race and gender. Overall, engineering students who completed their doctorates within our measurement frame averaged the least time to degree at 5.23 years. This was faster than the mean for science and mathematics (5.71), education (6.28), the social sciences (6.35), and the humanities (7.41). Although students in education were slower than those in two other fields, they showed the largest standard deviation (more than 3 units), indicating the widest variations among students' completion times.

In general, women in the sample who completed their doctorates within the period of the survey took nearly half of a year longer, on average, than their male peers (6.25 years, compared with 5.77 years). This pattern is similar to the pattern that Ibarra (1996) has observed among Latinos, where women had longer elapsed time to degree, which he attributed to their higher degree of part-time attendance. In our study, in the social sciences, male students averaged 6.11 years to the doctorate, while women averaged 6.59 years. With this exception, all fields were remarkably similar.

As might be expected given their faster rate of progress, international students who earned a doctoral degree were significantly ahead of all other groups in time to degree. They averaged 5.32 years, compared with 5.99 years for Asian Americans, 6.21 for whites, 6.26 for African Americans, and 6.34 for Hispanics. Examining these differences by field we found that international students in education (5.17) were ahead of both whites (6.50) and African Americans (6.27). In engineering, international students led at 4.89 years, compared with whites at 5.50 and Hispanics at 6.00. In science and mathematics, international students averaged 5.47 years, compared with whites at 5.76 years and Asian Americans at 6.02 years. In the social sciences, international students averaged 5.81 years to completion, compared with 6.46 for whites, 7.21 for Asian Americans, and 7.49 for Hispanics.

Several researchers have considered why time to degree might be protracted. It is not surprising that the reasons suggested for prolonging doctoral study are similar to those for failure to complete degrees. The type of financial support can hasten or lengthen time to degree (Abedi and Benkin 1987; Bowen and Rudenstine 1992; Ehrenberg and Mavros 1995; Gillingham, Seneca, and Taussig 1991; Hauptman 1986; National Research Council 1996; Nerad and Cerny 1991; Wilson 1965). Navigating the dissertation stage can also influence the time it takes to complete a degree (Council of Graduate Schools 1990; Isaac et al. 1989; Nerad and Cerny 1991; Rudd 1986).

What Contributes to Winning Student Experiences?

One bit of evidence that the three outcomes are distinctive is that they have variety in the factors that result in their variability. The following is an analysis of the factors that contribute to each of the three outcomes.

Rate of Progress

Rate of progress is our measure of students' median time through eight stages of their doctoral programs. This measure allows us to take a continuous snapshot of the factors that are important for students across the five fields of study. It is not surprising that, for all students in the sample, the largest predictor of steady progress in every field was continuous full-time enrollment (see table 4.1). As well, for students in education, engineering, and the humanities, having a mentor made a considerable positive difference in accelerating progress. Older students in education, engineering, the humanities, and science and mathematics appear to have made faster progress than younger students, and in the humanities and the social sciences, international students progressed faster than their white peers. In engineering, men made slower progress than

TABLE 4.1
Predictors of Rate of Progress in Doctoral Programs, by Field

Independent Variables[a]	Education[b]		Engineering		Humanities		Science/Math		Social Sciences	
	B	SE	B	SE	B	SE	B	SE	B	SE
Male	-0.024	0.065	-0.248**	0.087	0.058	0.065	-0.035	0.043	0.063	0.043
African American[c]	-0.077	0.108	0.058	0.189	0.144	0.144	0.105	0.134	0.069	0.086
Hispanic	-0.127	0.136	-0.187	0.189	-0.077	0.159	-0.112	0.137	-0.069	0.111
Asian American	-0.169	0.136	0.146	0.099	-0.004	0.144	-0.038	0.070	-0.181	0.095
International	0.118	0.128	0.136	0.077	0.315*	0.139	0.104	0.054	0.129*	0.063
Parents' SES[d]	0.089**	0.034	0.051	0.035	0.039	0.036	0.040	0.022	0.063**	0.024
Household income (in $1000s)	0.000	0.001	-0.003*	0.001	-0.001	0.001	-0.002*	0.001	0.000	0.001
Children under 18	0.013	0.065	-0.267***	0.089	-0.086	0.095	-0.176**	0.066	-0.228***	0.060
Age at start of doctoral program (in 1-year increments)	0.017***	0.004	0.053***	0.010	0.012*	0.006	0.022***	0.006	0.004	0.004
GRE Verbal (in 100s of points)	-0.222***	0.036	-0.086**	0.031	-0.033	0.045	-0.056*	0.023	-0.119***	0.025
GRE Analytic (in 100s of points)	0.103**	0.033	0.033	0.037	0.057	0.040	0.066**	0.025	0.055*	0.025
Master's upon entry	0.140	0.079	0.027	0.070	0.097	0.073	-0.030	0.060	0.134**	0.050
Private graduate school	0.165*	0.064	0.027	0.065	-0.020	0.071	0.158***	0.044	0.093*	0.045
Always full-time doctoral student	0.586***	0.068	0.315***	0.090	0.478***	0.086	0.356***	0.072	0.358***	0.059
Ever received a fellowship	0.101	0.066	-0.125*	0.063	-0.016	0.075	0.083*	0.042	-0.001	0.046
Ever was a teaching assistant	-0.166*	0.071	-0.027	0.061	-0.002	0.078	-0.013	0.046	0.027	0.047
Had some research productivity	-0.080	0.062	-0.121	0.064	0.004	0.067	-0.170***	0.040	-0.084	0.043
Incurred education debt as doctoral student	0.000	0.067	-0.068	0.094	-0.054	0.068	-0.047	0.060	-0.165***	0.046
Has a mentor	0.182**	0.063	0.176**	0.065	0.229**	0.075	-0.010	0.043	0.047	0.048
Constant	-0.482	0.271	-0.952	0.399	-1.097	0.359	-0.817	0.255	-0.242	0.234
n (unweighted)	2,419		861		1,309		1,806		2,426	
R²	0.108		0.091		0.094		0.062		0.120	

Source: Survey of doctoral student finances, experiences, and achievements.

[a] Married/domestic partner, selective undergraduate institution, GRE Quantitative, ever was a research assistant, and academic interactions with faculty were nonsignificant predictors in all fields and were dropped from the models.

[b] Unstandardized regression coefficients; dependent measure is standardized (M = 0; SD = 1).

[c] All racial groups and international students are compared to whites.

[d] Parents' SES is a composite of educational attainment and occupational prestige.

$*p < .05; **p < .01; ***p < .001$

women. In engineering, the social sciences, and science and mathematics students with children under the age of eighteen also made slower progress. For students in education and the social sciences, higher parental socioeconomic status was associated with faster progress; students in engineering and in science and mathematics with lower household incomes appear to have been slowed in their progress.

Counter to what one might expect, students with higher GRE verbal scores made slower progress in education, engineering, science and mathematics, and the social sciences. Students with higher GRE analytical scores made faster progress in education, science and mathematics, and the social sciences. Social sciences students who entered their programs having already earned master's degrees also made faster progress, as did those studying education, science and mathematics, and the social sciences at private graduate schools. Fellowship recipients in the field of engineering had a slower rate of progress, while those in science and mathematics progressed relatively faster when compared with nonrecipients. Students who held teaching assistantships in education, as well as students in science and mathematics who demonstrated some research productivity, appear to have made slower progress. Student debt burdens appear to be an impediment to progress only for students in the social sciences.

Doctoral Degree Completion

For our analyses of doctoral degree completion, only those students who had completed their degrees by 2001 (nearly 62 percent of the sample) were categorized as completers. Conceivably, as more respondents complete their degrees, some of the variables could increase in importance and others decrease, but for the moment, this glimpse of what has been happening is more extensive than any previous research. By analyzing the data for students who completed their degrees, we are able, at least, to provide a fresh look at the elements that contributed to their success.

Research productivity proved to be an important predictor of doctoral degree completion in all five fields (see table 4.2). Students in science and mathematics with research productivity were 3.9 times more likely to complete their doctorates than those without. In the other four fields, the effect was similar, although not as large: the humanities, 3.0 times; engineering 2.7 times; education, 1.8 times; and the social sciences, 1.6 times. With the exception of engineering, another key predictor of degree completion was maintaining full-time enrollment. In science and mathematics, students who maintained full-time enrollment were 4.0 times more likely than their part-time peers to complete their degree

TABLE 4.2
Predictors of Doctoral Degree Completion by 2001 for Students beyond the First Year, by Field

Independent Variables[a]	Education[b]			Engineering			Humanities			Sciences and Math			Social Sciences		
	Odds	Inverse Odds	Odds SE	Odds	Inverse Odds	Odds SE	Odds	Inverse Odds	Odds SE	Odds	Inverse Odds	Odds SE	Odds	Inverse Odds	Odds SE
Male	0.801	1.248	0.098	0.702	1.424	0.142	0.931	1.074	0.163	0.947	1.056	0.120	1.084		0.133
African American[c]	0.707	1.415	0.145	0.150***	6.686	0.061	0.936	1.068	0.373	0.511	1.956	0.197	0.790	1.265	0.197
Hispanic	0.704	1.421	0.169	0.407*	2.459	0.167	0.852	1.174	0.369	0.585	1.709	0.240	0.521*	1.919	0.161
Asian American	0.972	1.029	0.253	0.558**	1.791	0.122	1.110		0.404	0.645*	1.551	0.134	0.806	1.241	0.218
International	1.304		0.308	1.219		0.241	1.547		0.605	0.999	1.001	0.164	1.612**		0.282
Age at start of doctoral program (in 1-year increments)	0.993	1.007	0.009	0.931**	1.074	0.022	1.019		0.018	0.984	1.016	0.018	0.977	1.024	0.013
Married/domestic partner	1.294*		0.163	2.167***		0.346	1.247		0.228	1.306*		0.166	1.181		0.148
Children under 18	0.756*	1.322	0.101	1.031		0.246	1.333		0.371	0.889	1.125	0.190	0.860	1.162	0.156
GRE Verbal (in 100s of points)	0.831**	1.203	0.059	0.821**	1.218	0.062	0.870	1.149	0.107	0.979	1.022	0.069	0.814**	1.228	0.059
GRE Analytic (in 100s of points)	0.889	1.124	0.056	0.907	1.102	0.083	1.072		0.117	0.974	1.026	0.076	1.198*		0.086
Master's upon entry	1.433*		0.201	0.973	1.028	0.164	1.162		0.230	1.052		0.198	1.177		0.169
Private graduate school	1.025		0.120	1.092		0.181	1.355		0.266	1.500**		0.204	1.052		0.134
Selective undergraduate institution	1.149		0.153	1.213		0.222	1.303		0.247	1.365*		0.202	1.202		0.166
First/only choice of doctoral program	1.187		0.181	1.444*		0.223	0.919	1.089	0.163	1.503***		0.183	1.251		0.151

Variable	(1) OR	(1) SE	(2) OR	(2) SE	(3) OR	(3) SE	(4) OR	(4) SE	(5) OR	(5) SE
Always full-time doctoral student	1.649***	0.218	1.374	0.308	2.761***	0.723	3.984***	0.936	1.868***	0.337
Time in doctoral program (in years)	1.166***	0.028	1.261***	0.059	1.318***	0.053	1.624***	0.070	1.285***	0.042
Ever received a fellowship	1.381**	0.171	1.091	0.168	1.074	0.221	1.100	0.142	1.072	0.141
Ever was a research assistant	1.142	0.153	1.284	0.229	1.125	0.210	1.379	0.179	1.240	0.154
Ever was a teaching assistant	1.482**	0.193	0.757 (1.320)	0.110	1.877**	0.424	1.054	0.146	1.252	0.170
Has a mentor	1.390**	0.169	1.675***	0.249	1.352	0.290	1.185	0.152	1.491**	0.204
Expect first job to be faculty/postdoctoral fellowship position	1.285*	0.154	0.829 (1.206)	0.132	1.181	0.242	1.615***	0.194	1.356*	0.170
Had some research productivity	1.800***	0.215	2.733***	0.413	3.021***	0.555	3.895***	0.515	1.556***	0.197
Constant	0.964	0.509	11.004	11.221	0.014	0.015	0.044	0.035	0.132	0.035
n (unweighted)	1,436		769		1,107		1,581		2,105	
Likelihood ratio test	207.43***		219.33***		183.52***		552.10***		216.30***	
McFadden pseudo R²	0.101		0.144		0.185		0.235		0.114	

Source: Survey of doctoral student finances, experiences, and achievements.

[a]Parents' SES, household income, GRE Quantitative, and incurred educational debt as a doctoral student were nonsignificant predictors in all fields and were dropped from the models.

[b]Dependent measure is dichotomous. (No=0. Yes=1.) Odds ratio coefficients. Inverse odds ratio (1/odds ratio) are presented for odds ratios less than 1.

[c]All racial groups and international students are compared to Whites.

*p < .05; **p < .01; ***p < .001

programs; for the humanities, 2.8 times more likely; for the social sciences, 1.9 times; and for education, 1.6 times. Students who had spent more time in the program were slightly more likely to complete their degrees in every field except education. Education is also by far the field with the longest time to degree.

Having a mentor made a small but significant contribution toward degree completion in the fields of engineering (1.7), the social sciences (1.5), and education (1.4). Students in the fields of education, science and mathematics, and the social sciences who expected their first postdoctoral job to be as college faculty or a postdoctoral researcher were also slightly more likely to complete their programs ahead of their peers with other career intentions.

Various funding options played a limited role in predicting degree completion. Being a teaching assistant somewhat improved a student's chances of completion in both education and the humanities. Research assistantships made a slight contribution in science and mathematics. Holding a fellowship was significant only for students in education.

What role did admissions criteria play in predicting degree completion? Attending one's first-choice doctoral program made a small but significant contribution toward completion in engineering and in science and mathematics. Students in education, engineering, and the social sciences who achieved higher GRE verbal scores were less likely to complete their doctorates than their peers with lower scores. Students in social sciences with higher GRE analytical scores were also less likely to finish their degrees.

Gender did not influence degree completion in any field. In engineering, African Americans were 6.7 times less likely, Hispanics 2.5 times less likely, and Asian Americans 1.8 times less likely than whites to complete their degrees. Compared with those of their white peers, the odds of completing their degrees were also lower for Hispanics in the social sciences and for Asian Americans in science and mathematics. In engineering, older students were less likely than younger ones to finish their degrees. However, engineering students who were married or had domestic partners were twice as likely to finish their doctorates, as were married students in education and in science and mathematics, although the effect was less strong. The presence in the household of children under the age of eighteen appears to have been an impediment to completion only in the field of education.

Time to Degree

For the nearly 62 percent of the sample who completed their degrees over the four years of the study, we have been able to calculate time to degree by matching the individuals with the dates at which they started their programs. Aside from continuing full-time enrollment, which as we might expect was a significant predictor of faster progress in all five fields, the other significant predictors vary by field (see table 4.3).

Among the demographic characteristics found to be related to time to degree were a few race-ethnicity matters and socioeconomic status effects. Hispanics in engineering took three-quarters of a year longer, and Asian Americans one-third of a year longer in science and mathematics and nearly a year longer in the social sciences, than whites to complete their programs. In the fields of engineering and the social sciences, the higher the students' parental socioeconomic status, the less time it took them to earn their degrees. Engineering students with relatively high household incomes took more time to achieve their degrees, as did students in science and mathematics.

It appears that having a mentor in the humanities and the social sciences is associated with shorter time to degree. This is another example of how mentoring positively influences student experiences, but notably not in every field. How students financed their doctoral degrees played a limited role in determining time to degree. None of the three major forms of student support—fellowships, teaching assistantships, or research assistantships—predicted time to degree. Only in the social sciences was debt incurred as a doctoral student a factor in lengthening time to degree.

Students with higher GRE verbal scores took significantly longer to finish their degrees in the fields of education, engineering, science and mathematics, and the social sciences. Conversely, higher GRE analytical scores predicted shorter time to degree in education, science and mathematics, and the social sciences. Prior attendance at a selective undergraduate institution predicted longer time to degree for engineering students, as did attendance at a private graduate school for both engineering and social sciences students. However, attendance at a private graduate school was associated with a shorter time to degree for science and mathematics students. Earning a master's degree before entering a doctoral program also promoted a shorter time to degree in both education and engineering. While the presence in the household of a spouse or partner was a stronger predictor of a shorter time to degree for students in engineering, the humanities, and science and mathematics, the presence in the household of children under eighteen was a strong predictor of longer time to degree for students in engineering, the humanities, and the social sciences. Age was a factor only for students in education, reducing the time to degree.

TABLE 4.3
Predictors of Elapsed Time to Degree for Doctoral Degree Completers by 2001, by Field

Independent Variables[a]	Education[b]		Engineering		Humanities		Science/Math		Social Sciences	
	B	SE	B	SE	B	SE	B	SE	B	SE
Male	-0.071	0.221	0.155	0.139	-0.085	0.260	0.110	0.085	-0.265	0.154
African American[c]	0.200	0.387	-0.032	0.388	-1.155	0.615	0.249	0.329	-0.128	0.328
Hispanic	-0.239	0.466	0.695*	0.348	0.105	0.661	0.370	0.287	0.869	0.443
Asian American	-0.103	0.435	-0.172	0.168	-0.119	0.569	0.362**	0.139	0.877*	0.342
International	-0.114	0.422	-0.136	0.130	-0.147	0.557	0.012	0.114	-0.087	0.225
Parents' SES[d]	-0.217	0.113	-0.167**	0.056	0.062	0.147	-0.017	0.044	-0.243**	0.086
Household Income (in $1000s)	0.006	0.003	0.009***	0.002	0.009	0.006	0.012***	0.002	0.003	0.003
Married/domestic partner	-0.245	0.263	-0.375**	0.120	-0.670*	0.315	-0.345***	0.098	-0.107	0.177
Children under 18	-0.217	0.232	0.558***	0.148	0.863*	0.356	0.134	0.135	0.805***	0.213
Age at start of doctoral program (in 1-year increments)	-0.047**	0.015	-0.028	0.016	-0.017	0.026	-0.019	0.013	-0.016	0.016
GRE Verbal (in 100s of points)	0.691***	0.119	0.171***	0.050	0.081	0.176	0.255***	0.045	0.398***	0.088
GRE Analytic (in 100s of points)	-0.434***	0.108	-0.067	0.058	-0.097	0.156	-0.130**	0.050	-0.278**	0.089
Selective undergraduate institution	0.030	0.240	0.384***	0.123	0.210	0.289	-0.163	0.097	-0.248	0.177
Private graduate school	0.300	0.214	0.389***	0.103	0.272	0.276	-0.236**	0.087	0.339*	0.153
Master's upon entry	-0.768**	0.267	-0.304*	0.112	-0.164	0.283	0.064	0.123	-0.203	0.178
Always full-time doctoral student	-1.860***	0.225	-0.333*	0.146	-1.906***	0.338	-0.674***	0.151	-1.273***	0.220
Has a mentor	-0.294	0.220	-0.152	0.109	-0.762*	0.320	-0.111	0.090	-0.469**	0.176
Incurred education debt as doctoral student	0.111	0.229	-0.082	0.150	0.375	0.266	0.182	0.120	0.676***	0.163
Constant	7.866	0.911	5.442	0.606	9.725	1.372	6.068	0.519	7.392	0.816
n (unweighted)	1,304		650		610		1,299		1,281	
R²	0.179		0.113		0.189		0.079		0.203	

Source: Survey of doctoral student finances, experiences, and achievements.

[a] GRE Quantitative scores, ever was a research assistant, ever received a fellowship, ever was a teaching assistant, and had some research productivity were nonsignificant predictors in all fields and were dropped from the models.

[b] Unstandardized regression coefficients; dependent measure is standardized (M = 0; SD = 1).

[c] All racial groups and international students are compared to whites.

[d] Parents' SES is a composite of educational attainment and occupational prestige.

*p < .05; **p < .01; ***p < .001

IMPLICATIONS FOR PRACTICE

The pressures of efficiency and accountability in doctoral education cannot be ignored. Questions of time to degree, rate of progress, and completion rates will become as common as they are at the undergraduate level and will rival questions of publication rates, grant funding, and student qualifications for the attention of graduate faculty. We have introduced a new measure of efficiency that we call *rate of progress*, which we believe to be a reasonable barometer of time to degree, allowing both faculty and students to assess students' accomplishments and progress. Graduate faculty may eventually wish to set standards and expectations that can be conveyed to students about expected rates of progress and time to completion. We might then expect differences in the rates across disciplines to dissipate—or at least to be explained by differing requirements in different disciplines and fields.

5

CONFRONTING COMMON ASSUMPTIONS

Designing Future-Oriented Doctoral Education

MARESI NERAD

Tempora mutantur et nos mutamur in illis; one would think that this Latin proverb—"The times are changing and we are changing with them"—applies to all sectors of life and all societies. However, in the United States, doctoral education is, for the most part, still structured as if it were meant to prepare students for life as university professors— as if times have not changed and graduate students have stayed the same. This outdated assumption is one of a number of common erroneous assumptions that are still in the minds of faculty and higher education policymakers and are perpetuated by the dominant media. Others are:

1. All students who study for a PhD want to become professors.
2. Professorial positions are highly desirable, and the best doctoral recipients become professors.
3. The career paths of these people are linear and smooth traditional academic careers, moving from PhD completion to assistant professor, with perhaps two years of postdoctoral fellowship in between, then to associate professor, and on to full professor.
4. Everybody who successfully completes a PhD will most likely choose the very best academic job offer, unconstrained by relationship and family concerns.
5. Professors enjoy the highest job satisfaction compared to any other employment group.

Most of these assumptions are outdated and based on anecdotal information rather than empirical data.

Astonishingly, there is little actual knowledge of what happens to PhD recipients or of their employment status five to ten years after degree completion (National Research Council 2005b; Nerad 2004; Long 2001; Nerad and Cerny 1999 (b); National Research Council 1998; COSEPUP 1995; Nerad 1997). Until very recently we were left with a perplexing problem: How can we understand the effectiveness of our programs when we have no idea what happens to our PhD holders? How can the next generation of faculty improve doctoral education if we do not create a feedback loop from those who have applied their education and who, from the advantage of employment experience, can also evaluate the quality of their education (Aanerud, Homer, Nerad, and Cerny 2006)? Although currently enrolled students can evaluate their experience—as is increasingly done today in institutional exit surveys—they cannot adequately evaluate the quality of their education without having had an opportunity to apply it (Golde and Dore 2001). To shed light on the effectiveness of doctoral education, three national studies set out to fill in the gaps by providing empirical evidence to answer these questions. Nerad and Cerny undertook the PhDs-Ten Years Later study in 1996 and 1997 with funding from the Andrew Mellon Foundation and the National Science Foundation. In 2001 they surveyed art historians, PhDs in Art History–Over a Decade Later, funded by a grant from the Getty Foundation. Social Science PhDs—Five+ Years Out, fielded in 2005 and 2006, is the third national survey of doctorate recipients directed by CIRGE principal investigator Maresi Nerad. This study was funded by the Ford Foundation.

In this chapter the results of these three comprehensive national PhD career path and educational outcome studies are presented. These studies have been the basis for confronting common assumptions about PhD holders and questioning whether we prepare our doctoral students adequately for the present and future in an era of globalization and increasing national interest in the role of doctoral education for the knowledge economy. In addition, comparative research that the author has undertaken over the years into innovation in doctoral education in Australia, Germany, and Japan has made it possible to identify characteristics of future-oriented doctoral education (Considine and Marginson et al. 2001; Grant 2002; Marginson 2004; Mcwilliam and James 2002; Nerad and Heggelund, 2008; Nerad 1994). The author argues that we need to begin now to implement such forward-looking doctoral education. The next generation of professors will need to prepare their doctoral students not just to be expert scholars but also to become world citizens who are aware of the negative effects of globalization and who are equipped to operate as informed leaders and responsible citizens on the world stage (Banks 2004; Parker 1996). In the history of universities we have come full circle from universities being universal centers of learning in the ancient period, to becoming nation-state universities that pursued national interests, to again emerging as international centers of learning and scholarship (Kerr 1994).

EMPIRICAL FINDINGS CHALLENGE OUTDATED ASSUMPTIONS

The following findings come from three national career-path studies: PhDs—Ten Years Later, (Nerad and Cerny 1999a; Nerad and Cerny 1999b; Nerad and Cerny 2000; Nerad and Cerny 2002; Nerad, Aanerud, and Cerny 2004) PhDs in Art History—Over a Decade Later, (Sadrozinski, Nerad, and Cerny 2003) and Social Science PhDs—Five+ Years Out (Nerad, Rudd, Morrison, and Picciano 2007). The first study, PhDs—Ten Years Later, surveyed six disciplines at sixty-one U.S. universities, capturing 57 percent of PhDs awarded in these disciplines during three consecutive years, 1982–85. The survey had a response rate of 66 percent for U.S. citizens and permanent resident PhD holders and 51 percent for international PhD holders. The disciplines surveyed were biochemistry, computer science, electrical engineering, English, mathematics, and political science. The second survey, PhDs in Art History—Over a Decade Later, surveyed all art history PhD holders who completed their degrees between 1985 and 1991. This study had a 70 percent response rate. The third study, Social Science PhDs—Five+ Years Out, surveyed anthropology, communication, geography, history, political science, and sociology PhD holders who graduated between 1995 and 1999. This study yielded a 45 percent response rate.

The questionnaires used in all these studies collected information on the career path, the search for a first job, a retrospective evaluation of the quality of doctoral programs, an assessment of the usefulness of the doctoral degree, and recommendations for current doctoral programs and students. Since 2002, starting with the art history study, the survey instrument has also tracked the relationship and family path parallel to the career path (Sadrozinski et al. 2003).

ALL PhD STUDENTS WANT TO BECOME PROFESSORS

The PhDs—Ten Years Later study showed that the first commonly held assumption—that all graduate students strive to become professors—was true for only about half of the PhD recipients in the six major fields surveyed (Nerad et al. 2004; Nerad and Cerny 1997). Moreover, the variations among fields were great. When asked about their career goals at the completion of their doctoral studies, among PhD holders in English and political science, most (81 percent and 72 percent, respectively) wanted to become professors, while 19 percent of electrical engineering and 32 percent of those with PhDs in biochemistry had academic career ambitions. Among art history PhDs holders, upon degree completion 71 percent wanted to become professors (Sadrozinski et al. 2003). The Social Science PhDs—Five+ Years Out study found that the intent to become a professor ranged from a high of 78 percent of historians to a low of 57 percent of geographers at the start of PhD studies (Nerad et al. 2007). Upon PhD completion, 84 percent of historians and 65 percent of geographers wanted to become professors. The findings indicate that overall about one forth of the doctoral students and about half of science and engineering students did not intend to become professors at the time of degree completion.

TABLE. 5.1
Career Goal at PhD Completion and Percent Tenured or Tenure–Track 5+ Years Later

	(1) Wanted to Be Professor (%)	(2) Tenured or TT of (1) (%)	(3) Tenured or TT of All PhD Holders (%)	N of All PhD Holders		
				(1)	(2)	(3)
Anthropology	72	64	52	407	261	371
Communication	75	84	71	319	214	299
Geography	65	74	53	155	96	152
History	84	76	66	789	614	757
Political Science	76	80	66	674	489	647
Sociology	75	78	63	521	362	495

Source: Center for Innovation and Research in Graduate Education, University of Washington, "Social Science PhDs–Five+ Years Out."

TABLE. 5.2
Career Goal at PhD Completion and Percent Tenured 10–14 Years Later

	(1) Wanted to Be Professor (%)	(2) Tenured of (1) (%)	(3) Tenured of All PhD Holders (%)	N of All PhD Holders
Biochemistry	32	34	19	(605)
Computer Science	46	61	34	(282)
Electrical Engineering	19	67	22	(328)
English	81	64	55	(767)
Mathematics	54	73	54	(522)
Political Science	72	66	53	(455)

Source: Center for Innovation and Research in Graduate Education, University of Washington, "PhDs–Ten Years Later."

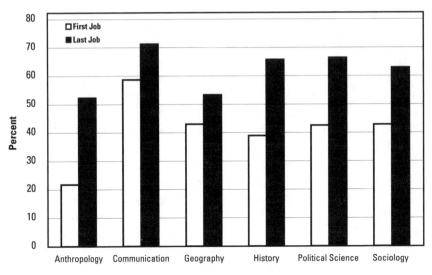

Figure 5.1. Percent tenure track and/or tenured in first and last job.

Source: Center for Innovation and Research in Graduate Education, University of Washington, "Social Science PhDs–Five+ Years Out."

The three national PhD outcome studies reviewed here find that, overall, between 50 and 65 percent of respondents, regardless of their career goals, held faculty positions at the time of survey completion. The other 35 to 50 percent of the PhD recipients were employed in business, government and nonprofit sectors (hereafter referred to as BGN). The largest proportions of PhD holders working outside academia were electrical engineers and computer scientists, followed by biochemists. In art history, 53 percent held faculty positions ten years after completing their studies and 47 percent worked outside academia, except for nine percent who were lecturers. The overall studies' findings revealed that not all doctoral students want to become professors and that among those who sought an academic career, not everybody realized their career goals.

The Best Doctoral Recipients Become Professors

The common assumption that the "best" people—measured by traditional standards of short time to degree and multiple publications at time of completion—become professors held true only for English and political science in the fields surveyed for PhDs—Ten Years Later. Logistic regression analyses indicated that short time to degree and number of publications was not associated with tenure status for PhDs in biochemistry, electrical engineering, and mathematics. Shorter time to degree was associated with tenure at the time surveyed for computer scientists. Higher-ranking PhD programs were associated with higher likelihood of holding tenure when surveyed. However, in fields with an attractive job market outside academia, such as computer science and electrical engineering, the association with the rank of the program was not significant. Among art historians time to degree was not associated with tenure status at the time of the survey, and the number of publications was positively associated with the likelihood of holding tenure for women only. The study findings indicate that traditional indicators of PhD holders' qualities such as short time to degree and multiple publications were limited indicators of predicting professorial career outcomes.

LINEAR AND SMOOTH CAREER PATHS

Another assumption that proved not to be true was that the career path from PhD to postdoctoral appointment (if expected in a field) to assistant professor to tenured professor is the dominant pattern for PhD recipients and its primary hallmark is its linearity. All three studies showed the same picture. About one-third of the PhDs began their careers in a tenure-track position, however over half of all PhDs had ended up in a tenured or tenure-track position at the time of the surveys. This finding implies that academic career paths are not linear. Many people start out in non-tenure-track positions and over a period of four or more years switch to tenure-track positions (Nerad et al. 2007; Nerad et al. 2004; Nerad and Cerny 1999 [a]). This finding underscores the need to observe PhD career paths for several years after graduation rather than relying on surveys on doctorate employment one or two years after degree completion, in order to gain an accurate picture of the career path and career outcomes of PhDs.

EVERYBODY CAN TAKE THE BEST ACADEMIC JOB OFFERED UNCONSTRAINED BY FAMILY CONCERNS

Embedded in the assumption of linearity is the fourth assumption, that a person is able to fully optimize her career options and take the best job offered after PhD completion. Among respondents to PhDs—Ten Years Later we found that the majority of women PhD holders partnered with someone who holds a PhD, MD, or JD, compared with one-third or fewer of the men. In biochemistry and mathematics the difference is even greater: 75 percent of the women biochemists had a partner with a PhD, MD, or JD, compared with only 24 percent of the men. In mathematics, 84 percent of women had a highly educated spouse, but only 25 percent of men did (Aanerud et al. 2007). Among art history PhDs, almost half (47 percent) of partnered women had spouses with a PhD, MD, or JD, while only one-third of partnered men had such highly educated partners (Rudd et al. 2008).

After degree completion, during the time of the job search, the challenges of being a dual-career couple emerge. Our survey included a question about the most important reasons for choosing the first job. The answers from women and men differed significantly. The women were far more concerned that their partners also had a good opportunity than were the men. The difference can be explained by the fact that the women tended to live with someone who could not easily give up one job and find another similar one in any location. The majority of men were partnered with someone who was more mobile; thus, men did not need to be concerned about the partner's ability to move. This finding implies that the pursuit of careers is far more complicated for women than for men.

The career-path study PhDs in Art History—Over a Decade Later allowed us to shed more light into the complicated situation of dual-career couples—a situation that needs to be addressed at present and in the future as the number of women PhD holders increases (Rudd et al. 2008). In the art history study we tracked career paths simultaneously with relationship and family paths. Both men and women named their partners as the major influence on their careers. However, the proportion of women who named their partners as the most influential on their careers was significantly larger than that of men. Women named children as the second factor that influenced their career. A third factor was the caretaking of a family member, including a parent, which overwhelmingly is done by women (Sadrozinski et al. 2003).

Comparing tenure status at the time of the survey by gender and family status among art history PhDs reveals the complex interaction of family, gender, and careers. Women and men who remained single had the same rate of tenure. Women in stable relationships with no children received tenure at the same rate as did single women. However, men in stable relationships received tenure at a significantly higher rate than single men or women in stable relationships. Women in stable relationships with children had a lower tenure rate than women in relationships with no children. However, men in stable relationships with children had the highest tenure rate. Stable relationships and children increase men's likelihood for a successful faculty career, while both factors decrease the chances of earning tenure for women. In sum, the marriage patterns of women PhD holders have a significant impact on their career paths. Historically, women PhD recipients were either barred from employment at the same institution as their husbands because of antinepotism laws or they took administrative rather than research and teaching positions to remain in academia (Shoben 1997; Stephan and Kassis 1997). Today, given the growing number of women earning PhDs, coupled with the changing economic structure of colleges and universities, the issue of an academic secondary labor market is especially acute. The reviewed studies indicate clearly that not all PhD holders can make career choices unconstrained by relationship and family considerations.

ACADEMIC FACULTY ENJOY THE HIGHEST JOB SATISFACTION

Another common assumption—that academic faculty enjoy the highest job satisfaction—also proved to be outdated. In the PhDs—Ten Years Later study, managers and top executives in the BGN sectors were the most satisfied with their employment, and not the permanent faculty (Nerad, Aanerud, and Cerny 2004). The reason for their high job satisfaction was not salary but the intellectual challenge of work and autonomy at the workplace. Both of these are job qualities that we traditionally have attributed to an academic work setting. Tenured faculty ranked fourth in job satisfaction among those surveyed for PhDs—Ten Years Later. The Social Science PhDs—Five+ Years Out study compared job satisfaction on three dimensions that were constructed from twenty items with a factor analysis: satisfaction with the work itself, with status, and with overall quality of life. Overall, social science PhD holders indicate high levels of satisfaction with their work in and of itself, but they are less satisfied with their status (a dimension that includes income and advancement opportunities). Satisfaction with the quality of life (a dimension including work and family balance) ranged between the high satisfaction of their work in and of itself and the low satisfaction with their status. Comparing tenure-track and tenured faculty to other academic employees (including non-tenure-track faculty and senior professional positions) and to people working in the BGN sectors reveals few differences in patterns of satisfaction. Most notably, however, ladder faculty are more likely to be very satisfied with their work in and of itself, while those employed in academia but not on a tenure track are more likely to indicate being very satisfied with their overall quality of life. Employees in the BGN sectors and those in tenure-track and tenured faculty jobs are equally likely to be very satisfied with status and with quality of life, although BGN employees are somewhat less likely to indicate being very satisfied with their work itself. All three surveys found that in all fields, including English, PhDs employed in the BGN sectors earned a higher salary than those in academia.

These findings have several implications: first, that the doctoral degree itself is put to many different uses in a variety of employment sectors; second, that doctoral education has been and can be the passport to a successful career path in many sectors; and third, that the university as a workplace is not the most attractive destination, as has been commonly assumed. Such empirical information is essential in our attempt to prepare doctoral students for the future. This information tells us that PhD education proves to be useful and valuable for doctoral recipients. However, it also reveals that doctoral education needs some modification as the erroneous, but influential, assumptions mentioned earlier are still shaping curriculum, research, and professional development activities.

CHARACTERISTICS OF FUTURE-ORIENTED DOCTORAL EDUCATION

The times are changing, and doctoral education will need to change with them. As we look into the future of knowledge-based societies, we can see that doctorate holders will increasingly be needed in a wider variety of societal roles. We need to consider whether existing and emerging doctoral programs are preparing students adequately to meet the challenges of working in and outside of academia, and across national and disciplinary boundaries within a context of globalization. Based on experiences with a decade of doctoral education outcomes studies, other CIRGE research, and previous evaluation work (Nerad 2005), the following characteristics for future-oriented doctoral education emerge:

1. Doctoral programs will prepare PhD holders for a variety of careers, both academic and nonacademic. Careers outside academia will need to be equally respected by faculty.

2. Doctoral programs will prepare students to work in interdisciplinary groups by providing epistemology courses that focus on the nature of knowledge, its foundation, and validity. As scientific, technical, or social problems become too complex to be solved individually or from a single perspective, research needs to be approached from a multidisciplinary perspective. Few scholars can master several disciplines, but all scholars need to understand and communicate with each other. A general graduate education introductory course, as Catherine Stimpson (2002) has advocated, should focus on what we know, how we know it, and what we regard as evidence.

3. Future-oriented doctoral programs integrate professional skill building into doctoral education by providing students with experiences in teaching, presenting research findings in front of a diverse audience, publishing, and writing for readers—in short, preparing doctoral students for a variety of future careers.

4. These programs introduce, when not already extant, collective supervision. The demand for one person to be the one and all—the ideal mentor—is unrealistic and contributes to faculty burnout. A panel of advisers can provide the students with more advice, insight, and consistent guidance.

5. Future-oriented programs introduce principles of effective teamwork and provide opportunities for practice. This can be in the form of collaborations on small research projects, or coauthoring of articles with other students or by students and faculty together.

6. These programs establish structured international collaborations with doctoral programs from other nations to develop research around global issues and problems.

7. These programs reintroduce foreign-language requirements, especially in English-speaking countries. The lack of foreign-language requirements for PhD education has negative consequences: first, much is lost by not being able to communicate directly with colleagues and collaborators and second, communicating solely in English privileges some and disadvantages others (Kerdeman 2003).

8. Future-oriented programs integrate cultural expertise and knowledge of international doctoral students and their needs into U.S. curricula.

9. These programs prepare students for leadership roles.

10. These programs initiate world citizenship education to revive awareness and obligation of civic engagement. They include the notion of a citizen who crosses national boundaries without seeking to assimilate and to homogenize, but instead to accept differences and embrace diversity.

In preparing for a knowledge-based society, higher education will need to make modifications. We recommend programs that focus on creating opportunities for doctoral students to become global citizens who can operate not only within academic circles, but are able to conduct socially responsible research and contribute to improving the quality of life on our planet. The next generation of faculty will need to implement doctoral programs in step with the changing times—programs that prepare graduates to work effectively in academic and nonacademic careers, to cross national and disciplinary boundaries, and to take on leadership roles in a globalizing world.

II

Attracting Undergraduates to PhD Study

6

GENERATING DOCTORAL DEGREE CANDIDATES AT LIBERAL ARTS COLLEGES

ROBERT J. LEMKE

Liberal arts colleges are an important source of PhD candidates. While these colleges award about 11 percent of all undergraduate degrees in the United States, almost 17 percent of all PhDs awarded to American students are to graduates of liberal arts colleges. The most recent data suggest that about 5.3 percent of all graduates from the best liberal arts colleges eventually earn a PhD, while only 2.2 percent of all graduates from the best universities do. There is also a substantial difference across liberal arts colleges, with the best colleges producing PhD candidates at three times the rate of lower-ranked colleges.

How is it that some liberal arts colleges are consistently more successful than other institutions at producing graduates who go on to earn a PhD? The answers to this question are inherently complex and difficult to isolate. This chapter is a first attempt to unravel parts of the story.

The social benefits provided by institutions of higher education in the form of having a highly educated citizenry are well understood. Society benefits from scientific discoveries, creative works of art, and informative policy analyses as well as from having a more knowledgeable electorate. Institutions of higher education, however, vary greatly in their approach toward education. At liberal arts colleges, where graduate degrees are seldom awarded, the primary mission is focused on educating undergraduates. Even though graduating students who will eventually earn a PhD is not the sole objective (and maybe not even a primary objective) of liberal arts colleges, the graduate school success of their students is important to liberal arts colleges. As socially conscious institutions, colleges value education and the benefits that a graduate education offers. Many faculty members at liberal arts colleges measure their contribution to society in part by the students they produce, including future PhD recipients who go on to undertake meaningful research of their own. More locally, the rate at which an institution's students pursue graduate study indicates generally how successful the institution is at fostering growth in its students' enjoyment of learning and a desire to pursue their own path toward understanding and discovery after college. Liberal arts colleges also have a preference, at least marginally, for hiring faculty with a liberal arts background. This suggests there is some consensus, at least among college deans, that liberal arts college graduates may have a greater appreciation, if not a greater affinity, for teaching (Astin 1999; Warch 2001). And more pragmatically, college rankings, the accreditation process, and granting agencies such as the National Science Foundation (NSF) all consider the graduate school success of alumni when evaluating institutions of higher education.

This chapter also provides insight into the relationship between faculty scholarship and the graduate school choices of students. Whether faculty scholarship should be required at liberal arts colleges has long been debated. Through the 1950s, college faculty were not expected to be engaged in research. Over the last forty years, however, scholarship expectations have changed. Presently, the most elite colleges require their faculty to be deeply engaged in research. Most lower-ranked colleges also consider scholarship in tenure decisions, though the quantity and quality of the scholarship requirements are less than at the top institutions and vary considerably across institutions (McCaughey 1994).

Some argue that imposing unnecessary research expectations on faculty detracts from high-quality teaching, the foremost stated mission of liberal arts colleges, as research competes for scarce funds and faculty time. Faculty who spend more of their time engaged in research, the argument goes, have less time to devote to teaching and advising, persuading fewer students to pursue a PhD.[1] In contrast, others maintain that engagement in scholarship, at least at the very best liberal arts colleges, helps faculty become better teachers (McCaughey 1994). Faculty research can engage students directly and foster excellent teaching. As a result, students are more likely to pursue a PhD.[2] The results presented herein suggest that both effects exist, with the positive effects of faculty scholarship being strongest at the best colleges.

Generating PhD Candidates

For our purposes here, the process of "generating" a PhD candidate occurs during one's undergraduate education. Specifically, an institution is said to generate a PhD candidate when a graduate from that institution receives a PhD from any PhD granting institution in the United States. Since 1970, American universities of all calibers (PhD-granting and non-PhD-granting) have generated between 20,000 and 24,000 PhD candidates annually, while liberal arts colleges have generated between 3,600 and 4,900 annually.[3]

The National Center for Education Statistics' Higher Education General Information Survey (HEGIS) and the Integrated Postsecondary Education Data System (IPEDS) Completions Survey provide the number of undergraduate degrees awarded by each institution each year, while the National Science Foundation's Survey of Earned Doctorates reports the number of PhDs earned each year by alumni of each institution.[4] Although the surveys contain information on thousands of institutions of higher education, the Carnegie Classification of Institutes of Higher Education system is used to focus on liberal arts colleges (institutions designated BA I or II) and universities (institutions designated Research I or II, Doctoral I or II, or Master's I or II). According to these definitions, there are 604 colleges and 732 universities. The discussion here, however, is restricted to the "top" institutions in each group. There are 165 colleges designated as BA I, and 87 universities designated as Research I. While the top universities and colleges alike account for about one-third of all undergraduate degrees awarded, the top universities consistently account for just under half of all PhD candidates generated by universities, while the top colleges account for more than two-thirds of all PhD candidates generated by liberal arts colleges.

Using data from the Survey of Earned Doctorates and the Completions Survey, the rate at which each institution or each type of institution that generates PhD candidates can be calculated and will simply be called the PhD generation rate. Two issues, however, are worth mentioning. First, the Survey of Earned Degrees does not report when the PhD recipient received her undergraduate degree. Thus, a five-year rolling window between undergraduate and graduate degrees is used.[5] Second, to smooth the data from year to year, the yearly PhD generation rate is calculated as all PhDs awarded within two years as a fraction of all undergraduate degrees awarded within two years. For example, the rate of generating PhD candidates for all liberal arts colleges in 1975 is calculated as all PhDs received by graduates of liberal arts colleges from 1973 through 1977 measured as a fraction of all undergraduate degrees awarded by liberal arts colleges from 1968 through 1972.

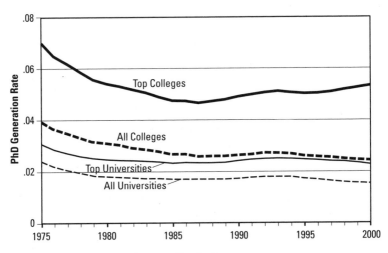

Figure 6.1. PhD generation rates by type of institution.

Source: Author's calculations using the NSF Survey of Earned Doctorates and HEGIS/IPEDS Completion Survey.

Note: Colleges are all BA I and II Carnegie classified institutions in 1994. Universities are all Research I and II, Doctoral I and II, and Masters I and II Carnegie classified institutions in 1994. Top colleges are the BA I institutions, while top universities are the Research I institutions.

Yearly PhD generation rates for the top liberal arts colleges versus the top universities and for all liberal arts colleges versus all universities are shown in figure 6.1. Rates of generating PhD candidates steadily fell from 1975 until 1985 for all types of institutions. Since 1985, however, only the top liberal arts colleges have experienced an increase in generation rates—from just under 4.7 in 1987 to over 5 percent by 1992 and in excess of 5.3 percent since 2000. Comparatively, the rate at which top universities generate PhD candidates fell below 2.5 percent by 1980, and has hovered between 2.2 and 2.5 percent ever since. A similarly persistent gap, though not as large, exists between all colleges and all universities. Whereas the rate of generating PhD candidates for all colleges fell from just over 3 percent in 1980 to 2.4 percent in 2000, it fell for all universities from 1.8 percent in 1980 to under 1.6 percent in 2000.

These differences in the rates of generating PhD candidates are substantial. Throughout the 1990s, for example, whereas liberal arts colleges graduated one person for almost every eight university graduates, graduates of liberal arts colleges earned one PhD for every five earned by university graduates. The ratios are even more striking for the top institutions. From 1985 to 1995, the top liberal arts colleges consistently generated PhD candidates at twice the rate of the top universities.

By 2000, as they had in the mid 1970s, the top liberal arts colleges were generating PhD candidates at a rate two and a half times greater than that of the top universities.

CHOOSING TO PURSUE A PHD

There are many possible explanations for why liberal arts colleges generate PhD candidates at a greater rate than their university counterparts. Liberal arts colleges might be more attractive to students who will later be drawn to graduate study. Students at liberal arts colleges also interact frequently with their professors, and typically at a deeper level than do students at universities. This closer relationship may lend itself to faculty members encouraging students to go on to graduate school more often, and/or that graduate school advice is more frequently followed. It may be that the occupation that students at liberal arts colleges are most familiar with, apart from that of their parents, is that of college professor. This familiarity may lead students to attend graduate school.[6]

Others argue that it is not so much advice given and received but that the experiences afforded by liberal arts colleges naturally foster a desire to further one's education. Warch (2001), for example, argues that the one-on-one undergraduate research experiences offered to students at liberal arts colleges are not only transforming but that such opportunities are rare to nonexistent at universities where graduate students have first claim to laboratories, equipment, and the professor's time. Astin (1999), Bourque (1999), Warch (2001), and others claim that it is only natural that one-on-one research experiences are likely to have a transformative effect on students and that liberal arts faculty are particularly suited to lead such experiences. Quantitative evidence to this effect, however, is lacking.

To try to begin to fill this void, a survey was sent to 850 current full-time faculty members at liberal arts colleges asking when they themselves knew they wanted to go to graduate school and what factor was most responsible for that decision. Surveys were returned by 358 faculty members for a response rate of 42 percent. Of those returned, 152 were from faculty who attended a liberal arts college as an undergraduate, while 206 attended a research university as an undergraduate. The tabulation of responses is given in table 6.1.[7]

The question of timing is addressed in panel A. Roughly 50 percent decided to go on to graduate school during their last two years of college, regardless of type of undergraduate institution. University students were more likely to make the decision before entering college or early in college, while liberal arts college students were more likely to make

TABLE 6.1
The Timing and Motivation for Graduate School by Undergraduate Institution

Type of Undergraduate Institution	Liberal Arts College (N = 152)		Research University (N = 206)	
A. When did you know you were going to go to graduate school?				
Before college	14	9%	30	15%
Freshman/sophomore year of college	14	9%	30	15%
Junior/senior year of college	83	55%	102	49%
After college	41	27%	44	21%
B. To what factor would you most attribute your decision to go to graduate school?				
Family	16	11%	15	7%
Undergraduate institution	89	58%	97	47%
Employment goals	43	28%	73	36%
Self-motivation	4	3%	21	10%

Source: Author survey. In the summer of 2006, the author sent the survey to 850 randomly chosen faculty members of elite liberal arts colleges, of which 358 were returned.

the decision after working for some time. None of these differences, however, are statistically significant at the 5 percent level.

The question of who or what most influenced the decision to go to graduate school is reported in panel B. The responses are broadly grouped into four categories: family, undergraduate institution (including a professor, classmates, a research experience, or a particular class), employment goals (including frustration with one's job, needing a PhD to do interesting research, or wanting to teach at the collegiate level), and self-motivation. Although much more research should be done on the motives underlying the decision to go to graduate school, this simple survey provides some evidence that liberal arts colleges connect with their students in a way that universities do not. Whereas 48 percent of graduates of universities attribute the primary factor in their pursuit of a PhD to something concerning their undergraduate institution, 58 percent of graduates from liberal arts colleges do. (The difference is statistically significant with a p-value of 0.032.)

The other statistically significant difference in table 6.1 concerns self-motivation. Whereas 10 percent of graduates from universities attribute their pursuit of a PhD to self-motivation, only 3 percent of graduates from a liberal arts college do (with a p-value of 0.005). This difference might be attributable to the difference in how students and professors interact on university campuses or simply to the number of students on university campuses. For a student to be an academic standout on a university campus, she must rise above thousands, not hundreds. To do this requires an inner desire for academic success. Whereas this desire undoubtedly exists in the standouts at liberal arts colleges, it may be more necessary on university campuses, and thus is more frequently noted by such graduates.

Although we are cautious of the small sample sizes and rudimentary survey method, it appears that liberal arts colleges deliver on their promise to interact closely with students. More research in this area, however, would be worthwhile. In particular, how engaging students in undergraduate research projects likely affects future decisions concerning PhD pursuits remains largely unknown. If liberal arts colleges have an advantage in this area, then calls for further funding, such as from NSF grants, to expand such opportunities at liberal arts colleges should be explored (Warch 2001).[8]

QUANTITATIVE ANALYSIS

We now turn our attention from comparing liberal arts colleges and universities to that of exploring empirically why some colleges generate PhD candidates more frequently than others. Attention here is restricted to BA I colleges as defined by the Carnegie Classification system in 1994. Using the number of graduates from each college from 1989 through 1998 and the number of doctorates earned by alumni of each college between 1994 and 2003, each college's PhD generation rate was calculated. The average college in the sample saw 4.2 percent of its graduates go on to earn a PhD.

To carry out a statistical analysis of PhD generation, additional data was collected from two sources. The 1995 edition of *America's Best Colleges* by *U.S. News and World Report* lists 161 top liberal arts colleges in 1994 and provides data on the 75th percentile Scholastic Aptitude Test (SAT) score of incoming freshmen (an average of 1235) and per-student expenditures.[9] Expenditures per student ranged from a low of $4,510 to a high of $23,715, with the average college spending $13,420 per student. Barron's 1994 *Profiles of American Colleges* reports enrollment, percentage of students who are female, student-faculty ratio, and the percentage of incoming students who scored above a 700 on the verbal and math sections of the SAT.

Finally, the Web of Science database was used to determine the number of articles attributed to each college in the Arts and Humanities Citation Index (A&HIS), the Social Science Citation Index (SSCI), and the Science Citation Index Expanded (SCI-Expanded) from 1989 through 1998.[10] Using each college's enrollment and student-faculty ratio, the number of articles per college was transformed into the number of articles per faculty member over the ten-year period. The average school had 0.3, 0.4, and 0.6 articles in A&HIS, SSCI, and SCI-EXPANDED, respectively, per faculty member for the entire ten years. These low rates reflect that they are calculated per faculty member and not per faculty member in each division. Combining the three indexes, the average college had almost 2.5 entries of any kind—not just journal articles—per faculty member over the ten years; put differently, the average faculty member contributed an entry to the index once every four years. Whereas the least prolific college had almost no entries, the most prolific college averaged just under one publication per faculty member per year.

When attention is restricted to only BA I colleges with an enrollment of between 500 and 3,500 students for which there is no missing data, there are 148 colleges in the sample. All the colleges used in the analysis, along with their PhD generation rate of students who graduated between 1989 and 1998, appears in table 6.2.

Explaining PhD Generation Rates

Using these data, the relationship certain factors have with generating PhD candidates from liberal arts colleges can be explored. To do this, two models were estimated using ordinary least squares regression—one for the 81 colleges in the first and second tiers and one for the 67 colleges in the third and fourth tiers, according to the *U.S. News* guide.[11] The dependent variable is each college's rate at which it generates PhD candidates as reported in table 6.2. The explanatory variables include the college's 75th percentile SAT score, log of enrollment, percent of students who are female (measured 0 to 100), per-student expenditures (measured in thousands of dollars), whether the college offered a business degree in the 1990s, whether the college is located in the Northeast,[12] and the number of Web of Science database citations per faculty member from 1989 to 1998.[13] Offering a business degree was included for two reasons. First, offering such a degree might indicate that the college attracts students who are more inclined to pursue professional degrees or who have more immediate job expectations after graduation. Second, a business major may compete with the more traditional majors offered at liberal arts colleges, which in turn may limit student options for pursuing a doctorate after graduation. Location has also been included because of the historical presence of many elite colleges, and clusters of elite colleges, in the Northeast. Kaufman and Woglom (2005) also account for location.

The results from both models are reported in table 6.3. The percent of students scoring in the top quartile of the SAT is positively related to generating PhD candidates for both groups of colleges, though the magnitude of the effect is much greater for tier 1 and tier 2 colleges than for tier 3 and tier 4 colleges. While neither enrollment nor the percent of students who are female is statistically significant in either

TABLE 6.2
List of Colleges and 1989–98 Generation Rates

College	Rate	College	Rate	College	Rate
Agnes Scott College	4.8	Gettysburg College	3.0	Oglethorpe University	1.2
Albion College	2.8	Gordon College (MA)	3.5	Ohio Wesleyan University	3.8
Albright College	3.2	Goshen College	4.6	Pitzer College	3.9
Allegheny College	5.9	Goucher College	4.4	Pomona College	11.4
Alma College	3.1	Grinnell College	11.1	Presbyterian College	1.6
Amherst College	9.3	Guilford College	2.3	Randolph-Macon College	2.3
Antioch University	1.8	Gustavus Adolphus College	2.9	Randolph-Macon Woman's College	4.0
Augustana College (IL)	3.2	Hamilton College	4.5	Reed College	18.4
Austin College	3.1	Hamline University	1.5	Rhodes College	5.9
Bard College	4.1	Hampden-Sydney College	1.9	Ripon College	5.1
Barnard College	7.4	Hampshire College	6.6	Salem College	1.0
Bates College	5.4	Hanover College	3.3	Sarah Lawrence College	3.3
Beloit College	7.5	Hartwick College	2.1	Scripps College	4.7
Bethany College (WV)	2.1	Hastings College	2.9	Shepherd College	0.6
Birmingham Southern College	2.5	Haverford College	12.1	Siena College	1.1
Bowdoin College	6.5	Hendrix College	6.4	Skidmore College	2.2
Bryn Mawr College	7.5	Hiram College	3.7	Smith College	5.3
Bucknell University	4.1	Hobart and William Smith College	3.2	Southwestern University	2.8
Carleton College	14.6	Hollins College	1.8	Spelman College	2.6
Central College (IA)	2.6	Hope College	4.7	St. Andrews Presbyterian College	2.5
Centre College	4.5	Houghton College	3.5		
Chatham College	3.4	Huntingdon College	1.9	St. John's University (MN)	4.0
Claremont McKenna College	2.2	Illinois College	1.2	St. Lawrence University	3.3
		Illinois Wesleyan University	3.5	St. Mary's College of MD	1.4
Coe College	2.7	Juniata College	5.1		
Colby College	4.5	Kalamazoo College	11.2	St. Olaf College	7.1
Colgate University	4.3	Kenyon College	5.1	Swarthmore College	18.0
College of St. Benedict (MN)	1.7	Knox College	7.5	Sweet Briar College	1.9
College of Wooster	7.7	Lafayette College	4.1	Transylvania University	2.5
College of the Holy Cross	3.6	Lake Forest College	2.6	Trinity College (CT)	3.8
		Lawrence University	7.7	Union College (NY)	
Colorado College	5.0	Lewis and Clark College	1.6	University of Dallas	3.4
Concordia College (MN)	2.3	Luther College	3.4	UNC at Asheville	1.6
Connecticut College	3.5	Macalester College	7.3	University of Puget Sound	1.3
		Manhattanville College	1.8	University of the South	1.7
Cornell College	3.2	McDaniel College	1.5		
Davidson College	7.0	Middlebury College	4.3		4.5
DePauw University	3.4	Mills College	2.1	Ursinus College	2.4
Denison University	3.5	Millsaps College	2.7	Vassar College	6.8
Dickinson College	3.5	Monmouth College	2.7	Virginia Military Institute	2.0
Drew University	2.6	Moravian College	1.9		
Earlham College	8.3	Morehouse College	1.2	Virginia Wesleyan College	1.1
Eckerd College	2.5	Mount Holyoke College	7.4		
Erskine College	2.0	Muhlenberg College	3.6	Wabash College	7.9
Franklin College Indiana	1.0	Nebraska Wesleyan University	2.6	Wartburg College	2.2
Franklin and Marshall College	5.7	Oberlin College	13.4		
Furman University	4.3	Occidental College	7.0		
Georgetown College	1.3				

TABLE 6.2—cont.

College	Rate	College	Rate	College	Rate
Washington College	1.8	Westminster	1.7	Willamette University	1.5
Washington and	2.2	College (PA)		William Jewell	1.7
Jefferson College		Westmont College	2.5	College	
Washington and	2.0	Wheaton College	2.4	Williams College	8.2
Lee University		(IL)		Wittenberg	3.5
Wellesley College	8.2	Wheaton College	5.1	University	
Wesleyan University	6.9	(MA)		Wofford College	2.5
Westminster	2.4	Whitman College	6.3		
College (MO)		Whittier College	1.4		

TABLE 6.3
OLS Regression Results

	Tier 1 and Tier 2 Colleges	Tier 3 and Tier 4 Colleges
SAT 75th percentile score	0.0203***	0.0037**
	(0.0049)	(0.0017)
Natural log of enrollment	0.3578	–0.0782
	(0.8361)	(0.3464)
Percent students who are female (0 to 100)	0.0048	–0.0069
	(0.0172)	(0.0066)
Per student expenditures in $1,000	0.0721	0.1484**
	(0.1271)	(0.0673)
College offers a business degree (0/1)	–1.9485***	0.2123
	(0.6893)	(0.3922)
College is located in the northeast (0/1)	–3.0178***	0.8110*
	(0.6677)	(0.4451)
Citations per faculty member, 1989–98	0.4497**	–0.0161
	(0.2289)	(0.1856)
Constant	–24.3854	–2.8280
	(8.6792)	(3.6664)
Number of observations	81	67
R-squared	0.5615	0.2482
Adjusted R-squared	0.5195	0.1590

Notes: The dependent variable is each college's overall PhD creation rate measured, 0 to 100, and is calculated as the number of PhD's earned by alumni of the college from 1994 to 2003, measured as a percent of the college's graduates from 1989–98. Standard errors are reported in parentheses.
***Significant at the 1 percent level.
**Significant at the 5 percent level.
*Significant at the 10 percent level.

regression, the most important point to be taken from table 6.3 is how different generating PhD candidates is for the colleges in the top two tiers than it is for the colleges in the next two tiers. There are meaningful differences between the generation of PhD candidates and college expenditures, offering a business degree, college location, and faculty scholarship. Each of these is discussed in turn below.[14]

While expenditures per student are not statistically significant in explaining the generation of PhD candidates from tier 1 or tier 2 colleges, expenditures are statistically significant at the 5 percent level at tier 3 and tier 4 colleges. The magnitude of the effect, however, is very small. A $1,000 increase in per-student spending is associated with less than a 0.15 percentage point increase in PhD generation. For the typical college, this suggests that increasing the annual budget by over $1 million annually would be associated with one additional graduate going on to eventually earn a PhD every other year.

Among colleges in the top two tiers, those that offer a business degree generate PhD candidates at a rate that is almost 2 percentage points lower than those that do not offer a business degree. Offering a business degree by colleges in the bottom two tiers, however, is not statistically associated with generating PhD candidates. One interpretation of this finding is that not only are good students at the best colleges attracted to nontraditional liberal arts majors like business, but also that students who choose these majors develop less interest in graduate school or find it more difficult to pursue a graduate degree.

Tier 1 and tier 2 colleges located in the Northeast are predicted to generate PhD candidates at a rate that is 3 percentage points lower than comparable colleges not located in the Northeast. In contrast, tier 3 and tier 4 colleges in the Northeast are predicted to generate PhD candidates at a rate that is almost 1 percentage point higher than comparable colleges not in the Northeast. Wall Street and the U.S. financial/banking industry could be an explanation for this pattern if the financial sector of the United States, which is located predominantly in the Northeast, has a preference for hiring the best students from the best regional colleges.

Finally, the relationship between generating PhD candidates and faculty scholarship also varies by tier. Among tier 1 and tier 2 colleges, faculty scholarship is positively related to generating PhD candidates, while faculty scholarship is unrelated to PhD generation rates at tier 3 and tier 4 colleges. This suggests that both arguments mentioned earlier— that increased faculty scholarship might detract from a professor's time to advise and teach or it might add to faculty interactions with students— hold, but that they are realized to varying degrees at different colleges. Faculty at the best colleges who are engaged in scholarship may affect their students positively toward graduate school. At lower-ranked colleges, however, faculty scholarship does not appear to be a catalyst for encouraging students to pursue a doctoral degree.[15]

Explaining PhD Generation Rates across Disciplines

Using the same data as above, the relationship certain factors have with generating PhD candidates from within each division was explored. To do this, the previous models were estimated using seemingly unrelated regression (SUR), which allows for better estimation of parameters when error terms are correlated across equations. Each model estimates three equations, with the dependent variables being each college's PhD generation rates in the humanities, social sciences, and natural sciences.[16] The explanatory variables are the same as in table 6.3, except that each equation includes division-specific faculty citations.[17]

The regression results strongly suggest that PhD generation rates at liberal arts colleges are correlated across academic divisions. The correlations of the error terms are greater than one-half and are positively correlated at the 1 percent level. Moreover, if the errors were randomly distributed, one would expect roughly ten colleges (one in every eight) to have all positive or all negative errors in each of the three equations. Instead, of the 81 tier 1 and tier 2 colleges, 21 had all positive errors while 28 had all negative errors. Similarly, of the 67 tier 3 and tier 4 colleges, 14 had all positive errors and 22 had all negative errors.

The estimated relationships between generating PhD candidates and college enrollment, per-student expenditures, offering a business degree, being located in the Northeast, and faculty scholarship largely support the results from table 6.3. A notable difference, however, concerns the percentage of female students. Although the percent of a college's student body that are women was unrelated to PhD generation rates originally, having a greater percentage of women students on campus is associated with generating more PhD candidates in the humanities and social sciences when compared to the natural sciences.

The results concerning test scores are roughly the same under the SUR model as they were in table 6.3. A college's 75th percentile SAT score is positively associated with PhD generation rates for both groups of colleges, but a 100-point increase is associated with between a 0.6 and 0.9 percentage point increase, depending on discipline, for the top two tiers while a 100-point increase is associated with only a 0.1 percentage point increase for the bottom two tiers. The model can be expanded by replacing the 75th percentile SAT score with the percent of students who scored above a 700 on each subject test of the SAT. Almost 20 percent of the colleges, however, fail to report these variables. Consequently, many estimated coefficients are statistically insignificant, as they are associated with large standard errors given the smaller sample sizes. That said, the results suggest that student abilities matter in their choices of major and graduate study. The percentage of students who score above 700 on the verbal portion of the SAT is positively associated with generating PhD candidates in the humanities and social sciences but unassociated with generating PhD candidates in the natural sciences. Conversely, the percent of students who score above 700 on the math portion of the SAT is positively associated with generating PhD candidates in the natural sciences but unassociated with generating PhD candidates in the humanities or social sciences.

A final test of robustness is also worth mentioning. The Completions Survey data are not disaggregated enough to calculate the number of graduates in each academic division for each college. When a student has a double major, for example, only one of her majors is recorded in the data. Accurate division-specific PhD generation rates can be calculated, therefore, only if every double major always had a double major in the same division. Making the heroic assumption that the Completions Survey data accurately reflects the distribution of undergraduate degrees, division-specific PhD generation rates were calculated along with division-specific shares of undergraduate degrees. The model was reestimated, once using the division-specific generation rates as dependent variables and once including each division's share of undergraduate degrees as an explanatory variable in that division's equation. Both sets of results qualitatively match the original SUR results, but estimates are much less stable across equations and models, and standard errors are larger.

College Policies and Generating PhDs

Generating PhD candidates from elite liberal arts colleges remains a mysterious process, but this chapter has begun to shine some light on the differences across colleges. First, within colleges, PhD generation is highly correlated across academic divisions. Second, college characteristics and student traits matter. Most important is student ability (as measured by test scores) upon entering college, but location, the percentage of students who are women (positively related to generating PhD candidates in the humanities and social sciences; negatively related in the natural sciences), and curriculum (colleges that offer a business major generate PhD candidates at a slower rate) also matter. Third, faculty research plays an important but selective role: PhD generation is positively related to faculty scholarship, especially in the social and natural sciences, but only among the top eighty or so colleges.

Although the above mentioned factors are important, they do not tell the entire story. The regressions only explain about 50 percent of the variation in PhD generation rates among the top two tiers of colleges, and even less so in the next two tiers. To try to better understand the process of generating PhD candidates, the regression results were used to identify twenty-one colleges that consistently generate more PhD candidates than regression analysis predicts and twenty-six colleges that consistently generate fewer PhD candidates than regression analysis predicts. Using these two groups of colleges, a search was undertaken regarding each college's career center webpage and the services offered pertaining to graduate school. Under the assumption that colleges with career centers in the 1990s that focused attention on student applications to graduate school would continue to do so, a present-day comparison between the career centers between these two groups of colleges could be fruitful. Although quantitatively comparing web pages across colleges is difficult, the overall assessment shows that career centers at colleges that consistently generate more PhD candidates than expected are about twice as likely to offer a greater amount of information and provide access to multiple web resources to students who are interested in graduate school than are career centers at colleges that consistently generate fewer PhD candidates than expected.

The directors of the career centers at the top performing colleges were also asked their opinion concerning how their centers meet student needs. The overriding theme given by directors of career centers is that they do not focus on funneling students toward graduate school; rather, when students come to them for advice, the approach is to present the student with many options—job, graduate school, professional school, volunteer work, and so on. Although graduate school is not the focus, it is discussed and presented as a viable option. All of the centers also had resources available to students to help with the process of applying to graduate school—from providing practice Graduate Record Examination tests, to offering a list of alumni to talk to at various graduate programs, to helping write a personal statement. Of course, it is unclear if the mission of career centers and the services provided result in greater interest in graduate school or if the students at colleges that generate many PhD candidates require the career center to serve their needs.

In addition to career centers, these colleges can also be compared using the previously discussed faculty survey. Of the 358 responses to the faculty survey, 31 faculty members attended one of the colleges that consistently generate more PhD candidates than expected while 17 attended one of the colleges that consistently generate fewer PhD candidates than expected. Although the sample size is very small, some interesting patterns emerge. Compared to students from colleges that consistently generate fewer PhD candidates than expected, students from the colleges that consistently generate more PhD candidates than expected were more likely to make the decision to go to graduate school in their last two years of college (61 percent vs. 47 percent) and were less likely to make the decision early in college or even before college (16 percent vs. 35 percent). There are also notable differences to what the respondents most attributed their decision to go to graduate school. Compared to students from the colleges that consistently generate fewer PhD candidates than expected, students from the colleges that consistently generate more PhD candidates than expected were more likely to attribute the decision to a professor (36 percent vs. 24 percent) and less likely to attribute the decision to a particular class (7 percent vs. 18 percent) or not enjoying work (3 percent vs. 18 percent). Response rates were more equal in attributing the decision to an undergraduate research project (7 percent vs. 6 percent) or not wanting to stop with schooling or having a love of learning (7 percent vs. 12 percent).

Finally, it is interesting to hear from the colleges directly as to what they think the source of their college's success is. The dean of faculty (or equivalent) at each of the colleges that consistently generated more PhD candidates than expected was asked to "describe why you think it is that your college is successful at having its students go on to earn PhDs." The common theme from all deans was curriculum. Although the abilities and talents of incoming students matter in terms of which colleges are most likely to produce future PhD candidates, the academic experiences of students while in college also play a role. Providing a serious curriculum, encouraging students to take on challenges, and developing a campus environment that respects intellectual curiosity all contribute to the development of students. The idea of a campus culture in which graduate school is well thought of was articulated by many deans. Two examples stand out: Kalamazoo College and Scripps College.

Kalamazoo College has long been successful at generating PhD candidates. Its generation rate was 9.2 percent in the 1970s, 10.6 percent in the 1980s, and 12.2 percent in the 1990s. It is also at or near the top in per-capita volunteers to the Peace Corps. In the 1960s, Kalamazoo undertook a substantial curriculum change, called the K-Plan, that frames each student's entire four years of college. All students participate in a first-year seminar and in an off-campus internship during their second year. Study abroad is strongly encouraged in the third year, with over 80 percent of students participating. And all students are required to complete an individual research project during their senior year, many of which are yearlong endeavors.[18]

Scripps College is the only all-women's college in the consortium of Claremont Colleges. Scripps has long offered a humanities focus to its students, but it intentionally widened its curriculum and recruited students in the 1980s in order to match that curriculum. The required humanities curriculum was developed into the Core Program,[19] in which all faculty are expected to teach regularly. The Core Program is a three-course sequence with a shared theme of "culture, knowledge, and representation." In addition to a more interdisciplinary curriculum, a new science building opened in 1990, and the number of science faculty was substantially increased. The number of science majors increased from just a few each year in the 1970s to its present numbers of between thirty and forty graduating science majors each year. These developments, however, have helped to vastly increase Scripps College's PhD generation rate across all academic fields—not just in the sciences. The PhD generation rate at Scripps was 2.4 percent in the 1970s and 4.2 percent in the 1980s; it has since increased further, to an average of 5.7 percent in the 1990s.

This chapter has begun to explore why some colleges are better than others at generating PhD candidates. Much more research is needed. In particular, a careful analysis of why individuals choose to go to graduate school would be fruitful. Do the best colleges generate future PhD students or are the best colleges simply the best at recruiting future PhD students to their campuses? Do undergraduate research experiences push students toward graduate school? If so, are these experiences different at colleges than at universities? Is the academic lifestyle at liberal arts colleges appealing to its students so that this exposure explains why graduates of these colleges pursue doctoral degrees at about twice the rate of graduates from large universities? The answer to these and many other questions would help us better understand the connections between an individual's undergraduate experience and her decision to go on to graduate school, possibly helping colleges better target this outcome.

7

Undergraduate STEM Research Experiences

Impact on Student Interest in Doing Graduate Work in STEM Fields

Myles Boylan

Does participation in undergraduate research in science, technology, engineering, and mathematics (STEM) affect the likelihood that participants will enter STEM graduate programs and succeed? This is one of many questions addressed in the literature on the effects of undergraduate research (UGR). Typically such studies examine the impact of UGR on a number of factors: the completion of a bachelor's degree in a STEM field; the probability of transitioning to graduate school after earning the bachelor's degree; changes in the depth of commitment to or level of interest in continuing into graduate school (because many UGR participants have already planned to attend graduate school); the decision or plan to pursue a career in STEM, especially in research; the research skills learned (operating lab equipment, applying appropriate statistical analyses, reading and synthesizing prior research papers, finding key prior research papers in a library, working independently, writing in appropriate scientific styles); the ability to think like a scientist; and the acquisition of communication skills (presentation; working effectively with faculty, graduate students, and undergraduate peers on teams).

Some studies also have considered the costs and benefits of UGR as well as its limits, such as the percentage of majors who can be effectively provided with quality UGR experiences given department size.

The Limitations of Empirical Studies

The quality of the extant research is affected by the problem of a relatively heterogeneous treatment group, of finding high-quality, affordable assessment data, and of obtaining long-term data on actual decisions as undergraduates transition to postbaccalaureate studies and full-time employment. Short-term assessment studies rely heavily on survey questionnaires. Fortunately, some long-term data exists, and the majority of actual UGR experiences studied were of fairly high quality and effectively designed for their clients, undergraduate students.

At many colleges offering UGR experiences, the students selected to participate were already high-achieving and oriented toward graduate school. For example, this is typically the case for National Science Foundation Research Experiences for Undergraduates (REU) projects. Only a few studies look at the impact of UGR on average or typical STEM students. Broadening the evident range of student capability would be a more useful and powerful test of the impact of UGR on student achievement and continuation into graduate programs.

The lack of a control group matched to the treatment group forces most studies to use a pre- and postexperience evaluation of UGR experiences, relying on student and faculty mentor responses to survey questions. In addition, most studies do not actually observe student choices long enough to determine the possible effects of UGR directly. Direct observation avoids the problem that students' plans to attend graduate programs and their career intentions will not actually be realized in a number of cases. We know from data provided by decades of surveys conducted by the Higher Education Research Institute at the University of California–Los Angeles and published in the annual *American Freshman: National Norms* that the formative intentions of first-year students for attending graduate programs—particularly doctoral study—are quite optimistic when compared to what actually happens years later. (This indicates the value of surveying the depth of student commitment to graduate school or embarking on a science and engineering career.)

Larger-scale studies such as program evaluations have incomplete controls and data on the nature of the UGR experience itself, other than some built-in quality-control procedures (such as peer review in the case of REU awards). However, while the experiences and the disciplines covered do vary, most experiences covered by published studies appear to be carefully constructed.

Virtually all of the data are survey based. When questions are not about factual events, student and faculty respondents code their answers using 5-point (or 4-point) Likert scales. Item construction can be critical in this context. The difference between a 5 and a 4 on a 5-point scale can be influenced by the way these numbers are represented verbally, and there is little hope that the studies in this review are fully comparable.

The mix of undergraduate disciplines seems to matter a great deal. In the absence of UGR opportunities, bachelor's graduates in mathematics are much less likely to attend graduate school in the near future compared to bachelor's graduates in, for example, physics. The measurement construct itself (change in the percentage of UGR participants planning graduate study) is tricky to compare across studies when some include only the best students and others also include average students.

Interventions such as UGR have been found in other studies to lower undergraduate student attrition. This reduced attrition can be attributed to a mix of cognitive and affective gains and, in many cases, financially competitive summer stipends. Examples are students in summer research programs sponsored by the National Science Foundation (NSF) or the Howard Hughes Medical Institute (HHMI) who earn attractive stipends. This creates a larger post-UGR survivor pool responding to the survey, but one that may have a lower proclivity to engage graduate work initially and a bigger potential for gains.

Synthesis of Findings

A reassuring discovery is that the observations and findings of empirical studies are broadly consistent (with occasional exceptions) across studies. Many of these studies have examined, in some detail, the increased learning and improved affect (deeper commitment) of UGR participants. They report compelling qualitative findings that indicate convincingly that most UGR participants derive strong intellectual growth and development benefits, a renewed commitment to engage in further STEM research, and a much broader sense of career options as a STEM professional. The measured benefits of student participation in UGR are plausible—often impressive—and in some cases based on very careful and detailed interview data.

Paradoxically, the more knowledge gained about career options as a result of participating in UGR the more uncertain students are about their career plans. However, this uncertainty is primarily the result of much richer knowledge. Another factor likely contributing to the uncertainty is that UGR experiences connect students to academic (basic) research—only a small part of the career options open to graduates. More often than not, faculty members guiding UGR projects are themselves not informed about nonacademic careers.

Increased intentions to enter graduate school in a STEM field following UGR experiences are quite large for those students who were not in the highest-achieving cohorts at their undergraduate institutions. Most of the highest-achieving undergraduate STEM majors were planning to do graduate work in STEM or in medical school prior to participating in an UGR experience. Several other enriching experiences are commonly rated by undergraduates as highly as (or even more highly than) UGR as sources of intellectual growth: internships in public agencies, nonprofit organizations, and private firms; cooperative activities (typically for engineering students), and writing senior theses.

Summary of Empirical Findings

The effect of UGR on the transition rates of students who are enrolled in highly selective colleges or in highly competitive summer UGR programs, or both, is evidently modest in quantitative terms. Four pre- and post-UGR studies of this nature—Wilson Gonzalez-Espada and Daphne Zaras (2006), Douglas Gould and Brian MacPherson (2003), Anne-Barrie Hunter et al. (2006), and David Lopatto (2004)—generally conclude that that there is virtually no gain in the already large fraction of students planning postbaccalaureate STEM studies but a large gain in the strength of many students' commitment to enter graduate STEM programs.

Lopatto, for example, found that 27 percent of the participants in UGR projects at institutions with at least one HHMI-funded summer research project had greater commitments toward attending graduate school. Only 4 percent more, however, had definitely decided to enter graduate school, which is offset by another 5 percent who decided this career track was not attractive. The Lopatto study summarizes the survey responses of 1,135 undergraduates out of 1,526 who participated in forty-one UGR programs in the summer of 2003.

Hunter et al., in a study of seventy-six students doing UGR in four selective liberal arts colleges in the summer of 2000, found no students who changed their plans in favor of attending graduate school (despite impressive developmental gains identified by both the students and fifty-five faculty guides), and found instead an attrition rate of 9 percent who learned through the UGR experience that this career track was not for them. Similar to Lopatto, however, Hunter et al. found that, for the remaining students, "the role of UGR was to increase student interest in [STEM research] and [raise] the probability of going on to graduate school...and to clarify which field of interest to pursue" (2006, 28). These seventy-six students were reinterviewed a year later (just before graduation) and again as alumni in 2003–04. A comparison group of sixty-two students who had not participated in UGR were interviewed

TABLE 7.1
Summary Characteristics of Published Studies

Study ID (Lead Author)	Disciplines; Types of UGR; Control Group?	Loci of UGR projects	Number of Students, Origins, and Response Rate	Time Period Covered
Lopatto	Biology related (primarily); NIH funded and other; no control	41 research and teaching institutions (unnamed)	1,135 from more than 41 institutions; 74%	2003
Hunter	Natural sciences; formal UGR; control group	4 liberal arts colleges (unnamed)	76, from more than 4 institutions; 100%	2000
Gonzalez-Espada	Meteorology and physics; no control	National Weather Center; 38; 100%	38, from more than 30 institutions; 100%	2001–05
Gould	Interdisciplinary neuroscience; no control	University of Kentucky	80 gross/66 net from 75 institutions; ~90%	1998–2003
Fitzsimmons (contractor report)	All STEM: NSF-sponsored REU projects; no control	Hundreds of institutions funded by NSF	1,915 from hundreds of institutions; ~70%	1987–90
Zydney	Engineering; formal and informal UGR; control group	University of Delaware	245 from U–DE; 38%	B-level grads: 1982–97
Bauer	All STEM; formal UGR and other UGR; control group	The University of Delaware; 986; 42%	986 from U–DE; 42%	B-level grads: 1982–97
Russell (contractor reports)	All STEM: NSF-sponsored UGR projects; other UGR; some controls	About 700 institutions funded by NSF	4,500 (76%) 3,300 (56%) 3,400 (~20%) 3,200 (~20%)	Summer 2002 Academic year 2002–03 B-level grads in STEM: 2005
Price ; Becker and Price	Economics; REU for minority students; some control	1 institution, moves every few years	821 from many institutions; particularly minority-serving institutions	1973–2006

Abbreviations used in this table:
UGR = undergraduate research
NIH = National Institute of Health
NSF = National Science Foundation
REU = Research Experiences for Undergraduates (an NSF program)
U–DE = University of Delaware

on the same schedule. Only the results of the first survey/interviews were available for the initial paper, however.

The study by Gonzalez-Espada looked at thirty-eight high-achieving undergraduates from a mix of research and teaching institutions who were doing research at the National Weather Center during 2001–05 and found a significant deepening of commitment to attend STEM graduate programs (37 percent) compared to a reduced commitment or change of plans (11 percent). However, when the focus was on *career* plans, gains (32 percent) were nearly offset by losses (29 percent).

The Gould study focused on high-performing undergraduate students from seventy-five institutions, fifty-three of which were deliberately chosen non–tier 1 research institutions (using the 2000 Carnegie Classification of Institutes of Higher Education system) who participated in an "interdisciplinary neuroscience research experience for undergraduates" 2003, A24) supported by the NSF. This annual REU was designed deliberately to increase the transition rate to graduate programs and interest in neuroscience careers. From 1998 to 2003, eighty students participated. One-third of the students were drawn from underrepresented minority groups, and about two-thirds were women.

As a result of the REU experience, many students reported a deeper commitment and a higher probability that they would apply to the University of Kentucky to study neuroscience. A high percentage of students admitted to the REU were already planning on applying to graduate programs. As of 2003, 19 students were still in undergraduate programs, and data was not provided by 14 students. Of the remaining 47 students who had graduated as of 2003, 32 were either in graduate school or were applying to graduate school (68 percent), 8 others were in professional schools, and the remaining 7 were employed in science careers as teachers and technicians. It is possible that some of the 32 students attracted to graduate work were convinced by the REU experience (and that some of the 14 not in graduate school were also convinced by the REU experience that a research career was not for them).

In situations where institutional selectivity, student selectivity, and project or program selectivity were less stringent, with resulting broader ranges of student achievement, the gains in transition rates to graduate school were much higher. Five published studies have some of these elements: Karen Bauer and Joan Bennett (2003); Stephen Fitzsimmons, Kenneth Carlson, Larry Kerpelman, and Diane Stoner (1990); Gregory Price (2005); Susan Russell et al. (2005); and Andrew Zydney, Joan Bennett, Abdus Shahid, and Karen Bauer (2002).

In 1990, Fitzsimmons and his colleagues at Abt Associates Inc. reported small but significant effects on student plans to do doctoral work following participation in the NSF Research Experiences for

Undergraduates program. This study was an evaluation of the early years of the NSF REU program, when the community was still adjusting to it. Almost 2,000 student participants were surveyed. The selectivity of grants and students was somewhat lower than in later years (after the higher education community became fully aware of the program). Unfortunately, this study also did not report gains and losses separately, but only net gains. The net gain in students planning to do doctoral work after their REU experience was 12 percentage points. This study also found that 17 percent of the students reported they were more likely (or had decided on a greater commitment) to attend a graduate program. The exclusive focus of this study on REU UGR and its findings actually place it in between the low-effect and high-effect groups.

The Zydney et al. (2002) study of engineering graduates from the University of Delaware during the years 1982–97 examined the impact of UGR programs that were open to all students. Of the 651 graduates Zydney selected for his survey sample, 229 had participated in formal UGR programs; this figure was based on registrar data. The survey response rate was 38 percent (245 responses)—a low rate, but at least there does not appear to be a response bias based on the type of UGR experience; of the 245 respondents, 91 were formal UGR participants, 66 were informal participants, and 88 were nonparticipants. The fraction of the alumni who had participated in formal UGR programs and subsequently enrolled in graduate school was 30 percentage points higher (at 80 percent) than the group who chose not to participate in UGR (50 percent) and 13 percentage points higher than the graduate school enrollment of the group who had experienced other forms of UGR (67 percent). The fraction of formal UGR participating alumni who engaged in PhD-level studies (35 percent) was 8 percentage points higher than alumni who had participated in other forms of UGR and 27 percentage points higher than alumni who had no UGR experiences.

In Zydney's study, the mean grade point average (GPA) of participants in formal UGR programs was highest (3.52), followed by the 27 percent who participated in other forms of UGR (GPA 3.37). The GPA of non-UGR participating alumni was 3.33. Could these GPA differences explain the difference in graduate school and PhD program attendance? There appears to be significant colinearity, because the average student rating of formal UGR was also significantly higher than the average rating of informal UGR. It is both likely that the best students tended to pick formal UGR options and that formal UGR experiences helped to bolster their GPAs. (The Bauer study, discussed below, tried to adjust for all confounding effects.)

The Zydney study shows that other major activities, as well as UGR, were judged by the graduates to be effective and valuable. Highest rated were internships related to the engineering major. (Edward Hackett reported a similar finding in a 1992 study that compared the effect of coop internships on undergraduates to UGR; the students were drawn from several cohorts of undergraduates enrolled in a large technical institute.) Studying abroad and doing a senior thesis were rated about as highly as formal UGR experiences.

Finally, the Zydney study also shows that the impact of UGR was higher (and on par with the very highly rated internships in engineering) in cases where four or more semesters of UGR were done. However, this could be an example of self-selection bias as well.

The Bauer study (2003) is an extension of the Zydney study, reporting on all alumni (not just engineering alumni) of the University of Delaware in the years 1982–97. It attempted to adjust for total effects—including discipline effects—in estimating the effect of UGR alone. The results of the study are roughly comparable to Zydney's. The response rate was 42 percent (986 usable responses from a target group of 2,444 alumni), who were matched by major and GPA in 2 groups—those who had and had not undertaken UGR. Of these 986 responses, 418 had participated in the formal UGR program, 213 had engaged in other types of UGR, and 355 had no UGR experience. A much larger fraction of respondents (56 percent) were women than in the Zydney study.

Bauer estimated that 67 percent of the typical STEM alumni (with a 3.5 GPA) who had formal UGR experiences subsequently did graduate work, compared to 57 percent of alumni who had no UGR experiences. Similarly, the probability of STEM alumni with formal UGR experience pursuing a doctoral degree was 43 percent, compared to 36 percent for alumni with informal UGR experience and 23 percent for remaining alumni. These differences at the PhD level are among the largest discussed found in the literature.

The Russell study (2005), performed under NSF contract to SRI International, had the largest survey population. It covered all of the UGR experiences that were sponsored by the NSF in 2002 or 2003. In addition to REU projects these included Research in Undergraduate Institutions projects and projects in six other NSF programs, including targeted programs. The survey population included a large number of minorities and women. Of the respondents 15 percent had a GPA below 3.0 and 28 percent were in the range 3.0–3.5. Thus, the evaluation looked at a significant fraction of average and moderately above average students.

The evaluation work done by Russell included four web-based surveys conducted between 2003 and 2005. The initial survey was of roughly 4,500 undergraduate participants in NSF-sponsored UGR programs. The response rate was 76 percent. Two years later there was a follow-up survey of these 4,500 UGR participants; usable responses were received from 3,300.

In addition, to get baseline data Russell conducted two nationally representative surveys of STEM baccalaureate graduates in the age range twenty-two to thirty-five: one of natural science and engineering STEM majors (3,400) and the other of social and behavioral science majors (3,200), which the NSF also defines as STEM. About 50 percent of the respondents in each of these nationally representative samples reported some UGR experience. About 7 percent reported that their UGR experience had been supported by the NSF, the National Institutes of Health (NIH), or the National Aeronautics and Space Administration (NASA), and the outcomes reported by this group were similar to those reported by the 4,500 participants in NSF-sponsored UGR programs.

The rates of UGR participation did not vary by type of undergraduate institution in the two nationally representative surveys. (It was about the same for baccalaureate institutions, master's institutions, research intensive institutions, and research extensive institutions, as defined by the latest Carnegie Classification scheme). The rates of participation in UGR did vary considerably by baccalaureate major, from lows of 34 percent in mathematics and 37 percent in computer science to highs of 63 percent in psychology and 74 percent in environmental science.

On the one hand, Russell found in all three groups that participation significantly increased student interest in STEM careers (68 percent of the follow-up respondents who had participated in NSF-sponsored UGR, and about 60 percent of the nationally representative baccalaureate graduates). On the other hand, about 8 percent of the follow-up respondents were less interested in a STEM career, and 16 percent had discovered that research was not an attractive career. Measured in terms of PhD intentions, among the follow-up respondents 29 percent reported that they had not planned on doing PhD work before they started college but had since changed their mind. To provide some baseline for interpreting this result, the natural science and engineering STEM national sample had gains of 19 percent for graduates who had participated in NSF-, NIH-, or NASA-sponsored UGR experiences, 12 percent for all graduates with any UGR experience, and 5 percent of the graduates with no UGR experience. (It is quite possible that the 29 percent figure will shrink closer to the 19 percent figure as the follow-up cohort ages.) Some of the gain in PhD intentions of the follow-up respondents was at the expense of earlier intentions to go to medical school. In the follow-up group there was a drop of 5 percentage points among those who had, before their UGR experience, intended to go to medical school.

Russell found that most racial/ethnic group differences were small. Positive effects were modestly larger for minority groups than for non-Hispanic whites. She also found that effect sizes were virtually identical for men and women on any of the study variables. Finally, similar to Zydney's and Bauer's University of Delaware studies, Russell found that the greater the amount of calendar time spent in research the greater the probability that the baccalaureate graduate would plan to earn a doctorate.

In another study, Price (2005) found that 14.4 percent of the known 180 African American PhD economists teaching at U.S. colleges and universities during the 2000—2001 academic year had, as undergraduates, attended a summer program designed to teach a variety of technical skills important for graduate study and involve them in research projects guided by prominent faculty. This program, funded by the NSF REU program and run by the American Economic Association (AEA), is known as the AEA Summer Program (AEA SP); it has operated annually since 1973, moving every few years to a new host campus. Designed explicitly for underrepresented minority students, it aims to recruit them to graduate study and strengthen their technical skills. Because some of these 180 faculty members were too old to have had a chance to participate in the AEA SP, its impact is likely even greater than the 14.4 percent figure suggests.

As Price points out, however, there is no direct proof that the program is responsible for this effect. Yet he found that those faculty members who had participated in the AEA SP were more likely than their peers to publish in top journals and get NSF grants. Additionally, Becker and Price (in this volume) report that 64 of the 162 alumni of the AEA SP classes of 2001–06 have entered doctoral programs in economics, and 37 others "are preparing to do so," a total effect of 62 percent. Becker and Price estimate that typically only 15 percent of the 162 alumni (about 25 students) on average could be expected to enter doctoral programs. The fact that four times that number have entered or will enter doctoral programs seems to be a clear testament to the impact of the AEA SP. Becker and Price estimate that the net effect on minority PhD production is to raise the output of U.S. citizen PhDs by about one-third.

Summary and Implications for Federal Policy

In recent years educators and policymakers have paid increasing attention to the value of authentic research experiences for STEM majors. Such experiences have generally been found to increase the interest of undergraduate majors in STEM and often to increase their interest and commitment to continuing their studies in graduate programs.

Even though the data from the few published studies are difficult to compare and are often not ideally suited to address the question of the effect on students' decisions to enter graduate programs, the findings of these studies are qualitatively similar and replicated consistently in every major empirical study.

Many undergraduate students who are afforded authentic research experience working under faculty member supervision have been selected from the highest-performing STEM majors. This fact has made it difficult to measure the full potential effect of UGR because so many of these top students were planning ex ante to pursue graduate studies, and often a PhD. For the highest-achieving undergraduates, the effects have been primarily to shift a small percentage of their postbaccalaureate plans from medical school to graduate school and increase their determination to earn doctorates.

Fortunately, some published studies on the effects of UGR have looked at undergraduate STEM majors who are not at the top of their classes. In these studies the measured effect in attracting them to graduate work has been quite large, demonstrating the power of authentic UGR experiences with close faculty mentoring. Such power appears to work for women as much as men, and for students who are from demographic groups that have been traditionally underrepresented in STEM majors and STEM PhD programs. This suggests that Federal agencies supporting UGR programs should consider opening them to a broader ability group of undergraduate students. In particular, the evidence from these studies is that UGR provided to women and under-represented minority students would have a strong effect in convincing them to apply to graduate programs in STEM fields.

III

Increasing the Representation of People of Color in the PhD Pool

8

Minority Students in Science and Math

What Universities Still Do Not Understand
about Race in America

RICHARD TAPIA AND CYNTHIA JOHNSON

Why do so few Hispanics and African Americans enter science, technology, engineering, and mathematics (STEM) fields, which are essential to the economic and social health of the nation? Simply put, the educational system grows increasingly unresponsive to America's Hispanic and black populations as the degree stakes go up. Borrowing the pipeline analogy, the STEM faculty pipeline is just the last, smallest-diameter section of a system that eliminates large numbers of Hispanic and black students all along the way while providing little support to those who try to stay the course. Some universities are beginning to complain not only of a shortage of candidates for faculty positions in the sciences and engineering but also of a shortfall of graduate students, a situation mirrored in industry, where the demands for a technically skilled workforce are increasingly difficult to meet. With their strong market orientation, business and industry are asking for a diverse workforce to meet the needs of a diverse population; the university case for diversity is less straightforward, to say the least. Among other things, universities work for diversity so that students study in an environment that prepares them for life after graduation. But universities are academic institutions, with an increasingly strong orientation toward research. They want strong students with a good academic foundation. When it comes to admissions, university STEM faculty still strongly favor rank-ordering systems of students based on test scores and tend to rate underrepresented minority candidates below white men in ability and potential. Women have made considerable inroads, but their situation is only marginally better than that of underrepresented people of color.

American education is on two separate trajectories serving two populations, one of which is growing rapidly. In the next fifty years, the Hispanic population is projected to reach 102.6 million (U.S. Census 2004). As educators we need to learn how to reach minority students unless we intend to shut ourselves off from what will soon be half of the population. We might think about the K–12 teachers' refrain, "You teach the kids you get."

Dwindling numbers in the STEM workforce pipeline generally and in the STEM academic pipeline in particular is not a new problem. In the past, the solution to a shortage of academic candidates was to bring in talent from overseas; the United States has reaped enormous benefits from the importation of talent. It is difficult to imagine U.S. technology in the middle decades of the twentieth century without the scientists who fled Adolf Hitler, or those who immigrated to this country for a variety of other reasons. In past decades we have also imported considerable numbers of faculty members of color. And of course, the United States is fortunate in that many international students remain in this country after completing their education here.

The importation solution is becoming a less viable option, however, as other countries strive to keep their talent at home and/or bring scholars back from the United States when they have completed their graduate work here. And just as it is becoming more difficult to import and keep international talent, the United States is requiring far larger numbers of scientists and engineers than ever before. Like other nations, we are increasingly dependent on technology and the foundational disciplines that produce it. Better technology is, in fact, a result of better science, not just more technology.

Yet another consideration as we face this deficit is that science and technology continue to develop in complexity. Whereas in the past many people obtained adequate job training for careers in technology through high school or vocational training programs, society now depends on universities to produce this labor force. And we should not forget that our country also needs large numbers of K–12 teachers with a strong science background.

So we have a shortage, and the old solution is no longer viable, or adequate to our needs. But we do have resources—the untapped talent of minority Americans. This should mean we have the answer to the problem: welcoming large numbers of minority students into STEM education.

But this is not happening. In fact, we now have a problem of demand as well as a problem of supply. Black and Hispanic students not only drop out of higher education in STEM fields at a significant rate, but many are opting out of science and math long before they go to college by avoiding these subjects in high school. While there is growing awareness that the United States stands to lose its competitive edge in science and technology (sectors critical to the health of the economy) if we do not produce more scientists and engineers, foreign students—not U.S. minority students—are still suggested as the solution. There seems to be little real concern that the United States might be wasting valuable resources of its own. Indeed, black and Hispanic minorities are viewed as having little to offer to science, mathematics, and technology.

In 2004, there were 73,327 African American undergraduate students enrolled at four-year, Title IV (using the 2000 Carnegie Classification of Institutes of Higher Education system) degree-granting institutions in biological/life sciences, mathematics, physical sciences, and engineering. The corresponding number for Hispanics was 55,725, and for Native Americans, 10,987.[1] The combined population of these groups was 83.5 million people. The number of these minority students who will complete the undergraduate degree is even smaller, for attrition from the university as well as from the scientific and technical disciplines is a serious problem for these population groups.[2]

By itself, then, the underrepresentation of minorities in the STEM fields—which leads to their underrepresentation in the critical technical workforce—represents a tremendous waste of talent, the scale of which is increasing as minority populations grow. But there are also repercussions for universities themselves if they do not reach and teach far larger numbers of minority students: they stand to lose support on many fronts—political, social, and financial. As we have noted above, universities have been active in civil rights advocacy and, to a lesser extent, support for equal opportunity and affirmative action policies; nonetheless, things have changed very little within higher education itself—especially graduate education and faculty composition. Universities are out of step with other key sectors of our society.

To understand the current situation in higher education, we have to look at the education process as a whole for underrepresented minorities. When we do, we see that there are problems all along the way, from elementary schoolchildren who think they can't learn math to high school seniors counseled into "soft" disciplines and away from science. But the greatest problem that minority students face in higher education is poor preparation at all prior levels of schooling.

Much has been said and written about the plight of U.S. public education. The problems that beset our schools have especially serious consequences for minority students, who are nearly always enrolled in public education and whose families are among the most vulnerable sector of the population. Parental levels of education still tend to be proportionately low among Hispanic and African American families when compared to white families. This means more than parents not being able to help students with their homework, although that, too, is a problem. It also means that Hispanic and black parents cannot successfully guide their children through the educational process—especially postsecondary education.

Many minority families are simply not acquainted with higher education, its language, its processes, its demands, or its advantages. They are not aware of the far greater opportunities open to students with baccalaureate degrees, much less the career options for those with PhDs. They are not aware of what has to be done to prepare for college—from selecting the right courses in high school to signing up to take the Scholastic Aptitude Test. Recent immigrants from Mexico have been schooled in a very different system, one in which parents participate little to not at all; these students and their parents may be limited by weak English language capabilities. An apt analogy for not only many Hispanic but also many African American students is to think of higher education as a foreign land, where the lifestyle and language are different—and in fact they are, from matriculation and dormitories to commencement. All in all, many minority parents are not able to give their children informed support through the trials of education—trials that all students experience but that may be devastating in their consequences for these students, as Bowen and Bok point out in their 1998 study of minorities in higher education.[3]

Although many public K–12 schools are extending their social mission and providing extensive services to students and parents, from tutoring to food programs, their resources are limited and demands are increasing. The burdens on urban schools are particularly heavy. These institutions are typically viewed as unattractive work environments, where challenges are great and rewards few. Consequently, they face daunting problems in staffing alone. Recruiting good teachers is a challenge for these schools, as is teacher burnout.

Communities under stress, parents with few if any resources, overworked teachers, and underfunded schools have a hard time producing good scholars. So do teachers ill-prepared or unqualified to teach the subjects they are assigned—a problem in U.S. schools generally. Increasingly, U.S. students are not competitive with students from overseas at all levels. Foreign students who enter our universities continue to expose (by comparison) the deficits in the academic preparation of many of our students, majority and minority alike.[4]

Ironically, although universities and politicians are quick to point out the inadequacies of K–12 teachers and schools for their part in the poor performance of students, similar performance issues in the academy are rarely ascribed to professors and universities.

Further complicating the situation for poorly prepared students going into STEM fields is the importance of mathematics in these disciplines. A weak math background is hard to correct because of the cumulative nature of mathematics. Lack of a good foundation in math, then, puts students at risk not only in math courses but in all of science and engineering. No matter what a student's level of talent, it is nearly impossible to succeed in a doctoral program in mathematics or a math-based field without excellent preparation, and excellent preparation is not the norm for most underrepresented minorities. Other skills less directly (but still significantly) related to professional achievement (e.g., writing, the development of an argument, understanding research methods) are also likely to be poorly developed in minority students who have not had a good K–12 education.

Educational deficits, then, loom large as a problem for Hispanic and African American minority students. Unfortunately, attempts to remedy these deficits, such as support programs or "catch-up" courses, often stigmatize the students enrolled in them. If not carefully designed and implemented—and sometimes in spite of careful design and implementation—these programs are typically viewed as remedial, and that is a sore point for minority students. The programs may even engender negative feelings by majority students who perceive this assistance as a form of favoritism extended to minorities.[5]

Hispanics and African Americans are, in fact, caught between a rock and a hard place when they try to compensate for their poor preparation. If these programs were designed to bring majority Americans up to the level of their international peers, would they "taint" participants in the same way that programs designed to help minority students have tended to do, or would they be viewed as "enrichment"? If programs designed for minorities are viewed differently, it may be explained by the fact that minorities are viewed differently.

Although progress has arguably been made toward a less racist society in the United States over the last fifty years, minorities still must cope with forms of bias and prejudice. One of the most pernicious of these in the academic environment is low expectations of success—a serious obstacle to academic achievement. Although it is good to be able to say that today's minority students very seldom complain of outright racism on campus,[6] the issue of low expectations is perhaps more acute at the university level than in K–12 education; so, also, is the specter of affirmative action—still. Minority students express both anger and hurt at the implication that they have been admitted to the university as an act of charity and have not earned the right to be there, for that is the attitude they sense in others.

A third set of problems exists for these students, and they are arguably the most difficult to address because they deal with the beliefs minority students carry within them. More than fifty years after *Brown v. Board of Education of Topeka*, the minority internalization of the experience of race in the United States is still a challenge to the well-being of black and Hispanic students on our campuses.

Race is on the minds of Hispanic, African American, and Native American students—and Asian students, for that matter—a great deal of the time. They think about how they are perceived as minorities, not how they are perceived as students or individuals. Indeed, a minority student often feels that she leads two lives—one personal and unique, the other as a representative of her race. For Hispanics and African Americans, failure carries the perceived risk of failing for *all* Hispanics or *all* African Americans. It is not difficult to see how the assumption of this symbolic role may adversely affect performance—especially the risk taking that is so important in creative research. Minority students most emphatically do not want to "let their race down," and this is a source of inner conflict as they reconcile the demands of their work with their need not to place themselves in jeopardy.

University faculty may find this deep, constant awareness of race on the part of minorities hard to comprehend—unless they are minorities themselves, of course. Indeed, one frequently hears faculty say, "I do not care what color my students are," presumably thinking that the issue of race has been laid to rest. Telling a minority student that race does not matter means little. Minority youth will identify forms of bias that people in the majority do not observe; they may, in fact, sometimes believe there is prejudice where none exists. But their feelings are, in the words of sociologist W. I. Thomas, "real in their consequences." These feelings and their consequences thus cannot be dismissed out of hand.

It is not hard to understand, then, why moving into the upper reaches of academe in the STEM fields has been beyond the reach of all but a few. The fact that comparatively few minorities undertake science and math—and in a climate of skepticism about their abilities based on performance on standardized tests—contrives to create a negative environment, or at least one that does not enable them to feel that they belong (as other students do even at the undergraduate level). Not surprisingly, they may doubt their chances of success. When they overcome these reservations sufficiently to venture into graduate education, their advantages—unique perspectives on problem-solving honed through life experience, distinctive forms of creativity, the potential to serve as role models to other minority students, and their interest in fields where science and human problems intersect, to name only a few—may be undervalued. At the same time, their probability of failure is exaggerated. They are evaluated by standards developed for a different student population; they find few peers; and there are not many people, including faculty, who understand their challenges and want to talk about them. There is not much energy in evidence on our campuses when it comes to minority underrepresentation issues, in spite of the expansion of programs focused on diversity.

Overturning segregation laws was not sufficient in and of itself to establish equality; affirmative action programs were created with the purpose of continuing the process of achieving a level playing field. The same optimism, naïveté, and expectation of rapid results that greeted the end of legal segregation also surrounded the early years of affirmative action. But while the ending of legal segregation and the creation of affirmative action programs were the sine qua non of equality, they were nonetheless only the first of many steps needed to complete the long process of righting very old wrongs and creating equal opportunity for all Americans. However, when progress seemed slow (or in some cases virtually nonexistent), frustration grew, fueling a backlash. That backlash continues.[7]

Cultural change is a slow process. More than fifty years have passed since the great social upheavals of the early civil rights movement; it has been more than thirty years since the creation of the first affirmative action programs. We are now in what could be called a third stage of the civil rights movement, working through the problems that are deeply rooted in our society and in the races and ethnicities of which it is composed. What better place to do this work than in the university? It is not at all clear, however, that universities are doing the work necessary to bring U.S. minorities into the economic mainstream—at least where this involves science and technology—or if indeed such universities are even able to meet this challenge.

There are, of course, departments with a good climate for minorities, and there are minority students thriving in excellent programs throughout the country, but all too often these situations are serendipitous—depending, for example, on a department chair, faculty member, or supportive dean who works successfully with minority students. There is no assurance that the next chair, adviser, or dean will show the same level of interest or provide the same level of support. In addition, there may be no model for institutionalizing effective programs; unless initiatives are properly institutionalized they merely become a drain on faculty time and energy, dying out as a professor, adviser, or dean burns out.

Without institutional change, there will be no lasting improvement in the climate for minority students.

Institutionalizing change is challenging in an academic setting. Faculty both need and demand considerable autonomy and tend to resist top-down management. There may in fact be not only considerable resistance to change but no good organizational model for change or effective leadership as institutions contemplate a different role with regard to the student population in our country or reevaluate long held beliefs about student aptitudes and the mission of the academy.[8] But this is not to say that universities cannot or do not change, even in the way they view themselves; witness the recent trend of institutions identifying themselves as *research universities* or *urban research universities* rather than simply universities. Institutes, centers, and consortia at which faculty work with other faculty and less often with students are proliferating, and new facilities house these enterprises. Outreach initiatives and mentoring programs—increasingly directed by staff, and seldom by faculty—proliferate as well, yet the line between K–12 and university education remains clearly drawn.

Universities grow, change, and redefine themselves. Demands on faculty increasingly emphasize research, expertise in getting funding, and scholarly publication. The subordination of teaching (and the skills it requires) to research and its benefits is by now an old story on most university campuses. This shift has had serious repercussions for underrepresented minority students, for whom mentoring has particular significance. Of the many ways in which top administration officials could change the climate for African Americans and Hispanics, one of the most effective would be to put more emphasis on teaching, and to reward both good teaching and successful mentoring—especially in the tenure process.

Although colleges were mainly for the elite from colonial times through the early years of the twentieth century, the nation's leaders showed considerable wisdom and foresight in also establishing some specialized institutions to meet teacher training needs or serve other populations of students, as in the case of agricultural and technical schools. It might also be worthwhile to note the dramatic gesture of Columbia University in the early years of the twentieth century, when it removed the Latin requirement in order to serve a growing and different population of students.[9]

The second era for universities in America began with the GI Bill; as a result of this legislation, education became the great equalizer in our society. The GIs returning from World War II sixty years ago brought a very different kind of life experience to university classrooms; many of them were significantly different from the youth who matriculated in the late nineteenth and early twentieth centuries. These former soldiers most likely would not have earned a degree without the stimulus and assistance the government provided.

The inclusion of large numbers of students who have a cultural and racial history that defines them in a very different way from the students of the past would create a third era in U.S. education. In many ways, this shift in campus demographics, if it occurs, will parallel the changes that the introduction of the GI Bill produced, or what happened when Columbia decided to serve the immigrant population. As the students of the 1940s did, great numbers of Hispanic and African American students will transform the landscape on our campuses, especially in disciplines on which the nation's economy depends.

Clearly, then, when we ask why there are so few minorities on university faculties in the STEM fields, we are beginning at the end. The problems begin with the all-too-often substandard early education of minority students, and they do not end there. Many of the challenges these students face are also to be found in America's universities. These challenges may not be as obvious as the clear deficiencies in K–12 education, and indeed most are not. The ambivalent relationship that exists between America's largest minority populations and the STEM disciplines in universities has its roots in how universities define themselves and view their role in society; how faculty members describe themselves and their professional responsibilities; academic institutional competition that affects the choices made by administrators and department chairs; and universities' ability to assess potential and nurture talent in students significantly different from those of the past. At present most universities are majority enclaves, and majorities do not experience race in the same ways that minorities do—not emotionally, not personally, not intellectually. Is there, finally, anything positive to say?

Although we do not have systems in place to address all of these issues in a coherent manner, and there are certainly no solutions that work in every case for specific challenges in educating and supporting Hispanic and black students as well as we do other students, we have collected a good deal of information about what it takes to recruit, retain, and graduate minority scientists, engineers, and mathematicians. Good models have been developed by faculty at a number of institutions,[10] and these models generally include:

- new approaches to assessment and re-evaluation of the use of standardized tests in evaluating performance
- strong mentoring and advising, from matriculation of undergraduates through early career development
- establishing a critical mass of minority students in order to counter feelings of isolation

- building community and creating support networks; in fields where student numbers are exceptionally low, it is helpful to create these communities across departmental lines
- development of a departmental mission statement and/or plan to ensure faculty commitment to the success of underrepresented minority students
- programs to help students overcome deficiencies in preparation that are designed with care so that participants are not stigmatized

In addition to these components of successful models, we would add that for minority students, points of transition are especially critical. One of the most critical points—especially as we consider increasing the number of faculty of color in the sciences—is the transition to graduate school. All models should emphasize support at points of change from one academic setting to the next.

The transition from undergraduate school to a graduate program poses challenges to most if not all students. Yet while minority students increasingly have friends or relatives who have undergraduate degrees, PhD programs and careers for PhD holders may still largely constitute unknowns. In fact, for many if not most minority students, the transition from undergraduate school to graduate education is nearly as significant an adjustment as going from high school to college. Like most undergraduates, they may talk of "going on" for a master's degree or PhD as if they were going from a hypothetical grade 16 to grade 17. It is important for students to understand the difference between undergraduate and graduate education—a distinction made in no uncertain terms by faculty.

Graduate study is intense, because it is difficult and because there is no "relief" from it—days are not broken up by a variety of courses and activities as they are in undergraduate school. And graduate school can often be characterized by isolation; the relative solitude of graduate study is exacerbated for underrepresented minorities by the fact that graduate minority populations in the STEM fields are generally small. It is not unusual for an African American or Hispanic student to be the only minority student in a department. Minority students repeatedly cite racial isolation as a problem, a good illustration of how universities are failing to put into practice what we have learned about supporting minority students. While it is important to do further research to increase our understanding of minority issues in general and student attrition versus persistence in particular, most universities would do better now to shore up mentoring and student support programs than to create yet another task force. After a certain point in time, doing further research on minority student issues begins to look like an avoidance tactic, or at best a lack of leadership. As has been noted herein, good models exist, and it is time to use them.

University presidents have influence and power both within their institutions and beyond as public intellectuals, and it is difficult to make substantial changes in higher education without the leadership of these presidents. With support and direction by university administration and accountability built into the process at every level there could be many more success stories for Hispanic and black students. But universities are also highly decentralized places. In spite of all that a president can do, without comprehensive buy-in (particularly at the departmental level) there will be no real change in how universities support minority student education and view faculty composition.

Decisions on admissions, recruitment, testing, hiring, and tenure—activities that lie at the heart of the academic enterprise—are largely and in some cases almost exclusively controlled by academic departments. Indeed, we learn much about the interpersonal skills and goals of faculty by observing their behavior in departments.

The university as a whole may have any number of policies on equal opportunity hiring, discrimination, and so forth, but the individual department is the site where policies are or are not implemented. Initiatives such as the development of a more effective mentoring program or the creation of a student support group must be implemented at the departmental level. We need these sorts of middle-range activities, and the department is the crucial middle ground between administration and classroom.

The talents that individual professors bring to the tasks of advising or sponsoring student support groups, which are of course essentially social activities, are critical to the success of these programs. They often require not only interpersonal skills that span a difference in age, but also the ability to communicate effectively across cultural lines. Of course, not all educators are good communicators. Teaching in one's area of specialization is different from talking across racial and ethnic divides. But an awareness of the need to establish a dialogue goes a long way toward creating that dialogue, and it is an important first step.

We hear about diversity every day on our campuses. Universities have been successful with diversity in the sense that they work hard at showing openness to all types of people, and this is certainly the way things should be on a campus. But this kind of diversity is not the antidote to minority underrepresentation. It is easier to create a diverse campus, with people from many religions, nations, and ethnicities, than it is to successfully integrate large numbers of U.S.-born minorities into higher education. Without significant numbers of Hispanics, Native Americans, and African Americans, our universities are diverse in letter but not in spirit. The problem of underrepresentation was behind the drive to create a diverse university, but underrepresentation itself has slipped below the radar. Hiring a professor from Buenos Aires is not a diversity achievement; hiring a Chicano from East Los Angeles is. Hiring one black professor and giving him six titles is a new form of tokenism; it does not change the composition of the faculty. Black faculty clustered in African studies programs and Hispanics clustered in Chicano studies programs, but with neither represented in the STEM fields, is not a good model for minority representation on campus.

In the United States we like things to happen quickly; we are known for that—all of us, minorities included, for we are alike in many ways. Achieving racial fairness, however, takes time. It calls for profound change in everyone involved in the process, including minority students themselves. Perhaps the frustratingly slow pace of change accounts for the fact that in the past few years there has seemed to be less energy in the drive to deal with underrepresentation and to create a university that mirrors our society more accurately from a demographic standpoint, especially in the fields that drive the economy. But we cannot afford to lose, or not regain, our momentum. When one-third of this country's population remains on the outskirts of science and technology in the university, what does it say about the university and its understanding of human potential?

The challenges are there, but so are the accomplishments. We have learned a great deal about what works; now it is time to put that knowledge to work. Until we see far greater numbers of minorities enrolled in higher education, embarking on graduate study, and represented on our faculties in not only the humanities and the arts but also the STEM fields, diversity will be mere window dressing and universities will have little to do with the world beyond the campus. It would be hard to estimate the harm that will continue to be done to the minority population and to our nation if that should happen.

9

THE MATHEMATICAL AND THEORETICAL BIOLOGY INSTITUTE

A Successful Model for Increasing Minority Representation in the Mathematical Sciences

CARLOS CASTILLO-CHAVEZ AND CARLOS CASTILLO-GARSOW

William Yslas Velez—a distinguished professor of mathematics at the University of Arizona, a past president of the Society for the Advancement of Chicanos and Native Americans in Science, and a recipient of a White House President's Award for his documented efforts to mentor and support minority students—has often challenged elite institutions to find ways of increasing minority representation in the mathematical sciences.[1] At Cornell University we have taken up this challenge. In 1996 Velez introduced us to James Schatz, who was at that time the chief of the Division of the Mathematical Sciences at the National Security Agency, and who is now the agency's deputy director of research. To Schatz, the absence of minority groups of Americans in the mathematical sciences is a matter of national security as well as of deep personal concern. Thus, with the advice of Velez and the encouragement of Schatz, in 1996 Javier Rojo (University of Texas el Paso) and Carlos Castillo-Chavez drafted a plan for a mentorship model that would be tried at a Hispanic-serving institution. The University of Texas–El Paso, home of Javier Rojo at that time, seemed like the ideal place. We began to plan how to make UT–El Paso a national model for the training of U.S. underrepresented minorities in the mathematical sciences.[2]

Velez also introduced us to Herbert Medina—a professor of mathematics at Loyola Marymount University—whose interests in undergraduate education and diversity were known to Velez.[3] We were now ready to submit a National Science Foundation (NSF) proposal that would support ten students in our undergraduate research experience program in applied mathematics. The summer research experience would be held at UT–El Paso. Unfortunately, the Mathematics Department at UT–El Paso did not find the model compelling. Facing an NSF grant deadline in less than twenty-four hours, we called Cornell University's provost, Don Randel,[4] and requested his support for a version of our effort that included a change in site from UT–El Paso to Cornell. Randel instantly provided the economic support needed to get this project off the ground and had no doubt that our plan would set up a national mentorship model in the mathematical sciences. The Mathematical and Theoretical Biology Institute (MTBI) was established with the strong institutional support of the Cornell Office of the Provost in 1996. In 2004 MTBI moved to the nation's largest Hispanic-serving research institution, Arizona State University. The Office of the Provost at Arizona State University and that of its president, Michael Crow, have enthusiastically supported the MTBI program and its expansions.

MTBI: A BRIEF LOOK AT THE NUMBERS

Over the course of eleven years the MTBI has mentored, through its sequential summer research experiences, a diverse group of 277 undergraduate and 31 graduate students. This population includes a high percentage of underrepresented U.S. minority students. The MTBI recruits primarily juniors and/or seniors from mostly "nonselective" colleges and universities—students who might otherwise not have considered graduate school as a real possibility for their future. MTBI participants have either a solid, very good, or outstanding academic record. Most if not all applicants have a clear desire to find out what role if any mathematics plays in solving problems of importance to our society. Naturally, mentorship programs that take advantage of the deep social concerns of U.S. minority students are bound to be extremely attractive to students from underrepresented U.S. minority communities.

MTBI alumni have contributed to the establishment of successful minority student graduate communities at Arizona State University, Cornell University, and the University of Iowa.[5] MTBI alumni have helped the faculty at these institutions establish and maintain a critical mass of U.S. underrepresented minority students in their graduate programs, and has also sent a small number of minority graduate students to such major research institutions as Harvard, Princeton, and Stanford Universities and the University of Michigan. The first "large" crop of MTBI alumni completed their PhDs in the mathematical sciences in 2005, and are now pursuing careers in scientific research—primarily through the postdoctoral route. Their numbers, however small, represent a significant perturbation of the past equilibrium. In 2005, MTBI alumni received ten PhDs in the mathematical sciences, seven of which were awarded to members of underrepresented minority groups.[6] Seven 2005 graduates hold postdoctoral positions at selective institutions (among these are six underrepresented U.S. minorities) and one holds a tenure-track faculty position at the University of Puerto Rico in Mayaguez. The 2005 class of MTBI PhD holders includes four Latinas and one African American woman. In other words, a program that has served 277 undergraduates has dramatically increased the national production of mathematics scholars among U.S. Latinos who primarily held undergraduate degrees from nonelite institutions. These graduates now have a solid opportunity to join the faculty ranks of research universities if they choose to do so.

CHALLENGES IN IMPLEMENTATION

Despite decades of failures, a great percentage of the academic mathematics community believes that the problem of underrepresentation is either easy to solve or not really a problem. It is not uncommon to hear faculty members express the view that recruiting students who are not graduates of elite institutions is not productive (a "natural selection" theory). Institutional change in academia is difficult. The implementation of models that work relies entirely on the participation of committed individuals. A large percentage of faculty members fail to acknowledge or even grasp the importance of differentiating between U.S. minorities and foreign nationals. Systemic change will not take hold until U.S. minority representation becomes a national priority.

THE MODEL

In this section we will expand upon our study "The New American University: Mentorship in the Mathematical Sciences" (Castillo-Chavez and Castillo-Garsow, forthcoming) in order to highlight key elements of the MTBI's successful model with the hope that its large-scale portability becomes the norm.

Common Language

The MTBI program assumes that students are familiar with elementary calculus (two semesters); have been exposed to linear algebra (eigenvalues and eigenvectors); and have some familiarity with probability, basic statistics (probability densities and distributions, random variables, Bayes's Theorem, and expectation), birth and death stochastic processes, as well as some familiarity with a computer programming language. The cooperative nature of MTBI's environment is such that weaknesses in some of these areas are not critical. The first three weeks of the program are devoted to the study of dynamical systems in the context of ecology, epidemiology, immunology, and conservation biology. Students also learn how to use the MATLAB and XPP programs through carefully prepared computational laboratory activites, while also becoming proficient with the Maple, Minitab, and LaTeX programs.

Students are responsible for sixteen extensive complex sets of problems closely tied into lectures. Review lectures are provided on the essentials of linear algebra and probability. The preparatory phase ends with a small directed project that forces the students to go beyond the material covered in class. Typically, the project involves the study of a biological system with identified dynamics at two highly distinct temporal scales. Bifurcation analysis, simulations, and the interpretation of model results are at the heart of the exercise. Students are involved in lectures, problem and modeling sessions, and computational labs for an average of five hours per day.

Mentorship in Modeling

Relevance seems to be the key to motivation and success. Students often encounter difficulties when they insist on using a specific methodology without taking into consideration its appropriateness for their question. As a method of addressing this difficulty, MTBI builds a culture in which students interact with mentors who demonstrate, assign, and assist the development of highly relevant mathematical modeling problems.

During the first weeks, distinguished researchers provide sets of two or three ninety-minute lectures on a single topic supplemented with relevant problem sets. These lectures highlight interesting "pure" mathematics or nontrivial applications.

A modeling seminar is conducted twice a week by program alumni (undergraduate and graduate students). These alumni discuss their own experience as program participants in identifying and selecting their own projects as well as in convincing a group of colleagues (three to four) to work on their proposed joint project. The alumni put an emphasis on identifying a key question, a process that precedes the selection of methodology.

Participants are assisted by the resident faculty and graduate students, and are encouraged to work together with other students throughout the summer. Generally following the Oberwolfach model,[7] the lectures, seminars, and talks are followed by a community dinner at which students interact with faculty and graduate students. Paper tablecloths serve a double function as writing or drawing pads; napkins are not sufficient in these learning communities!

The Absence of Hierarchies

By design, the research agenda of this summer institute is set by the undergraduate participants. This tradition was begun in 1997 when the institute was in its second summer. Today it is not uncommon to see students arrive with their own projects at the start of "math camp." Such students try to "sell" their projects to two to three additional participants during the first three weeks. There are no rules regarding the formation of such groups except that they be made up of three to four individuals. Once the groups have been formed (without faculty supervision) students begin to orally present their projects to a dynamic group of faculty, graduate students, and visitors. The initial role of these sessions is to help students narrow the scope of their projects. Efforts to identify a workable question are at the heart of these sessions, but no effort is made to alter the overall goal of the students' projects. Typically initial suggestions are along the lines of: What is the impact of alcohol on brain activity? What are the dynamics of eating disorders? What conditions will guarantee the survival of the monarch butterfly? What are the effects of social structures on the spread of HIV in Nigeria? Once a question that captures the essence of the students' project is selected, the next step is to build a model. These modeling efforts have moved us into the world of networks or dynamical systems (broadly understood to include stochastic processes) or simulations. During this process the students are assigned faculty advisers and provided with reliable graduate student support. The incorporation of these individuals is based on the desire of the faculty to get involved in the enterprise and the interest of the graduate student in the project. The project dynamics, including forming a group, deciding on a research question, and selecting a model, are in the hands of undergraduate students. Participants work on problems for which faculty participants do not have the answer. Faculty, graduate students, and undergraduate participants become partners in the processes of exploration.

Meeting Expectations

The following three weeks are driven by the intensity of the participants in providing an answer to a relevant question. Regular open meetings are conducted at which each group presents and defends its efforts. (On some occasions, students have had to make dramatic changes to their models near the end of the summer research experience.) After three weeks of intense collaborations, a series of results (numerical, analytical, and statistical) that shed some light on the question are delivered. Students then work hard on writing a technical report of twenty-five to forty-five pages that captures the problem and its background, the model, the methods, and the group's results.

The Product

The participants conclude their efforts with a technical report (of which there have been 111 in eleven summers), prepare a thirty-minute presentation, and highlight their research on a poster. In 2006, for example, the program began on June 6 and concluded on July 29. Seven groups of participants made oral presentations of their results at the joint meeting of the Society for Industrial and Applied Mathematics (Life Sciences Group) and the Society for Mathematical Biology, which was held in Raleigh, North Carolina, from July 30 to August 4, 2006. Seven posters were presented. These posters were also presented at the annual meeting of the Society for Advancement of Chicanos and Native Americans in Science in Tampa, Florida (October 27, 2006) and at the annual American Mathematical Society meeting in January of 2007. Students regularly present their research at their own institutions and local conferences during the academic year that follows the completion of the project. An average of two to three awards per year have been given to MTBI projects.

Increasing Diversity in the Sciences

The first step in achieving the goal of the MTBI and the Institute for Strengthening the Understanding of Mathematics and Sciences (SUMS) is to increase the number of underrepresented minorities in the mathematical sciences at the graduate level.[8] The MTBI and SUMS have sent 138 students from underrepresented minority groups to graduate school over its first eleven years, and 169 students overall. Furthermore, 52 percent have been women, including 65 women from minority groups. In the years 2001 and 2002, prior to the MTBI producing PhD graduates, the United States awarded an average of ten PhDs to U.S. Latinos.[9] In 2005, MTBI alumni earned ten PhDs in the mathematical sciences, seven of which were awarded to members of underrepresented minority groups. That is, almost one-fourth of the national output of minority doctoral students who earned their degree in the mathematical sciences for that year came from MTBI alumni. In 2005, MTBI alumni included one-third (five out of fifteen) of the total female underrepresented minority PhDs in the mathematical sciences for 2005. Four of those five were Latinas—over half (four out of seven) of the national production of Ph.D. degrees in the mathematical sciences. The 2006 class of former MTBI participant PhD holders includes ten equally successful individuals, most of whom are members of underrepresented minority populations.

MTBI/SUMS alumni are prolific, having coauthored 111 technical reports over the past eleven summers. These reports are often continued or extended during the academic year. Several reports have served as instigators of highly innovative research projects. In this book's bibliography are references to ten refereed publications in which MTBI alumni played a fundamental role and where their interests in the use of mathematics to address issues of social equity and opportunity—the promises of our democracy—are obvious. The articles co-authored by Song et al. (2006); Gjorgjieva et al. (2005); Kribs-Zaleta et al. (2005); Chowell et al. (2006); Yakubu et al. (2004); Rios-Soto et al. (2006); Sanchez et al. (2006); Del Valle et al. (2004); Gonzalez et al. (2003); and Chowell et al. (2003) are but a fraction of the research instigated by MTBI/SUMS participants over the past decade.

The indicators of future and current successes are visible. Twenty-four MTBI alumni have enrolled in a mathematical sciences program at Cornell University since 1996 and nearly 90 percent of those who enrolled in the PhD program have completed or will complete it.[10] The mathematics department at Arizona State University has enrolled twenty-four Latino and five African American students in its graduate program in the mathematical sciences. There are now thirty-four MTBI alumni at ASU. Fourteen underrepresented minority students (all MTBI alumni) have enrolled in a mathematical sciences program at the University of Iowa;[11] this number does not include MTBI alumni enrolled at Iowa who are not minority students. These three subpopulations of MTBI alumni form the nuclei of a close-knit community of minority and non-minority scholars at three research institutions.

MTBI alumni stay in touch with each other and get together at annual professional meetings. Their alumni network is already affecting the training of future mathematicians, particularly those from underrepresented minority groups.

The MTBI's move to a state institution has allowed for the expansion of its mission. MTBI/SUMS mentorship efforts now begin at the high school level. SUMS staff has mentored 2,095 high school students through its Mathematics Science Honors Program (MSHP) over the past twenty-one years. MSHP students are diverse; 60 percent of its participants have been young women. Hispanic and Native American students account for the largest ethnic minority groups, at 51 and 18 percent, respectively. Thirty-one percent of the students who participated in the MSHP attended two or more summers consecutively, earning up to twelve credits in the three summers prior to attending ASU as freshmen. Almost 60 percent of MSHP participants have attended ASU after graduation from high school over the past four years. There are currently over 350 former MSHP students attending ASU, with 56 percent female students and 49 percent Hispanic students representing the largest gender and ethnic groups, respectively. The Ira A. Fulton School of Engineering at ASU has the highest percentage of enrolled MSHP students (at 34 percent), followed by ASU's College of Liberal Arts and Sciences (at 24 percent). Additionally, students who participate in the MSHP tend to have higher grade point averages and retention rates than students who did not participate in the program: the standard grade point average (GPA) for a current non-MSHP student at ASU is 3.01, while the average GPA for a current MSHP student is 3.15.

Four White House President's Awards for Excellence in Science, Mathematics, and Engineering Mentoring have been associated with the MTBI and SUMS: the first (1996) to the late Joaquin Bustoz Jr., founder of SUMS; the second (1997) to Carlos Castillo-Chavez, director of the MTBI/SUMS; the third (1998) to Armando Rodriguez, professor of electrical engineering and a strong contributor to the MTBI/SUMS programs; and the fourth (2003) to SUMS itself. The American Mathematical Society has just recognized the MTBI and SUMS as a "Mathematics Program that Makes a Difference."[12]

MTBI/SUMS alumni are beginning to take on faculty positions, and evidence of future patterns of secondary recruitment have begun to emerge. The establishment in 2005 of the Applied Mathematical Sciences Institute by MTBI alumni Erika Camacho and MTBI graduate mentor and former summer director Steve Wirkus provides a vivid example.[13] One of the most distinguished SUMS graduates is Trachette Jackson, who is now a tenured associate professor of mathematical biology at the University of Michigan.

CHALLENGES

Creating Infrastructure to Sustain an Increase in Diversity

As successful as the MTBI has been at increasing diversity in the mathematical sciences, it is but one program. Unless the changes that the MTBI has created become self-sustaining and self-generating, its impact will be short-lived. To this end, we believe that creating a large community of minority scholars that is committed to the issues associated with the problems of minority underrepresentation in the mathematical sciences is but one way. Such a community will provide the environment where minority success and minority recruitment into the sciences is natural—the norm rather than the exception.

Encouraging the Development of the New American University

The MTBI/SUMS philosophy adheres to the principles of the "new American university"—that is, the MTBI is an institution that, like its home institution, ASU, wants to be judged by the quality of the research and academic accomplishments of its students and alumni rather than by academic pedigree or prior access to selective educational settings on the part of its participants.[14] Encouraging the development of this perspective is critical to the goals of the MTBI because it directly addresses the disadvantages that many underrepresented minority students face. The MTBI wants to be an institute whose alumni, while pursuing their scholarly and scientific interests, also consider "the public good." The MTBI wants to be an institute whose students, alumni, faculty, and staff transcend the concept of community service to accept responsibility for the economic, social, cultural, and environmental vitality of the communities they serve.[15]

The success of the MTBI in creating excellence in the context of social responsibility is best illustrated by the work of Camacho and Wirkus who, only a few years after graduation, have begun to give back generously to the mathematical community. Camacho and Wirkus have set up a model learning community in just two years.[16]

Costs

The issue of the costs of a program like the MTBI was omitted from the first draft of this manuscript. David Burke, a professor of human genetics and a member of the Michigan Center for Genomics and Public Health headed by Mike Boehnke at the University of Michigan, brought it to our attention and suggested that we include it. The Michigan Center for Genomics and Public Health faculty has given a three-day workshop on genomics, as well as long-distance mentorship to MTBI participants for the past five years. All mentorship activities involve intense faculty participation—that is, the participation of highly trained individuals. So what is the cost? Who pays for their time? When it comes down to research, universities pay for most of the research time of their mathematical sciences faculty. Typically, nine-month appointments (composed of

50 percent research and 50 percent teaching and service) mean that in general, the NSF will decide who does paid summer research and who does it for free. This has become an accepted practice in academia—albeit unwillingly. Training undergraduates to be ready for graduate school is not less costly than other programs and practices, and their training provides no tangible rewards. Typically, there are *no* immediate publications, no grants and no recognition when it comes to mentoring undergraduate students, particularly at research universities. Those in charge of salary increases or promotions do not value mentorship activities and so it would seem suicidal to devote time training U.S. students to do research. There are plenty of academicians at research and undergraduate research oriented universities who would gladly shift a great deal of their time to the mentorship of undergraduates, but such a decision would bring negative responses by university administrators. The NSF and the National Institutes of Health need to put forward the meager funds required to support the careers of individuals who choose to train undergraduates to do research. Mentorship success would be measured by the ability of a program to place these students in graduate programs. Top research groups, with obvious priority differences, cannot do the job that is required at the scale that it is needed, but there are plenty of researchers and professors who would do it if the rewards were there.

At the MTBI the cost per student per summer is high—about $10,000. However, this is not the real cost per student, as we do not account, in dollars and cents, for the time and effort put out by individuals and groups (like the time given to the MTBI by the Michigan's Genomics Group faculty) in these mentorship efforts. The "cost" of each student who has been successfully placed in graduate school—that is, if we only consider students who have actually *received* an advanced degree—would be more like $25,000. This amount includes room, board, stipend ($3,000 per summer), and paid mentorship efforts over an average of two and a half summers (five months). If we remove the stipends, then the cost per student is about $17,000 or $18,000. This amount is equivalent to tuition paid at an elite university for one semester!

Support

MTBI and SUMS efforts have not been carried alone. The MTBI received extraordinary support from the Cornell University administration, the Cornell Center for Applied Mathematics, and Cornell's departments of Biological Statistics and Computational Biology. And the MTBI and SUMS have had no less support at ASU, having established a highly effective partnership with ASU's Hispanic Research Center; and

ASU's Mathematics and Statistics Department has not only embraced our efforts but has actively contributed to them. MTBI and SUMS successes have been possible because of the leadership and hard work of all our partners, supporters, staff, and summer faculty. However, at the end of the day it is the continuous funding by the NSA, the NSF, and the Alfred P. Sloan Foundation that have kept this effort alive long enough to make a difference.

10

CURRICULUM INTENSITY IN GRADUATE PREPARATORY PROGRAMS

The Impact on Performance and Progression to Graduate Study among Minority Students in Economics

CHARLES BECKER AND GREGORY PRICE

Considerable resources are devoted to preparing students for doctoral study, particularly in quantitative disciplines. This is especially true in the United States, where most domestic students come from the liberal arts, which have not given them the complete background necessary for success in doctoral programs with substantial prerequisites. The United States also suffers from a legacy of discrimination against many minority groups, especially African Americans, Native Americans, and Hispanics. American minorities continue to experience inferior primary and secondary education on average, and are disproportionately likely to attend nonresearch, largely noncompetitive colleges and universities that neither encourage nor prepare students for rigorous academic graduate programs. The combination of historic discrimination, lack of encouragement, and weaker preparation has resulted in low representation of American minorities within the science, technology, engineering, and mathematics (STEM) disciplines. As a result, many disciplines have taken proactive steps, creating programs aimed at reducing minority underrepresentation.

These programs have been subject to little serious analysis of their design or effectiveness. The need for such programs is particularly great in economics in light of a confluence of forces. First, there is a huge gap between undergraduate study in economics—which is in part a service program for business and other fields, and one with modest quantitative requirements—and doctoral study, for which a bachelor's degree in mathematics is ideal preparation. Second, most American MA programs still leave a substantial gap in terms of quantitative preparation between themselves and doctoral study, and generally are not regarded as a stepping stone to PhD work. Thus, few American students enter leading doctoral programs in economics with MA degrees. However, most international students who join U.S. PhD programs in economics *do* have highly quantitative master's degrees, thereby further extending the gap between them and American liberal arts undergraduates, especially those from nonelite institutions.

In response to the underrepresentation of American minorities in economics, in 1973 the American Economic Association (AEA) set up the American Economic Association Summer Program (AEASP) and Minority Scholarship aimed at encouraging and preparing minority students to embark on doctoral study and ultimately to enter the economics profession. The program started the following year, spending its first year hosted by the University of California–Berkeley, and then moving to Northwestern University for five years. Yale University (1980–82) and the University of Wisconsin–Madison (1983–85) followed, each with three-year stints. Temple University (1986–90), Stanford University (1991–95), and the University of Texas–Austin (1996–2000) all served as hosts for five years. Most recently, the program moved to the University of Colorado–Denver (2001–03) in affiliation with North Carolina A&T State University, and then to Duke University (2004–07), also in affiliation with North Carolina A&T. The program moves to the University of California–Santa Barbara, its tenth host, for the summers of 2008–10.

In light of the pattern of switching hosts (and hence modest but nontrivial design changes) and its chronically tenuous funding situation, the AEASP never has been formally evaluated for its effectiveness, save for one striking exception. Gregory Price (2005) has created a data set of black economists teaching at U.S. colleges and universities during the 2000–2001 academic year and matched it with an AEASP alumni list. Since some 93 percent of AEASP alumni before 2000 were African American, the exclusion of other minorities has little impact on the results—and the number of U.S. citizen Hispanic and Native American economics faculty is small, even relative to the numbers of black faculty. Of the 180 black university economists Price has identified, 14.4 percent had attended the AEASP. This sampling does not make it possible to determine whether the program has an impact on applying to graduate school, earning a doctoral degree, or entering the profession thereafter, but it does allow Price to examine the treatment impact of exposure to the AEASP on scholarly productivity. Econometric results indicate that AEASP participation raises the likelihood of publishing in top journals, securing National Science Foundation grants, and membership in the National Bureau of Economic Research. The likelihood of being employed at a research university, a liberal arts institution, or a selective liberal arts institution does not appear to depend on program participation, nor does one's total number of publications.

In this chapter we will evaluate the effectiveness of the new curriculum treatment of the AEASP and examine the extent to which the selection of less-prepared and less "advantaged" students affects performance. Specifically, a recent design shift enables us to draw initial conclusions as to which sort of interventions are most effective. The largest questions—whether and to what extent the AEASP increases flows into and through economics doctoral programs—are left to subsequent analysis as part of a project undertaken by the authors together with economists Cecilia Rouse of Princeton University and Sue Stockly of Eastern New Mexico University.

While the AEASP has never been formally evaluated, casual review of survey data suggest that the program has mattered. The AEASP has had some 854 alumni during its thirty-four-year history, with an average of twenty-five new participants per summer. The program currently enjoys growth and renewed energy: during the past seven years there have been 195 minority alumni, including thirty-nine students who participated in two summers; the average enrollment has been thirty-three. Since the program expanded to a two-level (Foundations and Advanced) structure in 2001, some seventy-three alumni from 2001–07 have entered doctoral programs or will soon do so, and dozens more are preparing to do so. Five 2001–07 alumni already have earned their PhD degrees. To emphasize the obvious, having a likely 110–125 minority students enter doctoral programs from the 2001–07 classes is not a small number, and reflects a significant effort by the economics profession toward diversification.

The AEA Summer Program: An Inadvertent Experimental Design

For its first twenty-seven years, the AEASP conducted a single program of roughly eight weeks in duration. Then, starting in 2001, a second level was added, enabling the program to sort participants into the Foundations and Advanced levels. Moving to two levels offered several advantages. Most immediately, it reduced classroom heterogeneity, thereby making the experience less demoralizing for those relatively underprepared. It also made it possible to offer more rigorous study at the advanced end, a fortuitous development in light of the growing technical demands of graduate economics. More important still, the second level made it possible to focus recruiting efforts on students at institutions other than major research universities and selective liberal arts colleges, thereby enhancing the social diversity of the program. The program's move in 2001 to a nonelite state university, the University of Colorado–Denver, further emphasized the desire to recruit students from a broad range of institutions.

The redesigned program also held out the possibility that participants could return to the AEASP for a second summer. Although doing so is costly in that each returning student displaces a potential new student, the two-summer option has the advantages of providing additional training and enabling the program administrators to strongly influence students' course selections in the intervening year, since readmission is not automatic. At the outset, the program administrators had no idea whether students would return, but thus far more than 24 percent of participants have done so.

The combination of multiple levels and a two-summer option makes for a natural experiment, since there are now three types of AEASP experience: Foundations study, Advanced study, and both. A superficial reading of the data might easily lead one to conclude that two summers are better than one, and that Advanced study dominates Foundations study. However, simple descriptive statistics do not account for the possibility that group characteristics are different, and that returning for a second summer is a nonrandom event. Thus, the more interesting question is whether the multilevel and multisummer options increase the likelihood of progression to graduate school, conditional on student attributes. A second question of interest is whether there are differential effects for certain groups, which we handle in statistical analysis by adding interaction terms. As noted, the AEASP's two-tier design was added largely to increase the potential applicant pool, and to draw in less-prepared students. On the surface, the program would appear to be successful in this regard, but there has been no formal analysis of the two-tiered approach's impact. Taken together, answers to these questions should offer insights into what sorts of strategies might best reach the "hard-to-reach"—students with little exposure to research, little encouragement to enter academe, and little incentive to take advanced mathematics and statistics courses.

The empirical analysis that follows is based on data from the 2003 program at UC–Denver and the 2004 and 2005 programs at Duke University. It is important to emphasize the continuity of the program as it moved from UC–Denver to Duke. The course structure has been virtually unchanged—the only substantive difference being the addition of a game-theory component to the Foundations level in 2004. Thus, in all three years of the study, students were expected to take a grueling load of twelve academic credits in an eight-week period. Three credits are devoted to mathematics (with a focus on economics applications), three are devoted to statistics and econometrics, and microeconomics and game theory courses each receive 1.5 credits at the Advanced level, while they are combined into a three-credit course at the Foundations level. In addition, students are required to participate in a three-credit research seminar in which they produce a major paper. The continuity between UC–Denver and Duke is further strengthened by the presence of two instructors who have taught for all of the years in both programs, by several teaching assistants at Duke who participated in the program when it was at UC–Denver (three in 2007 alone), and by having the same program director at both institutions.

The AEASP included thirty minority scholarship students in 2003, and thirty-six in both 2004 and 2005. In 2005, a typical year in terms of admissions, just over forty minority students were admitted to the AEASP. More than 90 percent of those who were admitted accepted the admission offer. Of the thirty-nine who attended, thirty-six received a need-based AEA Minority Scholarship, though precise amounts varied according to need. All students completed the program. As in 2002–04 and 2006–07, the 2005 AEASP did not have the capacity to admit all of the qualified applicants, and many excellent students were turned away. The years 2003 and 2004 were exceptional in that the majority of participants were women. To our knowledge, these two years were the first time that the program has been predominately female, though the underlying applicant pool in 2002–04 was approximately 50 percent women for each year. The 2005 class swung sharply in the other direction, and the historic gender pattern for the program at Duke is now similar to that at other recent hosts.

ESTIMATION STRATEGY

There are two interrelated questions we seek to answer. First, does the AEASP's two-level, two-summer option make a difference in terms of progression to graduate school? Second, what factors explain performance within the AEASP itself? Understanding this second question is important in part because we need to control for selectivity, and in part because performance allows us to infer otherwise unobserved attributes.

Thanks to a fairly intrusive set of questions on the application form, we have considerable information on the applicant and actual participant pools, including gender, age, race/ethnicity, citizenship, and prior academic record.[1] Beyond estimating an overall grade point average (GPA) from past schooling, we also compile estimates of the number of courses in economics, mathematics, and statistics; we further calculate separate GPAs for economics and mathematics courses. Our information also includes the students' parents' education and occupation; it is possible as well to infer (imperfectly) whether the applicant comes from an intact family. Applicants are required to furnish income data, but this turns out to be of little use, since a large number of students are self-supporting and thus we do not have complete data on parental incomes. Since we have transcripts from previous academic institutions, we make rough inferences as to the nature and quality of prior schooling (such as whether the student attended a public or private university, a minority-serving or traditionally white institution, or a research university or elite liberal arts college). Finally, we have information on the level into which a student is placed (Foundations or Advanced), and whether or the student is returning for a second year. In terms of dependent variables, we know the student's performance in the AEASP, whether the student has actually entered a master's or doctoral program, and whether the student has indicated an intention to enter a master's or doctoral program (and is taking steps to fulfill that intention).

As economists typically evaluate performance outcomes within a general human capital framework, we follow the same approach in assessing the determinants of success in the AEASP. This allows us to condition actual student performance in the AEASP on those variables in our data that serve as proxies for an individual's stock of human capital, ability, and socioeconomic characteristics that may condition endogenous performance variables that cannot be observed. The findings discussed below are based on Ordinary Least Squares (OLS) estimates of the effects of these variables on performance in the AEASP.

Our approach to estimating the impact of the recent AEASP curriculum innovation is to view the participant's intentions and actual decisions to apply to a doctoral program in economics as latent decision variables that are a function of observable and unobservable characteristics. This allows us to condition the decision of a participant to either plan to apply or actually apply to a doctoral program on a particular treatment—having completed both the Foundations and Advanced curricula—and estimate its effect. We report bivariate probit parameter estimates of the treatment effect of having been exposed to two years of coursework in the AEASP on the intended decision to apply to a doctoral program in economics, as well as on completed applications.[2]

The Determinants of Performance in the AEASP

We tried a large number of alternate regressions, as many measures are problematic in some way or another. Representative OLS regressions appear in table 10.1. The coefficient estimates for the most part are surprisingly insensitive to specification, especially given the small sample size (just over one hundred observations).

Considering first demographic variables, gender has no impact on performance. Asian minority students (Vietnamese Americans or Filipino Americans) perform 0.3 to 0.4 grade points higher than their African American and Hispanic counterparts.[3] The few nonminority students also do better, but they tend to be a highly select group. While U.S. citizenship is not significant, its sign is consistently positive, and it will be interesting to see whether permanent residents and refugees continue to do somewhat worse as we expand the sample in future work. In most regressions, GPA declines with age: being thirty-four instead of twenty-one years old costs about one-third of a grade point.

This last result reflects several features of the AEASP. Older students have several disadvantages. Some have been out of a full-time schooling situation for several years. Some have weaker math skills than their younger peers, while others have taken lots of mathematics, but not recently. Several older students have children and families, and whether they are present or not, children compete for attention. Above all, we sense that the effort required to succeed in the program favors younger students, who are simply more energetic than at least some of the older students. This is not to say that older students never do well or that ability declines linearly with age. When we replace age with completed schooling variables, it appears that very young students are also at a disadvantage, even though the program tends to pair them in roommate assignments with older, prospective mentors.

Our measures of past achievement and effort do not have a strong effect. The only variable that tends to be significant is undergraduate GPA, with a coefficient ranging from 0.3 to 0.4, virtually the same as that found by Leeds (1992) in an analysis of the AEASP at Temple University fifteen years earlier. GPAs in mathematics and economics courses do not appear to matter, regardless of whether taken separately or together; nor does the number of math and economics courses taken have an apparent impact. There are several possible forces at work here. Students who do poorly in one mathematics course, for example, may repeat it or take a nonidentical but similar course, thereby biasing estimated coefficients downward. Many students take a large number of low-level courses (and typically do well), while math grades tend to decline in higher-level courses. The rigor of mathematics and economics

TABLE 10.1
OLS Parameter Estimates: Determinants of AEASP Grade Point Average

			Regression				
	(1)	(2)	(3)	(4)	(5)	(6)	(7)
Regressors							
Constant	0.743	2.013[c]	1.545	3.892[a]			
Elite college or university	0.107	0.024	-0.006				-0.007
Male	-0.069	-0.058	-0.005				
Father's education		0.052[c]	0.066[b]	0.046[c]	0.046	0.051[c]	0.046[c]
Mother's education		-0.003	-0.005			-0.034	
Mother's education (African American students only)	-0.008						
Undergraduate GPA in math and economics courses					0.195		
Undergraduate math GPA		0.241	0.357[c]				
Undergraduate GPA (all courses)	0.094						
Intact family (two parents living together)	0.065		0.029				
Hispanic race/ethnicity	0.069	0.039	0.329[b]				
Asian race/ethnicity	0.403[a]	0.404[a]					
Other nonblack race	0.485[a]						
Foundations level	-0.129	-0.252[b]	-0.199				
Advanced (nonreturning)				0.267[c]	0.223	0.239	0.268[c]
Full course load	0.109	0.104	0.145				
Foundations plus some advanced courses		0.192	0.116				
U.S. citizen		0.312	0.359				
Age	0.175			-0.026[c]	-0.025[c]	-0.027[c]	-0.026[b]
Age^2	-0.004						
Total number of undergrad math and economics courses taken		0.002	0.001				
Sophomore			-1.375[b]				
Junior			0.697				
Completed college			-0.358				
Taken graduate work			-0.397				
Enrolled in graduate program			0.076				
Program site (Duke = 1; UC–Denver = 0)				-0.328[b]	-0.379[b]	-0.321[b]	0.328[b]
Treatment							
Completed Foundations and Advanced curriculum				0.209	0.223	0.236	0.210
R^2	.092	.130	.238	.112	.179	.125	.112
N	102	103	103	104	104	104	104

N = Number of observations.

[a]Significant at the .01 level.
[b]Significant at the .05 level.
[c]Significant at the .10 level.

coursework also may vary markedly from one institution to another. We are working on alternative measures of effort and ability, but at present our measures are problematic. However, even if we do generate improved measures, it is possible that the effect will be null or modest. Since selection to the program weights math skills and economics background heavily, and since admission to the program is competitive, those with weaker skills who are admitted should have demonstrated some other drive or aptitude features in the application that the admissions committee noted. Since these features are not captured in the variables included, there is in effect an omitted variables' bias caused by a negative correlation between observed achievements and omitted drive and aptitude factors.

This same argument could in principle explain the lack of significance of the elite college variable. In practice, it is unlikely to do so, since the Admissions Committee favors applicants from nonelite institutions. One possible explanation is that participants from lesser institutions are more likely to stand out, and hence receive more faculty inputs; another is that the very best students from elite colleges do not need a program such as the AEASP, and hence do not apply.

Looking at family background, it turns out that only one variable—the students' fathers' education—has a consistent, positive impact on performance. Having a father who has completed college and two years of professional school rather than leaving high school in the tenth grade is worth about 0.4 grade points. Maternal education does not appear to matter, however. We had hypothesized that maternal drive and achievement may matter more in African American families than in other minority families, but this was not borne out by our regressions. Being part of an intact family did not appear to matter either.

What about the program itself? Grading appears to be stiffer at Duke than at UC–Denver: grades at the latter are about one-third of a grade point higher. Advanced-level students as a whole do better, but there are only tiny differences in coefficients for returning and new (nonreturning) Advanced participants. Moreover, while the coefficients for returning students tend to fall just shy of being significant at the 10 percent level, performance by those nonreturning Advanced students is significant.

Since there is considerable selection going on, these results are not surprising. New students placed at the Advanced level either have prior graduate school admissions or are placed there following a battery of entry placement exams. The returning students are also selected both on prior performance and demonstrated effort. It is also possible that there is an experiential effect from the first summer of the AEASP, but in the absence of effective control for selection, we have not identified it.

Taken as a whole, the striking result is not that several variables are statistically significant but that despite a large amount of information only a very small proportion of the variance in performance can be explained. From the program's perspective, this outcome is not disheartening. Rather, it reflects the highly competitive nature of the program: resting on laurels due to past knowledge gained does little good. The heavy workload also means that unobserved personal attributes (drive, ability to function with little sleep) and fortune (good health, an effective study group) will count for a great deal.

CURRICULUM INTENSITY TREATMENT EFFECTS

Our bivariate probit estimates aim to measure the so-called treatment effect of having completed both the Foundations and Advanced curricula. The correlated error structure of this econometric specification allows modeling the decision to complete both the Foundations and Advanced course sequence as endogenous. We condition both the probability of intent and actually applying to graduate school on whether or not the student attends or attended a historically black college or university; gender; citizenship status; having a mother or father with a high level of education, or both; the number of economics course completed to date at the student's undergraduate institution; the student's overall GPA in her major, and a binary treatment indicator measuring whether or not the student has completed both the Foundations and Advanced curricula in the AEASP.[4]

For intent to apply, the bivariate probit parameter estimates in table 10.2 reveal that for the AEASP participant, the treatment of taking both the Foundations and Advanced curricula has a positive and significant impact on the probability of applying to a doctoral program in economics. The instruments of age and its square are also significant, suggesting that our identification strategy is sensible. As the correlation between the error terms is significantly different from zero, a bivariate probit specification of the intent to apply to a doctoral program in economics is appropriate relative to a simple probit specification.

The bivariate probit parameter estimates of the effect of the treatment on the probability of actually applying to a doctoral program in economics are approximately the same as those for intent to apply. Being exposed to the treatment has a positive and significant effect on the probability of actually applying to a doctoral program in economics. The exception between intended and completed application is that a chi-square test for zero correlation between the error terms cannot be rejected in the latter case. This suggests that taking both the Foundations and Advanced

TABLE 10.2
Bivariate Parameter Estimates: The Treatment Effect of Curriculum Intensity
on the Probability of Pursuing an Economics Doctorate

	Outcome	
	Intent to Apply	Actually Applied
Regressors		
Constant	−.9217	−1.49
	(1.80)	(1.51)
HBCU student	.1337	.1318
	(.3217)	(.3454)
Male	.1839	−.0040
	(.2534)	(.2434)
U.S. citizen	−.4467	−.1184
	(.4155)	(.3676)
Mother's education	−.1565	−.2191
	(.3556)	.(3584)
Father's education	.0649	−.1543
	(.4477	(.4466)
Parent's education	.7263	.7390
	(.5578)	(.5360)
Number of economics	.0402	.0417
Courses	(.0277)	(.0276)
GPA in major	.2481	.2038
	(.4511)	(.3729
Treatment		
Completed Foundations and	1.34	1.64
Advanced curriculum	(.1932)[a]	(.2037)[a]
Instruments		
Constant	−.22.05	−16.33
	(4.12)[a]	(4.70)[a]
HBCU Student	.8812	.7971
	(.4014)[b]	(.4233)[b]
Male	−.2094	−.2827
	(.2842)	(.2861)
U.S. citizen	−.5332	−.5405
	(.4084)	(.4175)
Mother's education	.4565	−.5763
	(.4252)	(.4063)
Father's education	.5713	.5460
	(.4694)	(.5136)
Parent's education	−1.26	−1.29
	(.5972)[a]	(.6313)[b]
Number of economics	−.0009	−.0074
courses	(.0334)	(.0365)
GPA in Major	−.0687	−.1280
	(.4719)	(.4352)
Age	1.56	1.14
	(.2853)[a]	(.3366)[a]
Age^2	−.0270	−.0191
	(.0049)[a]	(.0061)[a]
Pseudo-R^2	.1973	.1386
X_1^2: ($\rho = 0$)	34.97[a]	1.19
N	99	99

Note: Standard errors in parentheses. N = Number of observations.
[a]Significant at the .01 level.
[b]Significant at the .05 level.
[c]Significant at the .10 level.

curricula has no effect on the probability of actually applying to a doctoral program in economics.

Of course, the difference between intending to apply and actually applying to a doctoral program in economics may be subject to a lag, rendering the treatment effect insignificant. For example, while the treatment effect of taking both the Foundations and Advanced curricula may have a positive effect on intentions, the administrative data may not cover a sufficient time horizon capturing the full execution of intents to apply to a doctoral program in economics. Some, while expressing intent, may actually apply at a later date. Conversely, some may change their minds and not actually apply.

In general, our bivariate probit parameter estimates suggest that the innovation of curriculum intensity in the AEASP has the effect on increasing the likelihood that minority participants make the transition to doctoral programs in economics. To the extent that one must have an intention before one actually applies to a doctorate program, the bivariate probit parameter estimates for the intent to apply probabilities are probably more relevant for assessing the treatment effects of an AEASP participant being exposed to an intense curriculum in economics. That the treatment parameter is the only significant one in the specification for intent to apply in the first stage of our estimates is even more suggestive of a positive treatment effect.

It is possible that the causal nexus presumed in our bivariate probit specification is the opposite of what is specified. That is to say, it could be that AEASP participants intend to or actually do apply to a doctoral program in economics, and then take both the Foundations and Advanced curricula to prepare for graduate school. This could particularly be the case if an AEASP participant has formulated an intention, or actually applied to a doctoral program after taking just the Foundations curriculum. If this is the case, the parameter estimates in table 10.2 are upwardly biased, as the causality is reversed—the decision to take both the Foundations and Advanced curricula is caused by a prior intent or decision to apply to a doctoral program in economics.

To check the sensitivity of the results to possible reverse causality, we reestimate the bivariate probit specifications on data that exclude those returning AEASP participants who had expressed an intention, or actually applied to a doctoral program in economics after they completed the Foundations curriculum.[5] In general, the results differ little from the parameter estimates of the full sample. This suggests that the effects of the treatment under consideration—an AEASP student taking both the Foundations and Advanced curricula—is indeed positive. As the estimated treatment parameters for the restricted sample are large relative to the full sample, this also suggests that while the effects of taking only the Foundations curriculum may be positive, taking both curricula has an even greater effect on the probability of an AEASP participant having a desire to pursue a doctorate in economics.

What Have We Learned?

The AEASP has many potential effects on its participants. One hopes there is a direct learning effect, resulting in improved performance in undergraduate courses and improved competitiveness in graduate study. For some this will translate into improved performance in a given graduate program; for others it will mean admissions to a higher-ranked and more competitive graduate program.

Beyond its direct instructional effect, the AEASP has the effect of recruiting into the profession and into academe people highly unlikely to consider graduate study in economics. In large part, this is due to lack of exposure: the AEASP raises the profession's visibility to a new audience. In part, the program offers a dramatic demonstration effect, with large numbers of minority students and professional economists at different stages of their careers. The AEASP thus builds self-confidence simply by creating a large group of like-minded people—a giant peer group effect. The AEA's Pipeline Program then builds on this and creates a supportive network. The AEASP also offers mentoring and placement assistance and, by providing credible recommendations and transcripts, makes participants more attractive to graduate programs. To the extent that participants realize the value of such support, it should further increase interest in going to graduate school, as the quality of graduate programs to which students are admitted will be improved.

These benefits are available to and recognized by all AEASP participants, regardless of whether they come for one or two summers. Yet the benefit we identify here is a different one: as our observations are limited to those who have participated in the AEASP, we cannot determine the value of the effects hypothesized above. However, we can ask whether attending for a second summer confers additional benefits—to the Economics profession, that is, in terms of its efforts to diversify. Our preliminary results suggest that it does matter, and further increases the likelihood of going on to doctoral study, even after controlling for the endogeneity of returning to the program.

At present we can only speculate as to the reasons for this effect. Additional learning and preparation, and hence additional confidence—in general, "more of the above"—are one such route. Strengthened peer effects almost certainly matter as well. We further suspect that increased enthusiasm for research is a critical contributor, which is consistent with

Grove, Dutkowsky, and Grodner's (2005) findings that experience contributes to graduate success, perhaps in part because it drives motivation. This avenue would also be consistent with those who observe the vastly disproportionate share of doctoral students coming from elite liberal arts colleges, as these, too, offer undergraduate research experiences.

11

ASSESSING PROGRAMS TO IMPROVE MINORITY PARTICIPATION IN THE STEM FIELDS

What We Know and What We Need to Know

CHERYL LEGGON AND WILLIE PEARSON JR.

In this chapter we focus on evaluations of programs designed to improve the participation of underrepresented racial/ethnic minorities (URMs) in the science, technology, engineering, and mathematics (STEM) disciplines in the United States (U.S.). Our goal is to review selected published studies and unpublished reports about the most effective and promising programs in increasing STEM diversity at the undergraduate, graduate, postdoctoral, and junior faculty levels. We seek to identify what is known and what needs to be known about programs, practices, and policies that are effective in diversifying workers in the STEM disciplines.

BACKGROUND

Within the past fifty years, the U.S. economic base has shifted from the manufacturing of durable goods to processing and analyzing information. In this information-driven economy, the most valuable assets are human resources. To compete successfully in the global economy, the United States needs citizens who are literate in terms of science and mathematics, and a STEM workforce that is well educated and well trained (National Academy of Sciences et al. 2006b; Pearson 2005).

Consequently, the nation cannot afford—literally or figuratively—to squander its human resources; the United States must develop and nurture the talents of *all* of its citizens.

Historically, the United States recruited its STEM workforce from a relatively homogenous talent pool consisting largely of non-Hispanic white men. However, this pool has decreased significantly due not only to the decline of white men as a portion of the U.S. population but also to declining interest among this group in pursuing STEM careers. The need to improve the participation of underrepresented groups— especially URMs—in the STEM fields is not solely driven by demographics and supply-side considerations. An even more important driver is that STEM workers from a variety of backgrounds improve and enhance the quality of science insofar as they are likely to bring a variety of new perspectives to bear on the STEM enterprise—in both research and applications (Building Engineering and Science Talent 2004; Jackson 2003; Leggon and Malcom 1994).

Over the last twenty years there has been a proliferation of programs geared toward improving and increasing the participation of URMs in the STEM fields. Yet, the proportion of STEM doctorates earned by members of underrepresented groups has shown only modest improvement (Committee on Equal Opportunity in Science and Engineering [CEOSE] 2004). These programs can be broadly categorized in a number of ways:

- *Level:* K–12, undergraduate, graduate, postdoctoral, entry-level professional.
- *Funding source:* colleges and universities, federal agencies (e.g., the National Science Foundation, the National Institutes of Health, the National Aeronautics and Space Administration), nonprofit foundations (e.g., the Alfred P. Sloan Foundation).
- *Institutional base:* an individual college or university (e.g., the Meyerhoff Scholars Program at the University of Maryland–Baltimore County); consortia (e.g., the Leadership Alliance, the National Consortium for Graduate Degrees for Minorities in Engineering and Science, the National Action Council for Minorities in Engineering); and professional associations (e.g., the American Chemical Society).
- *The STEM fields:* in broad terms (e.g., physical sciences) or in traditional fields (e.g., physics).

According to a report by Building Engineering and Science Talent, or BEST (2004), measurable objectives and formal evaluations are critical elements in assessing the effectiveness of programs. Evaluation represents the best strategy for providing information on what is effective and what is not. Moreover, evaluation can provide real-time continuous feedback to guide in design, planning, and implementation so that necessary changes can be made. Program evaluations continue to be limited and lack rigor. The few programs that do track participants report that academic benefits accruing to the students may actually diminish over time (Good, Halpin, and Halpin 2002). Other effects, such as the probabilities of persisting in basic math and science courses and of graduating, were assumed to persist (Barlow and Villarejo 2004). Much of the early funding of programs geared toward increasing the participation of URMs in the STEM fields did not include budgetary support for evaluation; consequently, evidence of program effectiveness was largely anecdotal, minimal, or absent. This situation has begun to change (CEOSE 2004). Although there seems to be more awareness and inclusion of evaluative components in programs, funding still lags and evaluation is frequently the first item eliminated or reduced when a requested funding amount is reduced (National Science Foundation [NSF] 2005).

Jackson (2003) points out that there is a lack of "authoritative, readily accessible information" on the most effective and promising programs, practices, and policies designed to broaden the participation of URMs in the STEM fields. She also argues that lessons learned from program successes and failures may provide critical insight into replicability, transportability, and scalability. Systematic formative and summative evaluation of the extent to which programs broaden participation in the STEM fields is essential to understanding what works for which URMs (and under what conditions) as well as what does not work, and why (CEOSE 2004).

BEST (2004) implemented a systematic process to identify and document effective programs that demonstrated promise in developing talent from among the populations that are currently underrepresented in the STEM workforce. Using a systematic search-and-nominate process, BEST identified a pool of 124 higher-education programs. Most of these programs were unable to provide any documentation on program outcomes. Generally, documentation consisted of little more than counts of the numbers of students participating in the intervention programs. Even decades-old programs lacked fundamental impact data; longevity does not ipso facto mean that a program is successful (BEST 2004).

BEST requested that each program complete a program profile covering goals, impact, growth, sustainability, and evidence of effectiveness. After developing criteria to "assess the soundness of the programs and practices that foster achievement in higher education" (BEST 2004, 5), thirty-six programs were rated by a subset of the BEST Higher Education Blue Ribbon Panel. This review panel process gave more weight to programs that had monitored their participants' progress and attempted to evaluate outcomes. Based on six of BEST's eight criteria, seven programs were rated as "exemplary" and five programs were categorized as "promising." Of the seven programs identified as exemplary, three focused on undergraduates, two on graduate students, one on faculty, and one on a statewide program in a single discipline.

What Works?

To systematically identify what works and why, in this chapter we build on the foundation of the BEST initiative to discuss selected programs that are either exemplary or promising in terms of increasing the participation of URMs in the STEM fields. Some of the programs discussed herein were included in the BEST initiative, while others were not. The focus here is to identify, illustrate, and summarize lessons learned from some promising programs whose goal is to increase participation of URMs in the STEM fields, and to identify extant knowledge gaps. The intervention programs selected for this discussion are disaggregated by the programs' focuses in terms of level of education and career milestone: undergraduate, graduate, and faculty.

Undergraduate Programs

In this section, the following undergraduate-level programs will be discussed: the Meyerhoff Scholars Program and the Leadership Alliance.

The Meyerhoff Scholars Program

One of the undergraduate programs identified by BEST as exemplary is the Meyerhoff Scholars Program (MSP) at the University of Maryland–Baltimore County (UMBC). The original goal of the program was to produce African American students who would continue their education beyond the UMBC to earn a doctorate in a STEM discipline and join a college or university faculty (Hrabowski and Pearson 1993). The program is now open to all students. The MSP is one of the few research-based intervention programs. It uses intense peer study groups as well as the total residential experience to focus on the needs of the whole student. The confluence of these and other practices creates a strong sense of community that, in turn, facilitates a high level of academic achievement and an environment conducive to intellectual exchange.

What the BEST Blue Ribbon Panel found most striking about this undergraduate program is the institutional commitment on the part of senior administration and faculty. This is consistent with evaluation findings indicating that successful interventions to improve the participation of URMs in the STEM fields must be institutionalized (National Research Council 2005b; NSF 2005). In this context, institutionalization means that the intervention is not a stand-alone or marginal component but an integral part of the standard operating procedures of an institution and, as such, a criterion on which the performance of faculty and administrators is evaluated (Leggon 2006). Moreover, institutionalization means that the intervention will not disappear when the funding that supported its inception ends.[1]

The MSP has undergone extensive internal evaluation. Maton, Hrabowski, and Schmidt (2000) have reported that MSP students achieved higher grade point averages, graduated with STEM majors at higher rates, and gained acceptance to graduate schools at higher rates than other students did in multiple current and historical samples. The authors were able to locate only one external evaluation of the MSP. Bridglall and Gordon (2004) have conducted what they call a "connoisseurial" evaluation of the MSP and conclude that the extraordinary commitment of the UMBC's leadership, faculty, and staff to minority students' academic achievement encourages them to constantly seek ways to enhance their students' academic performance.[2] Bridglall and Gordon have speculated that the MSP "is one of the few isolated efforts at bridging curriculum and teaching, social science, and cognitive science to more effectively apply this knowledge to the problems of nurturing talent in underrepresented students" (2004, 75). The authors believe that the MSP model is transferable to other institutions.

Leadership Alliance

The Leadership Alliance is a consortium of thirty-three of the leading U.S. research and teaching colleges and universities. This consortium includes institutions categorized as Ivy League, Research I (according to the Carnegie Classification of Institutes of Higher Education), and minority-serving institutions—historically black colleges and universities (HBCUs), Hispanic-serving institutions (HSIs), and tribal colleges (TCs). The purpose of the alliance is to provide students with opportunities to conduct research that would otherwise be unavailable to them. The LA's Summer Research–Early Identification Program (SR–EIP) provides intensive research experience and culminates in a national symposium in which students give formal professional presentations.

Pearson et al. (2004) have conducted rigorous, extensive formative evaluations of the LA and the SR–EIP since 2001. The evaluations have included both qualitative (i.e., interview and focus group) and quantitative (survey) components. In sum:

- *The SR–EIP works well for the clear majority of undergraduate students.* For example, 82 percent of the students surveyed in 2003 reported that their overall summer experience was "very good" or "excellent," and 76 percent reported that the program strengthened their commitment to pursue a research career.

- *A strengthened commitment to pursuing a research career is positively correlated with several other factors.* Specifically, those students who report strengthened commitment are also more likely to report that (1) the overall summer experience was excellent; (2) the program was useful in helping clarify future career plans; (3) the program improved their overall knowledge about the research process; and (4) the program's environment was socially supportive. The fact that these factors are all intercorrelated suggests that both satisfaction with the summer experience and strengthened career commitment can be enhanced by ensuring that students receive adequate information about the steps involved in pursuing a research career and adequate social support from mentors and other program representatives.
- *Instruction in methodological techniques is an important component of program pedagogy.* As the frequency of instruction in methodological techniques increases, so too does the student's satisfaction with the program, the perceived usefulness of the program, reported gains in research knowledge, and the perception of social support.
- *Many SR–EIP host sites have mechanisms—both formal and informal—for tracking students in their summer programs.* Several summer sites systematically track the success of the LA as a recruitment tool; at least three had data for as long as their institution participated in the LA.
- *The Leadership Alliance can be expanded.* The LA has accumulated critical program expertise both in its national office and among its senior campus directors that could be more broadly disseminated. The LA is well positioned to serve as a clearinghouse for programs concerned with broadening the participation of URMs in the STEM fields.

Graduate Programs

In this section we will discuss two graduate-level programs: the National Consortium for Graduate Degrees for Minorities in Science and Engineering and the National Institutes of Health (NIH) Minority Research and Training Programs.

The National Consortium for Graduate Degrees for Minorities in Science and Engineering

Also known as GEM, the National Consortium for Graduate Degrees for Minorities in Science and Engineering includes approximately 94 universities and corporations. Founded in 1976, GEM's primary goals are to enhance the value of the nation's human capital by increasing the participation of African Americans, American Indians, and Hispanic Americans at the master's and doctoral levels in engineering and science, and to prepare technical leaders for advanced careers in industry, academia, and government (Educational Testing Service News 2006). To achieve these goals, GEM provides its fellows with opportunities for mentoring, tuition remission (from member universities), stipends (funded by membership fees and contributions from corporate members), and paid summer internships. To date, there have been approximately three thousand GEM fellows, two hundred of whom have earned doctorates in the physical and life sciences and engineering. More than 450 GEM fellows are supported annually. GEM is the only student program at the graduate level that the BEST Higher Education Blue Ribbon Panel found to be exemplary. Survey data from alumni and employers indicated that GEM enhances the transition to both graduate study and the workforce. GEM's major contribution has been finding critical resources for students in need of funding for graduate degrees in the STEM fields. Financial support is strongly positively correlated with persistence in students' graduate studies and degree completion. Certain minority students are more likely than nonminority students to fund their education through personal savings and loans. Specifically, American Indian and African American doctoral students are more likely to rely on their own resources to finance their doctoral education than are whites and Hispanics; Asians are the least likely to do so (National Science Foundation, Division of Science Resources 2004b).

There are notable race/ethnicity differences in the use of various types of program- and institution-based support. For example, in the physical sciences and engineering, "Asians and whites are more likely than blacks and Hispanics to rely on research assistantships, and less likely to have fellowships or grants as their primary source of support" (National Science Foundation, Division of Science Resources 2004b, 26). Moreover, financial assistance eliminates time constraints caused by working and frees up time to focus on study. In sum, GEM not only identifies qualified students and provides them with resources, it also strengthens collaborations between universities and industry.

The NIH Minority Research and Training Programs

The Assessment of National Institutes of Health (NIH) Minority Research Training Programs was initiated in 1991 as part of the Minority Health Initiative. This assessment occurred in three phases. The first phase, completed in 1993, presented an overview of NIH extramural research training programs and documented an overall pattern of minority underrepresentation in the biological, behavioral, and clinical sciences. Phase 2, completed in 1997, assessed the feasibility of a trans-NIH assessment of minority research programs. In 2001 the National Center on Minority Health and Health Disparities contracted with the National Academies to determine whether the NIH minority research programs work, and to identify the programs and the specific features of those programs that have been successful. In 2001, there were 79 minority research training programs sponsored by NIH institutes and centers. The National Research Council's Committee for the Assessment of the NIH Minority Research Training Programs released its findings from the third phase of the assessment in 2005. One major finding was that although the primary goal of the programs was to increase the number of PhD-level minority biomedical researchers, "success in reaching this goal was not quantified among any of the program announcements" (NRC 2005b, 2). The lack of adequate definitions of what constitutes success and failure is an impediment to program evaluations; another impediment is lack of consensus among program participants on definitions of success and failure. One important principle concerning minority programs is that those program participants who exit the pipeline early to become part of the scientific workforce are not deemed program failures (NRC 2005b). Moreover, without extensive longitudinal data it is impossible to determine whether a program participant has exited the pipeline for good ("dropped out") or exited temporarily ("stopped out"). Given the time required to prepare for a career in the STEM fields, it might be appropriate to identify interim indicators of program success such as whether program participants had advanced to the next step in the career pathway. Longitudinal data on program participants must be collected in such a way as to facilitate distinguishing between students who are "stopouts" from those who are "dropouts." Moreover, it is crucial that longitudinal data are disaggregated by race/ethnicity and gender.

The NRC's 2005 evaluation of the NIH minority training programs severely criticized NIH–funded programs for failing to collect, keep, and analyze data on the outcomes of these training programs. In response to that criticism, the NIH division of Minority Opportunities in Research (MORE) inaugurated Efficacy of Interventions to Promote Research Careers grants to examine and analyze both the outcomes and assumptions of various NIH programs. To partially compensate for the lack of adequate longitudinal data, the NRC assessment committee conducted interviews with program administrators and minority trainees. Despite some methodological problems with the interviews (such as low response rates), the interview data indicated that for undergraduate, graduate, postdoctoral, and junior faculty trainees, the research experience itself was the best feature of the programs. Another positive outcome for program participants at all levels was the opportunity to network and collaborate with other scientists. Based on these and other findings, the assessment committee concluded that "underrepresented minorities are entering the biomedical workforce as a direct result of the NIH minority research programs" (NRC 2005b).

FACULTY PROGRAMS

Of the two programs concentrating on faculty diversity identified by BEST as exemplary, the Compact for Faculty Diversity targets racial/ethnic minorities, while Preparing Future Faculty focuses on diversifying faculty in terms not only of race and ethnicity but also gender and other characteristics.

The Compact for Faculty Diversity

In 1993, the Compact for Faculty Diversity (CFD) was formed by the Southern Regional Education Board, the New England Board of Higher Education, and the Western Interstate Compact for Higher Education. The CFD website describes the program as a "partnership of regional, federal and foundation programs that focus on minority graduate education and faculty diversity."[3] The only goal of the CFD is to increase the number of minority students earning doctoral degrees and becoming college and university faculty. To achieve this goal, the compact endeavors to (1) increase the percentage of minority students earning the doctoral degree in the STEM fields and seeking faculty positions; (2) diversify the pool of qualified faculty candidates; and (3) increase the participants' probability of success as faculty members.

The CFD creates a variety of intersecting support systems. It provides stipends that support full-time study for three years and one year of support to write the dissertation. In addition to financial support, the CFD provides extensive social support by facilitating sustained contact among the scholars, and between the scholars and the CFD. Each year, the Institute on Teaching convenes a forum for students and faculty mentors to engage in professional development, networking, and professional socialization. Not only does the institute benefit students, it also provides opportunities for mentors to enhance their mentoring skills and experience. The retention rate of program participants was 90 percent, as compared to retention rates of 37 percent for minority scholars in general and 40 percent to 60 percent for students of all race/ethnicity backgrounds.

Preparing Future Faculty

The Preparing Future Faculty (PFF) initiative began in 1993 as a partnership between the Council of Graduate Schools and the Association of American Colleges and Universities. Between 1993 and 2003, the PFF program was implemented at more than forty-five doctorate-granting institutions.[4] The program seeks to better prepare graduate students for the professoriate by exposing them to a variety of academic settings.

Such exposure enhances students' ability to make informed choices in terms of the academic setting in which they will seek full-time employment. PFF helps to socialize graduate students into the teaching profession, as well as to acculturate them into the academy. In addition, PFF encourages "graduate programs to integrate the professional development of graduate students more directly into education" (DeNeef 2002, 1).

An evaluation found that the PFF program has started to change the climate on the campuses of participating graduate schools. One change is that PFF has spurred graduate faculty to realize the importance of pedagogical issues to graduate students. Another change is that PFF has led to an expansion of the definition of success to include teaching in liberal arts colleges and community colleges, as well as in research intensive universities. PFF has further expanded the definition of a successful academic career to include administration as well as research and teaching. The evaluators concluded that "PFF not only smoothed the transition between graduate school and the graduate student participants' initial academic position, but it has also brought them into the larger conversation of academic reform and generally" (DeNeef 2002, 19).

What Do We Know?

The preceding review of programs identifies a commonality of elements and factors that are effective in increasing the participation of URMs in the STEM fields. These factors include

- enhancing substantive knowledge and technical skills (the Leadership Alliance, the Meyerhoff Scholars Program)
- providing and sustaining a comprehensive web of financial, academic, professional, and social support (GEM, the Leadership Alliance, and the Meyerhoff Scholars Program)
- facilitating the creation of networks (Compact for Faculty Diversity, GEM, Leadership Alliance, and Meyerhoff Scholars Program)
- providing extensive and intensive professional socialization (Compact for Faculty Diversity, GEM, Leadership Alliance, Meyerhoff Scholars Program, and Preparing Future Faculty)
- extensively and intensively tracking program participants, including faculty and mentors
- providing bridge experiences to facilitate transition from one education milestone to another (Compact for Faculty Diversity, GEM, Leadership Alliance, and Preparing Future Faculty)

In sum, the most effective and promising programs are based on a perspective that is holistic insofar as they address all of the needs of the participants. Effective programs address mentors' concerns about what is expected of them in their role as mentor, and provide ways to enhance their mentoring.

What Do We Need to Know?

Analyses of extant data enhance knowledge of what is effective in improving the participation of URMs in the STEM fields. However, these data are largely "snapshots" taken at different periods of time. Longitudinal data on program participants are needed to enable identification and assessment of the long-term impacts of these programs on all participants.

Students

The evaluation literature has documented the positive effects of students' participation in at least one intervention program. However, we need to know whether participating in a given intervention program increases the likelihood of participating in other intervention programs. In addition, we need to know in what ways the careers of the students who participated in a single intervention program differ from those who participated in multiple programs. Evidence from evaluations indicates that social support for URMs pursuing graduate degrees in the STEM fields is a critical element in increasing faculty diversity in the STEM fields. However, more needs to be known about the factors that enhance and sustain such support.

Longitudinal data may provide insight into the factors that account for differences in career outcomes, and are crucial to examine the extent to which participating in targeted intervention programs results in research collaborations during a participant's career. Although some programs and practices that work for URMs also work for all students, it is imperative that data be collected and analyzed by race, ethnicity, and gender to pinpoint those practices and policies that are especially effective for URM students (National Academy of Sciences et al. 2006b).

Faculty and Mentors

More data are needed on the dynamics of creating and sustaining social support networks not only among students and between students and faculty, but also among faculty and mentors. More information is also needed about effective mentoring in targeted intervention programs.

Institutions

Longitudinal data are needed to assess the long-term impact for institutions that have participated in targeted intervention programs. There is a paucity of adequate information or evidence on the scalability and transportability of successful programs. Although a few institutions are beginning to replicate some key features of effective programs, external evaluations appear to be either nonexistent or underreported.

A major knowledge gap concerns the degree to which targeted intervention programs impact one another. For example, does participating in a particular program increase the likelihood of participating in other targeted intervention programs and being awarded grants, fellowships, and prizes? To fill this gap, what is needed is a relational database with data on participants in all targeted programs by level (undergraduate, graduate, postgraduate) and by type of assistance (traineeships, fellowships, research assistantships, and teaching assistantships; see NRC 2005b). This database should also enhance the ability to track participants' professional careers.

IV

Increasing the Representation of
Women in Academia

12

First a Glass Ceiling, Now a Glass Cliff?

The Changing Picture for Women in Science and Higher Education Careers

M. R. C. Greenwood

Fifty years ago very few women chose careers in academic science or as leaders in higher education. Almost without exception, pictures and reports of major scientific events or societies depicted men—and mostly Caucasian men. Consequently there were few role models or exemplars for young women to emulate. Of course, there were some extraordinary exceptions such as physicist Marie Curie, astronomer Maria Mitchell, and, more recently, Nobel Prize–winning biologist Rosalyn Yalow. It is hardly surprising then that most women scientists at the full professorial level, now in their midfifties, sixties, or older, can easily recount experiences of being actively discouraged from pursuing an academic scientific career. With the advent of the women's movement, the use of affirmative action, and the enforcement of antidiscrimination laws, this next generation of educated women faces a greatly changed environment with respect to entry-level access to several fields in science. Today, more women than men receive baccalaureate degrees overall and although the production of science, technology, engineering, and mathematics baccalaureate degrees is low in the United States compared with many other countries, on a per-capita basis women are obtaining approximately 50 percent of these degrees. Thus, it can be argued that concern for the advancement of women in science and engineering is shifting from one of access to science careers to one of placement, followed by upward mobility leading to success. The question now is, Will access lead to success at the highest levels of the scientific pyramid or will obstacles—perceived or real—impede maximum use of the valuable, now critical, talent pool represented by the educated and scientifically credentialed women in the United States?

ASSESSING THE CURRENT STATUS

In the fall of 2006, the National Academies of Science (NAS) released a report titled *Beyond Bias and Barriers: Fulfilling the Potential of Women in Academic Science and Engineering* (National Academy of Sciences et al. 2006a). Donna Shalala, president of the University of Miami and previously the secretary of the U.S. Department of Health and Human Services, chaired the committee that prepared this report, and the committee included many prominent scientists. The report focused much of its work on the recruitment, retention, and advancement of faculty women— some of whom move on to administration and management. It made many useful recommendations for improving outcomes for scientifically talented women, and in addition served as a repository and synthesis of much of the important work on bias and unintended consequences.

The United States is facing a competitiveness challenge unlike any we have faced before. Friedman (2000) discusses this challenge in detail in the popular book *The World Is Flat.* In a world where brains, not brawn, will determine our collective future, we must ensure that we can draw on and maximize the talent that we now know resides in the pool of well-educated women. Since World War II, and particularly since the end of the Cold War, our nation's technological prowess and our national investments in fundamental research—with their huge economic benefits—have led to a national complacency, and an unwillingness to believe that we could be "beaten" by any other country or coalition of countries. But as another compelling NAS report *Rising above the Gathering Storm* has so clearly detailed (National Academies of Sciences et al. 2000b), the time to recognize our vulnerabilities and to act proactively has come.

The report has already had a substantial effect nationally. Senators Lamar Alexander and Jeff Bingaman commissioned the report in a bipartisan effort, in collaboration with the House Science Committee, to identify critical actions that federal policymakers could take to keep the United States competitive, prosperous, and secure in the twenty-first century. Furthermore, the report urges an implementation strategy.

Numerous reports demonstrate that U.S. students are performing at an unacceptable level in most international comparisons, such as the PISA 2003 study and the third international mathematics and science study (TIMSS)(Lemke et al. 2004; National Center for Education Statistics 1997). And at the college level, there is a growing shortage of students with degrees in science, engineering, and technology (National Science Board 2006). At the doctoral and advanced studies level we are becoming increasingly dependent on attracting students from other countries (National Science Board 2006). Although attracting the best students from around the world is something the United States should be proud of, it may not be wise or sustainable to consider it a workforce solution for the long run. Students are increasingly finding advanced education available in their own geographic areas, some of which are direct competitors of the United States. Indeed, the universities in the European Union and institutes in other countries that have immigration policies that are less offensive than those of the United States are recruiting international students. In addition, multinational corporations are moving research and development opportunities closer to international centers of excellence. Furthermore, students themselves are more inclined to return to their countries of origin. All of these factors should cause the United States to renew its efforts to stimulate international student interest in science, engineering, and other critical fields. Programs to accomplish this are among the recommendations of the NAS (2006b) report and several new programs are working their way through the tedious national legislative process and may represent a new imperative. Only time will tell if these efforts will succeed.

The "Rising Tide" of Women

Today, only about one-third of U.S. baccalaureate degrees are in science and engineering (National Science Board 2006). However, more than 50 percent of these baccalaureate degrees are being awarded to women (National Science Board 2006). The participation of women in science and technology has been increasing steadily since the early 1990s (see figure 12.1).

Although some fields of science and engineering lag in women's participation, the overall trajectory is impressive. There have also been increases in underrepresented minorities, which are crucial to our global competitiveness, but the numbers of minority scientists still remain small.

In this context it is worth emphasizing that substantially more women than men receive baccalaureate degrees in nonscience and nonengineering fields. Furthermore, women are rapidly approaching parity in master's degrees in science and engineering and dominate the master's

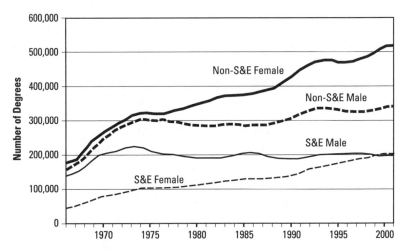

Figure 12.1. Bachelor's degrees awarded in science and engineering (S&E) and non–science and engineering fields, by gender, 1966–2001.

Source: National Science Foundation, Division of Science Resources Statistics 2004a.

degree recipients in the nonscience and nonengineering fields (see figure 12.2).

In short, the cadre of educated individuals in the United States is one that is increasingly female.

Although progress at the doctoral level has been slower, there is a steady, constant rise in female science and engineering graduates, while male participation is relatively constant and fluctuates largely as a consequence of our past ability to attract foreign graduate students, most often male (National Science Board 2006).

In some fields, women's share of degrees has risen above 50 percent. This shift is most apparent in the life sciences, such as the agricultural sciences and the biological sciences, and psychology (see figure 12.3). But it is notable that there is a recent significant rise in the participation of female doctoral degree recipients in the earth and atmospheric sciences and in engineering.

Glass Ceilings and Now a "Glass Cliff"?

Although this substantial progress in access is real and continuing, as the National Academy of Sciences report (2006a) notes, both published studies and more anecdotal evidence suggest that resentment and unexamined bias toward women in science and engineering continues. Ensuring a pathway to significant leadership positions is still a tenuous process.

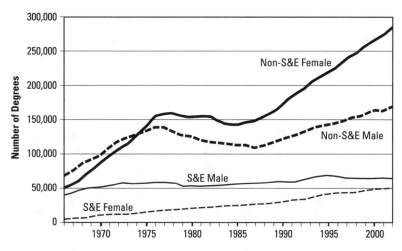

Figure 12.2. Master's degrees awarded in science and engineering (S&E) and non–science and engineering fields, by gender, 1966–2002.

Source: National Science Foundation, Division of Science Resources Statistics 2006.

One of the most significant issues is a lower-than-expected entry of women PhD holders into the tenure-track career path that begins the process of advancement to leadership roles. Several lines of evidence suggest that significant numbers of qualified women are not moving into university careers. The National Academies report (2006a) put it this way:

> Women who enter graduate school in science and engineering are as likely as men to earn doctorates, but give a poorer rating to faculty-student interactions and publish fewer research papers than men. Many women graduate students report feelings of isolation. More women than men report plans to seek postdoctoral positions. Among postdoctoral scholars, women report lower satisfaction with the experience and women are proportionately underrepresented in the applicant pools for tenure track faculty positions.

Although the reasons for this phenomenon are not yet clear, its existence should be of concern to those worried about the nation's long-term scientific prowess. If 50 percent or more of science and technology undergraduate degrees are being awarded to women and the trajectory is for graduate degrees to be increasingly awarded to women from some of the nations' finest institutions of higher education, the failure to draw such women into progressive academic careers and leadership roles will lead to decreasing quality at the highest and most strategic levels of the very organizations that have been the bedrock of our entrepreneurial success. In short, one can argue that the debate about the need to

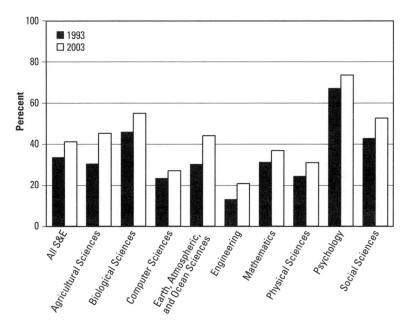

Figure 12.3. Female share of science and engineering graduate students, by field, 1993 and 2003.
Source: National Science Foundation, Division of Science Resources Statistics 2006.

encourage women to participate in science and technology careers has shifted from one of representation to one of necessity to maintain quality. But can current conditions support such upward mobility?

The disturbing pattern of women moving to top-level positions and then abruptly departing leads this author to suggest that in addition to the much-discussed "glass ceiling" a new phenomenon—a "glass cliff"—may be emerging. An article in the *Chronicle of Higher Education* (Lively 2000) can serve as an example of this possible problem. The article, a story of progress titled "Women in Charge," expresses the hope that the presence of women as chief academic officers in eleven of the sixty-one Association of American Universities (AAU) member institutions would lead to more woman presidents of these prestigious institutions.

The results have been mixed, at best. As determined by a subsequent World Wide Web survey of these eleven women in the fall of 2006 (Greenwood 2007), one had retired, six had resigned, four had became president (or the equivalent) of small colleges or smaller universities not in the AAU, and two were still chief academic officers in AAU member institutions. Although three had moved to a presidential position in a Research I institution (as designated by the Carnegie Classification of Institutes of Higher Education system), only two of those are still in place as of 2008. These are all women who by most standards have broken the glass ceiling but then suddenly disappear, as if encountering an unexpected glass cliff; this suggests that differential experience, treatment, or unexamined bias may still play a role when women leaders are rare and isolated and encounter difficulties.

The number of women in high-ranking academic and/or science and engineering policy positions is still rather small, and it fluctuates. Although the number of women university heads has increased, there are still fewer than one dozen in the prestigious AAU research institutions. And in too many institutions there are departments that have never had a female chair and divisions that have never had a female dean. At the national level, in some administrations the numbers of women in highly visible science and regulatory policy roles has been notable; in other administrations, however, women are barely visible. This is not to suggest that progress has not been significant and real, but that serious and sustained study and attention to the advancement and success of women in academic and policy leadership positions should be a high priority for the future. The study of the impact of the changing gender balance—in science and engineering, and in higher education generally—should be taken seriously and understood as a critical American issue. Our success in adequately capturing the talent that this shift represents and ensuring its full utilization should not be taken for granted. Much additional work remains before we can be assured that talented women will attain all that they—and the nation—have a right to expect.

13

INCREASING WOMEN'S REPRESENTATION IN THE LIFE SCIENCES

JONG-ON HAHM

In academic employment, women are not yet present in numbers that would be expected given the level of degree attainment over the past few decades. According to the 2003 Survey of Doctorate Recipients, women constituted 45 percent of junior faculty (assistant professors) and 29 percent of senior faculty, which included the associate and full professor ranks (survey data reported in National Science Board 2006). Among fifty research universities that receive that highest level of government research funding, the percentage of assistant professors is 30 percent, associate professors 25 percent, and full professors 15 percent (Nelson 2004).

The life sciences—including the biological and agricultural sciences—do not face the numerical challenges of the physical sciences and engineering in attracting women to their disciplines. Since 1996, women have earned more than 50 percent of the bachelor's degrees in the life sciences, a proportion that had grown to 59 percent in 2006 (National Science Board 2006). In 2003, women earned 46 percent of the doctorates in the biological sciences (National Science Foundation, Division of Science Resources Statistics 2004b). Thus, in postsecondary degree attainment, women are nearing or have exceeded parity with men.

However, the numerical advantage enjoyed by women in life sciences doctorates has not translated into similar gains in faculty ranks. This is particularly marked at the top research universities (National Research Council [NRC] 2001). As a group, the top research universities have the lowest percentage of women faculty, including those in the life sciences. This finding suggests that even in disciplines that have a significant supply of potential faculty, women's career development does not progress in a manner similar to men's.

Women face a number of challenges on their way up the academic career ladder. Women are less likely to receive tenure or be promoted than their male counterparts (NRC 2001). In a study of medical schools, the "fall off" of women from assistant to associate professor was nearly 60 percent (Nonnemaker 2000). It takes women longer to be promoted to senior faculty ranks. Valian (1999) has noted that women take much longer to advance from associate to full professor. Additionally, their rate of promotion from associate to full professor is lower than that of their male counterparts (National Science Foundation, Division of Science Resources Statistics 2004b).

The life sciences have had more women faculty for a longer period of time than other science disciplines; hence, it might be expected that there are significantly more senior women faculty. Despite the larger numbers, the level of female full professors in the life sciences in 1995 was under 15 percent (NRC 2001), and this number has not increased significantly since then.

Within the past decade a number of initiatives were launched to advance women faculty. In 2001 a group of nine leading universities began a well-publicized effort to promote women faculty on their campuses (Cox and Wilson 2001); the National Science Foundation introduced ADVANCE, a grant program intended to catalyze institutional transformation and systemic changes at awardee universities to advance women faculty; and the NRC's Committee on Women in Science and Engineering undertook a project to find common policies and strategies among institutions that have been successful in advancing women at different levels.

The nine leading universities assessed the status of women faculty on their campuses and initiated various programs to increase their numbers and improve career development.[1] To date a number of reports have been issued on the programs introduced as well as the progress achieved. Most of the findings have been reported at the institutional level, usually according to school. One reason for this is that for most universities, data collected at the departmental levels comprise too small a sample for meaningful statistical analysis. However, some universities disaggregate their data by department or by broad fields, which allows for examination of disciplinary differences.

In 2001 Princeton University convened a task force to examine the status of women faculty in the natural sciences and engineering. The task force conducted a survey of current and former faculty, and collected data from numerous university sources including departments and department chairs. As expected, there was uneven progress across the departments.

However, some of their findings were unexpected. In the life sciences, two of three departments experienced an increase in women faculty while the third experienced a decrease. The latter was surprising as the discipline—molecular biology—does not lack interested women scholars (Princeton University 2003). Although there are bound to be factors specific to the department or institution that may account for this unexpected finding, this surprising lack of progress in the life sciences was not unique to Princeton.

In 1999 the Massachusetts Institute of Technology (MIT) released its *Report on the Status of Women Faculty in the School of Science*. This report was the catalyst for the gathering of information on the nine leading universities. In 2006 MIT released a progress review, allowing analyses of gains since the initial spurt of activity following its 1999 report. Several of the findings were quite notable.

One finding was that action and activity did not occur in the absence of institutional pressure. For instance, in the schools examined, the hiring of women faculty increased significantly following measures adopted by the deans during the period of activity, but stagnated over time. In the life sciences, the percentage of women faculty and appointments of women to leadership positions increased in the years following the first MIT report, but such progress became neither institutionalized nor generalized.

MIT experienced an unusual period of expansion in the biological sciences in the past decade, with the establishment of several new institutes and centers. During this period of expansion, with its increased opportunities for faculty recruitment and advancement, women were not named to leadership positions (Hopkins 2006).

What the experiences of MIT and Princeton suggest is that simply increasing numbers of women is not sufficient to ensure that progress is achieved and sustained, and that the availability of a large candidate pool does not assure its actual use.

Harvard University took this and the experience of other universities into consideration when launching its initiative on women faculty. In 2005, in response to the reaction on campus to remarks by its then president Lawrence Summers, who in a speech at an economics conference alleged that women don't have the intellectual mettle needed to compete with men in the sciences, Harvard University convened two task forces to examine the status of women, one focused on women faculty and the other on women in science and engineering (Harvard

University 2005). The task force on women faculty collected information through focus groups and individual meetings. Institutional data was collected according to school.

In addition, the task force studied the experiences of peer institutions, conducting interviews with key individuals and identifying benchmark policies that could be adopted for use at Harvard. These were compiled and integrated into best practices and benchmarks among the task force's recommendations.

As part of its project to find policies and strategies successful in advancing women, the NRC's Committee on Women in Science and Engineering (CWSE) visited four top research universities.[2] Each had been recognized as being successful in its efforts to increase the number of women. The CWSE sought not only to identify successful strategies and practices but to determine how these strategies had been implemented. The committee focused on top research universities to address the widely held belief that women scientists were of lesser quality than men and that increasing their numbers among faculty and student ranks would degrade standards of academic excellence. It identified institutions that had successfully increased their number of women faculty as well as improved in quality on a number of measures including national rankings of academic excellence. Of the four institutions, one was selected specifically for its progress in the life sciences (NRC 2006).

In 2001 the NSF launched ADVANCE: Increasing the Participation and Advancement of Women in Academic Science and Engineering Careers.[3] The initial recipients of this program's grants have made significant progress at their institutions and provided guidelines, tool kits, and examples of programs, strategies, and procedures for other institutions to follow.[4]

Across these initiatives commonalities have arisen among the findings, despite the variation in institutions and data-collection methodologies. The following sections will present a discussion of efforts broadly grouped according to issue: the search process, institutional programs that differentially impact women, institutional or departmental "culture" issues, and a strong institutional leadership role in guiding these efforts.

THE SEARCH PROCESS

In general, the search for a faculty candidate originates in the department. The department ascribes the scientific expertise desired, develops the position description, and conducts the search. However, this traditional process is the route by which many departments have come to have few or no women faculty members. The university can institute measures to aid in the search process, and to intervene as necessary, to ensure that the department considers an appropriately broad pool of candidates for hire.

Increased hiring of women begins with increasing the number of women in the applicant pool. To accomplish this, one recommendation is to hold broad rather than narrowly focused searches. Because in any given subfield the number of women will likely be smaller than the number of men, searching among a larger set of subfields will create a larger pool of women candidates. A university can encourage its departments to adopt this approach to widen the net for quality women candidates.

A more diverse search committee that includes women will increase the outreach network to identify potential candidates as well as signal that the university is committed to diversifying its faculty.

Faculty members who have conducted searches in the traditional manner may need to be introduced to other methods of identifying potential faculty candidates. Providing training in methods of conducting a diverse search can help to introduce and institutionalize such methods universitywide. This may be especially critical for departments that have had trouble recruiting women.

Institutional Programs

Certain institutional programs have a greater impact on women than men. Of these, targeted hiring, tenure clock extension, and child care were the most frequently cited.

Targeted Hiring Programs

Targeted recruiting programs provide flexibility in hiring to capitalize on "targets of opportunity." Many institutions operate such programs, in which specific efforts are made to identify and recruit specific types of faculty such as women. These programs can be a source of concern, however. Some public universities cannot legally conduct targeted hiring along gender or racial lines. Others worry that the focus on a specific characteristic will yield hires that do not measure up to faculty hired in the usual manner. This is not an insignificant concern, as the perception of special hiring can convey negative implications that can cast a pall over a faculty member's future at the university.

MIT examined this issue by comparing external validations of faculty accomplishments—such as awards and election to prestigious societies—between faculty hired through a targeted program and those hired through the usual process. It found that the accomplishments of faculty hired through the targeted program matched or exceeded those of faculty hired in the usual manner (MIT 2006).

Dual-Career Programs

Many faculty face the "two-body problem" in that they are part of a dual-career couple. This frequently means that both partners must simultaneously search for employment, which is a difficulty in the academic job market. For women the difficulty may be more acute, as studies indicate a significant portion of female academics have spouses or partners who are also academics.

Dual-career programs have been instituted at many universities to specifically address this issue. Originally these programs were popular at rural universities, which found recruiting difficult due to the relatively limited employment opportunities in their environs. However, these programs have proliferated to more urban regions alongside the increase in dual-career couples in academia. Universities and colleges in California have formed two separate consortia to address this problem in the northern and southern parts of the state.

Harvard's task force recommended establishing a consortium for recruiting for the Boston and greater Massachusetts areas, modeled on the California consortia as well as on a similar consortium in New Jersey.

Tenure-Clock Extension Policies

Many universities have adopted policies to extend the tenure clock when a faculty member has increased family responsibilities, such as the birth or adoption of a child or care of an ailing family member. This provides a period of time of reduced teaching duties, and the assurance that the year in which the extension is requested is not included in the package for tenure consideration.

Use of this policy by women, however, may not be consistent. Some women may be afraid to request the extension for fear that they will be pegged as asking for special treatment; indeed, some institutions have found this to be the case (Bhattacharjee 2004).

For example, Princeton University has found in its review of the natural sciences and engineering that of seven requests to extend the tenure clock during a selected time period, six were from men. During this period fewer than 15 percent of women received extensions, despite the fact that women made up nearly one-fourth of the junior faculty (Princeton University 2003). Further, a survey of faculty found that more women were likely to view such extensions as detrimental to their careers. To obviate this problem, Princeton made the extension automatic with the granting of dependent-care leave (Bhattacharjee 2005). Harvard's task force rec-ommended adoption of this same policy (Harvard University 2005).

There are concerns among faculty that the extension year will not be truly excluded from consideration by promotion and tenure commit-tees, and that a faculty member who extends the tenure clock will be at a disadvantage. The institutional role is critical at this point to ensure that there is consistency in consideration of tenure packages universitywide, and that institutional policies will be adhered to in every case.

Child Care

The problem of child care has been addressed by nearly all institu-tions. The approaches to solving this problem are as varied as the in-stitutions themselves. Among the universities, many offer on-site child care through campus-operated centers. The CWSE has found, however, that multiple on-campus child care centers were not sufficient to meet the demand at one university, and that a single institution may not be able to meet the demand for the quantity and variety of care desired.

To provide flexibility in accommodating desire for different types of child care, many universities offer a financial benefit toward child care expenses rather than offering it on site. This flexibility was critical at one public institution whose perennial requests to establish an on-site child care center were denied by the state legislature. Based on a review of the costs of available child care in areas around Harvard's campuses, Harvard's task force recommended increasing financial support for child care expenses.

CULTURE ISSUES

The programs mentioned above may require significant resources. The CWSE has found some practices that are low-cost yet provide much benefit to the faculty and the institution. These, which might be called departmental culture issues, provided universities with tools to address the challenges that arise due to the unique nature of academia.

Awareness of Tenure Policy and Process

It may seem obvious, but the university should ensure that junior faculty are thoroughly familiar with the institution's tenure policy and process; at many institutions, however, this may not be the case. To avoid the "lore" that develops around the tenure process, the institution should ensure that all tenure-track faculty are aware of the formal tenure policy and the standards required to achieve tenure by making these public and by widely distributing the information.

Equally important is ensuring that faculty are aware of the informal guidelines for tenure in the department. It is important to make clear to junior faculty that certain parts of their performance will be weighted more heavily than others, but also that a tenure package with significant deficiencies in one area is likely to run into trouble.

The Faculty Mentoring or Guidance Committee

Some departments take care to make certain their junior faculty progress satisfactorily toward tenure by appointing a formal mentoring or guidance committee. Such a committee meets with the junior faculty member on a regular basis to review her progress toward tenure. This process is separate from the formal review process that many institutions undertake after some years in the department.

Protection from Excessive Service Demands

Service to the department and institution is an integral part of a faculty member's work. Most universities have a strong desire to have diverse membership on committees. If there are few women or minority faculty members in an institution, one individual can be inundated with requests to serve on numerous committees.

As women faculty are more plentiful in the life sciences, it is less likely that any one woman will be oversubscribed for committee service. However, it can be helpful to shield an individual from too many service demands if it is diverting too much time from research. In particular, a woman faculty member may find it difficult to decline service on a committee if the requestor is a senior administration member, so requests for service should be made judiciously.

It should be noted that shielding individuals from service must be balanced, as service on some important committees is important to advancement. Princeton has found that more men than women had been asked to serve on important committees within their departments, which was perceived to disadvantage the women faculty (Princeton University 2003).

Teaching Assignments

One area that has significant impact on a faculty member's progress is in teaching assignments. Course development takes much effort, and this may leach time away from research. For an assistant professor setting up a lab and starting a research program, the demands of teaching can mean significant periods of time away from research; this can lead to reduced publication productivity, a negative factor in consideration for tenure. Department chairs can be encouraged to minimize the impact by limiting the rotation of class assignments.

Lower Satisfaction

As a group, women faculty report lower satisfaction with their jobs, even when they feel they are compensated equally and allocated equivalent resources (Princeton University 2003). One reason for this finding may be isolation and marginalization within their departments. The CWSE has learned that at one institution, isolation was a major reason given by women faculty who left prior to achieving tenure.

The issue of marginalization has been prominently addressed in the MIT faculty report, which catalogs disparities between men and women faculty in the MIT School of Science (MIT 1999). Women faculty members cite marginalization and diminution of their contributions within their departments. Many universities have made efforts to combat isolation by setting up or supporting women's networks. Additionally, they formally recognize the accomplishments of women faculty by highlighting them in institutional literature.

INSTITUTIONAL LEADERSHIP

Perhaps the strongest agreement across initiatives is the importance of strong and visible institutional leadership on advancing women faculty, backed up by actions and resources.

Institutional collection and review of data is essential to all efforts. Collecting data aides institutions in assessing whether their efforts and investment to advance women are bearing fruit; it also helps to identify successes and failures, sticking points and bottlenecks. Data collection and examination on an institution-wide basis assure meaningful comparisons and better determination of whether the institution's resources are being properly utilized.

These studies have found that an institutional-level review is critical to achieving success on all fronts. For example, in the search process, a dean-level review helps to assure a more diverse candidate pool. There are additional benefits. One university has found that a dean's review at an earlier point in the search processes provides access to additional resources and incentives to offer to the candidates. Another has found that a dean's review guarantees a more concerted effort to find diverse candidates, and a more vigorous search process, resulting in higher-caliber candidates.

Institutional action, such as in the implementation of universitywide programs, is most effective in assuring that such programs are being utilized as intended, benefiting both the faculty and the institution.

LOOKING FORWARD FOR THE LIFE SCIENCES

For the life sciences, perhaps the most important finding from all reports and reviews is that even with its larger pool of potential candidates, increasing the number of women faculty requires concerted and continued effort. Because women are more visible in life science departments—as students, technicians, postdoctoral scholars, and faculty—it may be easer to make the assumption that women are advancing apace with men.

There is no single approach to improving the recruitment, retention, and advancement of women faculty in the life sciences. Institutions will discover as they launch initiatives that what was successful at another campus may not work as well on their own. They may also find that efforts that met with failure at different institutions excel at theirs. What all the programs discussed herein have in common are strong leadership from the top levels of the institution, a campus community genuinely committed to advancing women, and the will to take actions that effect lasting change.

14

Attracting and Retaining Women in Engineering

The Tufts University Experience

Linda Abriola and Margery Davies

In the United States, engineering is an academic field that has been, and continues to be, predominantly male. In recent years, only about one in five PhD recipients has been a woman. As the Congressional Commission on the Advancement of Women and Minorities in Science, Engineering and Technology Development notes,

> Now, more than ever, the nation needs to cultivate the scientific and technical talents of all its citizens, not just those from groups that have traditionally worked in SET [science, engineering, and technology] fields. Women, minorities, and persons with disabilities currently constitute more than two-thirds of the U.S. workforce. It is apparent that just when the U.S. economy requires more SET workers, the largest pool of potential workers continues to be isolated from SET careers." (Congressional Commission on the Advancement of Women and Minorities in Science, Engineering and Technology Development 2000, 9)

The relative absence of women from engineering also robs the field of the potential for additional perspectives and problem-solving approaches for a wide range of issues, and limits women's access to employment opportunities. (For discussions of gender and science/engineering, see Schiebinger 1999; Xie and Shauman 2003.)

TABLE 14.1
Women Receiving Engineering Degrees as a Percent of All Engineering Degree Recipients

	2001	2002	2003	2004	2005
Tufts University					
Bachelor's degrees	23.2 (194)	30.1 (193)	33.3 (195)	—	26.8 (164)
Master's degrees	45.1 (91)	31.7 (120)	31.7 (123)	32.5 (160)	21.9 (155)
Doctoral degrees	50.0 (10)	63.6 (11)	35.0 (8)	55.6 (9)	50.0 (8)
All Engineering Schools					
Bachelor's degrees	20.1	20.9	20.4	18.2	19.5
Master's degrees	22.1	22.2	22.3	21.9	22.7
Doctoral degrees	17.0	17.3	17.4	17.8	18.3

Source: American Society for Engineering Education, 2006.

Note: Total number of degrees in parentheses.

TABLE 14.2
Percentage of Faculty in Engineering Who Are Women

	Top 50 Departments in Selected Disciplines*			School of Engineering, Tufts University**		
	Assistant Professor	Associate Professor	Full Professor	Assistant Professor	Associate Professor	Full Professor
Engineering	16.94	11.17	3.68	50.0 (4 of 8)	6.3 (1 of 16)	8.0 (2 of 25)
Biomedical	—	—	—	100.0 (1 of 1)	0 (0 of 3)	0 (0 of 2)
Chemical	21.38	19.19	4.37	0 (0 of 2)	0 (0 of 2)	25.0 (1 of 4)
Civil	22.26	11.50	3.52	100.0 (1 of 1)	0 (0 of 6)	14.3 (1 of 7)
Electrical	10.86	9.84	3.85	50.0 (1 of 2)	33.3 (1 of 3)	0 (0 of 4)
Mechanical	15.65	8.89	3.17	50.0 (1 of 2)	0 (0 of 2)	0 (0 of 8)
Computer science	10.82	14.41	8.33	0 (0 of 3)	42.9 (3 of 7)	100.0 (3 of 3)

Sources: Handelsman et al., 2005; AS&E Office of Diversity Education and Development, 2006.

*Data on faculty derived from the same "top 50" departments for each discipline; ranked by NSF according to research expenditures in that discipline. Faculty data are from 2002.
**Data on SOE, Tufts University faculty come from the Faculty Retention Cohort Study. Data are from October 2005.

Tables 14.1 and 14.2 present data from the Tufts University School of Engineering (SOE) in Medford, Massachusetts. These data on women in engineering appear to deviate substantially from the national averages.

While at all U.S. engineering schools women earned 19.5 percent of bachelor's degrees in 2005, at Tufts women earned 26.8 percent of the degrees. Not only are the female undergraduates recruited and retained at Tufts SOE, they also do well academically—on average, better than their male counterparts. Combining the five graduating classes of 2001 through 20005, women made up 29.1 percent of a total of 973 graduates. The average grade point average (GPA) for women was 3.30, higher than the average GPA for men at 3.24.

In addition to a strong record of female undergraduate enrollment and academic achievement, the Tufts SOE also has a strong record of faculty retention. Of all tenure-track faculty hired in the SOE from academic year (AY) 1990–91 through AY 2004–05, 40.5 percent (seventeen out of forty-two) were women. To assess retention, we selected the cohort years from AY 1990–91 through AY 1998–99. All faculty hired within that period have been at Tufts long enough for their tenure review to have been resolved. Of the nineteen faculty hired during those nine years, the department has retained 50 percent (four out of eight) of the women, and 64 percent (seven out of eleven) of the men. Of the twenty-three faculty hired from AY 1999–2000 through AY 2004–05, nine were women. Three of these women have already received tenure, and the rest are still at Tufts. Fourteen men were hired during this same period; twelve are still at Tufts, and three of these have already received tenure (AS&E Office of Diversity Education and Development 2006.)

The Tufts SOE administration also has a high percentage of women. In 2003, Linda M. Abriola, previously of the University of Michigan, was appointed the dean of the School of Engineering. When she was appointed, Abriola was one of a very small number of female engineering deans at Division I (as ranked by the Carnegie Classification of Institutes of Higher Education system) research institutions. The SOE cabinet, which includes the top administrators assigned to various functional roles throughout the school, is 40 percent female (four women out of ten members).

Tufts is not the only engineering school that has a better-than-average record of employing and educating women. The percentage of women graduating with bachelor's degrees in 2005 from a number of other institutions were impressive as well: Yale University (41 percent of 54); Princeton University (36 percent of 181); the Massachusetts Institute of Technology (35 percent of 593); Brown University (35 percent of 66); the California Institute of Technology (33 percent of 96); the University of Pennsylvania (30 percent of 349); Washington University (29 percent of 309); the University of California, Berkeley (28 percent of 776); Harvard University (28 percent of 93); and Stanford University (27 percent of 388).[1] How has Tufts succeeded in being one of the handful of institutions that exceed the averages? What follows is a description of policies and academic climate factors that may contribute to Tufts' success in increasing the representation of women in engineering at all levels.

The Tufts Context: Fertile Ground for Recruiting and Retaining Women in Engineering

Tufts University is a small private institution, named by the Carnegie Classification system as a "Doctoral/Research Extensive" or "Research I" university. It enrolls some 4,800 undergraduates and 3,700 graduate students on three campuses. Founded in 1898, the Tufts SOE is located on the Medford campus and houses five engineering departments (biomedical; chemical and biological; civil and environmental; electrical and computer; and mechanical), as well as the Computer Science Department and the Tufts Gordon Institute for Engineering Management. The SOE supports fourteen undergraduate degree programs including bachelor of science programs in computer science and chemical, civil, computer, electrical, environmental, and mechanical engineering that are accredited by ABET, Inc. (formerly the Accreditation Board for Engineering and Technology). In AY 2006–07, the SOE awarded 174 bachelor's, 146 master's, and 11 doctoral degrees. Its faculty numbers some ninety-five full-time and part-time members, over sixty-five of whom are on a tenure track or already tenured. The SOE places particular emphasis on cross-disciplinary research and education programs, including some dual-degree programs with other schools at Tufts, as well as on educating engineering leaders (with a focus on communication skills, interdisciplinary technical preparation, management skills, globalization, and the societal impact of technology).

The Tufts SOE benefits from its close relationship with the School of Arts and Sciences. This close historic relationship between engineering and the arts and sciences has had a number of long-lasting implications for the inclusion of women in engineering. Undergraduate students can very easily transfer between arts and sciences (A&S) and engineering. No money changes hands between the schools when students cross-register or change majors, so there is no bureaucratic incentive for administrators to discourage students from taking classes in another school. Furthermore, a number of the required courses for SOE students are taught in A&S departments, and additional collaboration between the schools is institutionalized through joint majors. Last, but by no means least, the two schools are geographically cheek by jowl. This structural situation creates very permeable boundaries between the two schools, with beneficial effects for all students.

These permeable boundaries mean that the SOE is not isolated, and thus less likely to develop an exclusionary culture of male technical superiority.

One result of the ease with which SOE and A&S undergraduates can take courses and interact with students and faculty from the neighboring school is that the SOE has an almost zero net student attrition rate—that is, the number of students who transfer from the SOE to A&S is roughly equal to the number who transfer in the other direction. For example, in AY 2005–06, twenty-four SOE undergraduates (of whom six were women) transferred to A&S, while twenty-two A&S undergraduates (of whom seven were women) transferred to the SOE.

The two schools' close connection extends to all aspects of student life. Undergraduates from both the SOE and A&S are completely intermingled in terms of campus housing, student organizations, student services, and so forth. This allows students from both schools to get to know each other and facilitates administrator and faculty awareness of issues and opportunities in both schools. The schools share one office of admissions, one office of undergraduate education, one dean of students, one financial aid office, and so on.

Faculty can also intermingle very easily. The legacy of the many years of integration of the SOE and A&S under the overall umbrella of the joint School of Arts, Sciences, and Engineering (AS&E) is that much of faculty governance is integrated, including membership on advisory committees and promotion and tenure committees. Adjunct appointments for faculty members from one school to a department in another school are commonplace.

Another important academic climate factor is that there is a demonstrable commitment at the upper levels of the Tufts University administration to bring women into top posts. Four of the eight school deans are now women (in the SOE, the Friedman School of Nutrition Science and Policy, the Sackler School of Graduate Biomedical Sciences, and the Cummings School of Veterinary Medicine). Other top administrators are also women (the vice president for university relations, the vice president for human resources, the vice president for information technology, the vice provost, and the chief investment officer). This helps to create an overall atmosphere of inclusiveness and delivers a message that women's abilities and accomplishments are recognized at Tufts, even in fields in which men have historically predominated.

The integration of the SOE and A&S provides a supportive environment for women in engineering at Tufts. Women in the SOE are not isolated; both students and faculty have ample opportunity to get to know and to derive support from women in A&S, and vice versa. The ease with which students can move academically between the two schools has already been noted. If female students do not find a support group directly within the SOE, they have many places to go within the overall integrated structure provided by AS&E.

There is substantial anecdotal evidence from the faculty of the SOE crediting their contacts with faculty and administrators outside of the school as important sources of support. One example comes from an associate professor of computer science:

> Several faculty across the two schools have written proposals targeting the increase in representation and advancement of women in academic science and engineering careers. Two such programs have been funded in multi-year proposals involving several faculty. We have had several unexpected yet amazing outcomes. Interdisciplinary technical research discussions are common (e.g., between a female professor from Computer Science and a female professor from Math about modeling on-chip inductance. A student of the Computer Science professor also often approached the Mathematics professor for technical advice.) New friendships have formed among the faculty across the schools. Informal mentoring relationships between senior and junior women have evolved. (Soha Hassoun, e-mail communication with the authors, 2006)

Recruiting and Retaining Students

The joint Office of Undergraduate Admissions plays an important role in recruiting, as well as admitting, women into the SOE. The dean of admissions describes their efforts:

> Women in Engineering are a targeted group in our recruitment and selection efforts. While we do not run any specific programs for them on the recruitment side, we do proactively include women in our PSAT search parameters for engineers, feature them in our marketing work, and consider gender as a factor in our Engineering acceptance decisions. (Lee Coffin, e-mail communication with the authors, 2006)

In addition to these efforts by the Office of Undergraduate Admissions, Tufts' electronic and printed materials are designed to depict women at all levels in the SOE.

Once students are admitted to the SOE, many aspects of their education and experiences may contribute to the high retention rate. The goals of two SOE programs operated jointly with A&S—Computer Science, Engineering, and Math Scholarships (or CSEMS) and First Year Scholars—include increasing the number of women and members of underrepresented groups in engineering and the sciences.

CSEMS, originally funded by the National Science Foundation in 2002, provides scholarships to talented first- and second-year students with financial need at Tufts who are working toward degrees in computer science, engineering, or mathematics. Within this cohort, women and underrepresented minorities are given priority. Participating students are exposed to faculty and graduate student research, mentoring, and study skills through weekly meetings with research faculty, academic advisers, student mentors, and/or academic resource staff members. The program provides scholarships for an average of twenty-eight students in each class. Tufts provides additional financial support to enhance the programming.

First Year Scholars was founded in 2002 and is funded entirely by the university. This program provides an opportunity for students who meet certain eligibility criteria (e.g., being of the first generation in their families to attend college; coming from low-income families; coming from an educationally disadvantaged high school) to come to Tufts early and take two summer courses. This program helps them get a jump start on their coursework as well as providing a supportive environment in which to "learn the ropes." The program includes twelve to eighteen students a year. Since its inception, sixty-three students have participated; of these, twenty-eight were SOE students, of whom twenty-one were female.

There is evidence that programs that emphasize finding solutions to real-world problems are particularly attractive to women, many of whom tend to shy away from engineering courses in which the material covered seems too abstract or technical (Flora and Cooper 2005, 19). A number of aspects of Tufts' SOE formal curriculum, as well as extracurricular activities, provide just this real-world component.

In their first year at the SOE, undergraduates must take two half-credit courses in introductory engineering from two different departments. Many of these courses have syllabi that include, as substantial components, projects and other hands-on activities so that students are introduced immediately to the practical applications of the more abstract material that they will encounter in their engineering classes. Tufts faculty members have also founded and support engineering "academy" courses. These courses enroll both junior and senior engineering students, partnering them with mentors and students in the nonengineering disciplines to form multidisciplinary teams that are charged with problem-solving objectives in a particular area. In academy programs, students learn to work in teams, design for a client, interpret data, communicate their findings, and solve real-world problems. The robotics academy links child development majors with mechanical and electrical engineers and computer scientists to design and build next-generation robotics; since its inception in 2002–03, seventeen of the forty students involved have been women. The musical instrument–engineering academy brings musicians and engineers together to design, build, refine, compose for, and perform on a musical instrument. The Bringing Engineers into New Disciplines program partners engineers with students and mentors in psychology and nutrition in an effort to develop better approaches to the study of obesity.

A variety of extracurricular activities within the SOE also help to attract and retain women. Like most engineering schools, Tufts has an active chapter of the Society of Women Engineers, which is one of the official, funded student organizations. However, there are many less traditional extracurricular opportunities. Nerd Girls, an organization conceived of and advised by a female faculty member in electrical and computer engineering, involves female students in projects intended to showcase members' talents, diverse backgrounds, and engineering skills.[2] Each year, Nerd Girls team projects are undertaken, with local professional engineers and Tufts engineering faculty as consultants. In past years, projects have included building an energy efficient, solar-powered automobile and designing and installing a solar power system to operate one of the two lighthouses on Thacher Island off Rockport, Massachusetts. As another example of extracurricular activities, the Center for Engineering Education Outreach sponsors several programs that provide opportunities for K–12 students and teachers to be directly exposed to both male and female SOE students. The programs help stimulate precollege student interest in engineering, provide professional development for teachers, and give SOE undergraduate and graduate students practical experience in teaching, mentoring, and articulating why they are interested in the field. Tufts also has an active chapter of Engineers without Borders USA, which is a nonprofit humanitarian organization that was established to partner with developing communities worldwide to improve their quality of life. Founded by two SOE female students, the Tufts chapter now numbers some fifty students, and has sent sixteen students—of whom ten were women—on summer field projects. SOE faculty serve as mentors to the student teams.

In fall 2005, in its most recent accreditation visit at Tufts, the ABET, Inc. accreditation team was "particularly complimentary of the quality of the SOE's undergraduate advising" (Abriola 2007, 4). An associate dean of undergraduate education is dedicated 100 percent to advising SOE students, and the current associate dean is beloved for her warm, caring personality. The close attention that she gives to individual students complements the undergraduate advising structure in the SOE, where faculty members advise both premajor students and engineering majors. This advising structure ensures a larger degree of individual attention for students. The SOE's higher-than-average percentage of female faculty members also may have a positive impact on female student retention, with female faculty members often serving as formal and informal mentors and helping to provide concrete role models of women in engineering. In addition to its advising program, the SOE has a professional staff member whose primary responsibility is to arrange and supervise internships for SOE students, and a director of external relations whose responsibilities include developing contacts with SOE alumni/alumnae and local companies, and organizing career and graduate school fairs. At present, both of these staff members are women, another factor that may help the SOE retain female students. All of these contacts provide a network of potential mentors for students.

FACULTY RECRUITMENT AND RETENTION

In the School of Engineering at Tufts, 21 percent of the tenure-track/tenured faculty are women. Women comprise 36 percent (4 of 11) of Assistant Professors; 17 percent of the associate professors (4 of 23); and 18 percent (5 of 28) of the full professors (see table 14.2). While we hope to see these numbers increase, they exceed national averages, and they have not been achieved without effort. Since at least the early 1990s, the SOE has emphasized and put resources into increasing its numbers of female faculty.

The affirmative action officer (AAO)—Dr. Margery Davies, in a position shared by both the SOE and A&S—plays a central role in faculty recruitment. To highlight the importance of diversity, in 1996, the SOE and A&S created a dedicated, half-time AAO position for the two schools, instead of appending these duties to an already-existing full-time position. At the beginning of the academic year, the AAO meets with all of the search committees to go over procedures and to emphasize the importance of doing outreach to build a diverse pool of applicants. The SOE dean and the AAO monitor all steps of a faculty search very carefully, and departments must get approval from them at several points in the recruitment process before being permitted to proceed to the next stage. Each of these points is described briefly below.

Proposed position announcements are scrutinized carefully to ensure that their requirements are not overly restrictive and thus reduce the size of the eligible pool. Departments are strongly encouraged to place their position announcements in job listings that are targeted to diverse audiences, such as the Society of Women Engineers, the National Society for Black Engineers, and others, as well as in the standard disciplinary listings. Letting the position announcement do all the work is not considered adequate, however; search committees are also required to do outreach. The AAO provides departments with resource files of contacts that might help them build diverse applicant pools, and confers with individual search committee members when they have questions pertaining to how best to approach people for help. All of this advertising and outreach is intended not only to get the word out about a position but also to create a perception about Tufts that we are serious about building diverse applicant pools in the hope of building a more diverse faculty.

Faculty searches in the SOE and A&S do not have application deadlines, but do have a "review of applications" start date, after which the winnowing process begins. Hard-and-fast application deadlines were eliminated about ten years ago so that outreach efforts would have the maximum amount of time to operate and to ensure that promising candidates who surfaced later in the process would not be eliminated by an arbitrary deadline. After a search committee has made its "first cut" decisions, it must pause and have these decisions reviewed by the dean and AAO before continuing further with the process. The applicants who make it through the first cut are on the "preliminary list." Search committees are required to submit the demographics of their total pool of applicants, as well as those of the preliminary list. They also must answer an outreach questionnaire in which they detail the outreach that they have done. This allows the dean and AAO to assess the extent of outreach a committee has undertaken, the diversity of the total pool, and the comparability of the demographics of the preliminary list with those of the total pool. If a total pool is not diverse, and if the search committee cannot document much outreach, that committee is asked to go back and try harder. For example, in one recent search, the total pool had no women, and the outreach questionnaire indicated only that the position announcement had been placed in the standard disciplinary listings. The department was not permitted to proceed to the next step in the search until it had documented a substantial amount of outreach.

On the positive side, some search committees have undertaken extensive outreach without being asked. As the current chair of the Computer Science Department summarizes her very effective outreach approach,

(1) Look up highly regarded faculty in other institutions. (2) Call them, whether you have ever met them before or not. (3) Pitch the position you are trying to fill. Only after making the pitch for the specific position, ask them for any names. (4) After they give you a list of names, all of which you take down, then (and only then) say that you are trying to build a diverse as possible candidate pool and ask whether there are any *really good* women and/or persons of color whom they could recommend. Again, take down names. Then ask, of all of these candidates, whom they consider the most promising for the particular position. (5) Often, they will rank one of the second group of names higher than those in the first group. (6) Often, there is a lot of pointer chasing. Keep at it. (7) Then make a personal connection to the candidates. Listen to what will be the real deciding factors for them. Don't take an initial "I'm not interested" as the final word. Find out *why* they think that they are not interested, and what it would take for them to become interested, and then see if anything is feasible. (8) Be willing to call lots of people you have never met before and who don't

know you and pitch the job you are trying to fill. (Diane Souvaine, e-mail communication with the authors, 2006)

As a testament to the effectiveness of these techniques, in 2003–04, searches in computer science yielded four hires—three of whom were women.

Once the preliminary list has been approved, a search committee may proceed to the next step of proposing candidates for on-campus interviews. Again, the dean and AAO scrutinize those recommended for interviews very carefully. They will then often ask the search committee why a particular candidate is being recommended, or ask to see the applications of all the candidates on the preliminary list, so that they can examine in detail this all-important "second cut." The dean and AAO have on occasion denied permission to interview a candidate who did not seem comparatively strong enough, and have also requested that a department interview a candidate who was a woman or from an under-represented racial/ethnic group who had clear potential.

After the on-campus interviews have been approved, the dean and AAO try to ensure that the search committee is doing what it can to make the interview candidate feel welcome at Tufts and that the candidate is exposed to potential collaborators outside of the hiring department and, if appropriate, the school. If the candidate is a woman, female faculty from other SOE departments are often invited to informal receptions, meals, and/or interview seminars. When candidates come to campus for interviews, they always meet with the dean.

Finally, the dean confers with the department chair to share her impressions of the candidates. The department then sends its recommendation about which candidate should be offered the job to the dean and AAO, who then confer and decide whether to approve the hire or whether discussion with the department is needed. Once the department's recommendation is approved, the dean then takes over, offers the job, and handles the negotiations.

Obviously, the faculty search procedures at Tufts differ considerably from a department announcing to a dean that it is planning to offer a position to candidate X, have in fact made a verbal [and legally binding] offer, and just want to nail down how much salary and start-up money can be offered. The dean and AAO are very closely involved at every step in SOE faculty searches, and their input and decisions have a concrete effect on the outcome. In addition, these detailed procedures reinforce the understanding that the dean and AAO are really paying attention to what happens in a search, which helps to encourage departments to keep diversity in mind at all times while they are doing outreach and making choices.

Additional aspects of Tufts faculty hiring processes bear mentioning. The SOE has been quite willing to recruit, consider, and hire candidates who have not followed the "regular" academic career path or who have come from government or industry. This has resulted in the hiring of several faculty in recent years, most of whom have been women. We have also been willing to "go the extra mile" to recruit candidates and to win a positive response to position offers; encouraging calls from the dean; the offer of return visits to campus; competitive start-up funding; flexibility in start dates; a transitional housing program shared with A&S, as well as other informal help with housing and information about schools and local services; employment advice for "trailing spouses/ partners"—all of these have helped Tufts land candidates. The SOE has also been willing to hire two people out of a single search when the situation warranted it, and particularly if this would help diversify the faculty. We have also entertained proposals for window-of-opportunity hires if a department finds an outstanding potential faculty member who might be interested in coming to Tufts. The provost has been very helpful in this regard, and the overall Tufts administration is ready to "put its money where its mouth is" when it comes to diversifying the faculty.

A number of policies and programs in the SOE provide support for junior faculty in their quest for tenure. Dean Abriola has instituted a new course-load policy for all faculty hires: the nominal load is three courses per year. All new hires teach two courses in their first year (though this is sometimes extended to the first two years, depending on department flexibility). Prior to her arrival, the nominal course load for all new faculty was four courses per year. A junior faculty leave program gives faculty one semester of guaranteed paid leave during their tenure probationary period. This is often coupled with a grant or fellowship (some of which are funded by Tufts), so that the junior faculty member can devote an entire year exclusively to research.

The SOE also has a mentoring program that assigns two mentors to each new faculty member—one from that person's home department and one from outside that department. The concept is that the former can provide appropriate guidance on disciplinary issues and the latter more advice on general professional and personal developmental questions. The dean also sponsors a monthly networking brown-bag lunch of the untenured faculty in the school. The dean meets individually with all junior faculty once a year, both to get to know them better and to personally assess their progress. In addition to this informal check-in, all junior faculty must be reviewed by their departments and the dean in their second and fourth years. This is a formal, written review. While these review processes are understandably anxiety-producing for junior faculty, they do provide a structure for faculty to get formal feedback on their performance and progress and help to reduce faculty isolation.

Tufts University offers three months of paid maternity leave for biological mothers, and four weeks of paid paternity/adoption leave for all parents, regardless of sex or whether the new child is adopted or biological. The SOE and A&S also have a primary caregiver policy through which a faculty member who declares himself to be the primary caregiver of a child can stop the tenure clock for a year. This tenure-clock stoppage can occur twice during the tenure probationary period. While male faculty members have availed themselves of both the paternity/adoption leave and the primary caregiver tenure-clock stoppage, it is generally accepted that the fact that these policies are in place will prove more appealing to female faculty members as a group. The recognition of work and family balance issues—both the concrete programs themselves, plus the creation of an atmosphere that Tufts recognizes and supports people who are trying to combine work and family in balanced ways—can be attractive to women.

Finally, there are ways in which informal support afforded to female SOE faculty can make a tremendous difference in whether they have a positive experience. The integration of the SOE and A&S at the faculty level means that female SOE faculty have many opportunities to get to know colleagues in A&S who can provide them with advice and friendship. The presence of several senior female faculty in the SOE has had a powerful impact—both through direct help and through role modeling—on the careers of some junior faculty women. For example, in one department, the recruitment of a new female senior faculty member helped provide support to a junior female member who had felt isolated in her position. The senior woman sought out her junior colleague for a series of informal conversations pertaining to prioritization and choices in building a successful academic career. This informal mentoring process led to some tangible changes in the way the junior faculty member allocated her time and to some remarkable success in garnering external visibility and support for her research and service efforts.

Some departments have been able to provide a very supportive atmosphere and concrete support for faculty who are facing work and family balance issues. Faculty members with their own or their children's extremely serious health issues have had colleagues who taught classes for them, department chairs and a dean who have given them lighter teaching loads, and department chairs who have excused them from all committee work. These concrete instances of collegial support and caring have helped to create an atmosphere in several SOE departments that is deeply appreciated by faculty and seen as something valuable—an important factor in faculty retention.

IMPLICATIONS BEYOND TUFTS

The Tufts University School of Engineering has a better-than-the-national-average record of recruiting and retaining women as both students and faculty. The overall context of close integration with the School of Arts and Sciences and an array of programs and policies as outlined in this case study of the SOE may help to explain this. However, without a carefully constructed control, it would be difficult to maintain that the SOE has hard-and-fast *proof* that these aspects have led to a more diverse student and faculty body. Nonetheless, the SOE is proud of its record to date, and will strive to improve it further in the future.

Because the Tufts SOE is smaller than most of its peers, it is not clear how transferable its approaches and programs may be to the larger schools that are graduating many of the country's future engineers. Some aspects of the Tufts SOE education, however, should not be difficult to duplicate. These include: the integration of hands-on, real-world problem solving in the curriculum; the creation of team projects that involve nonengineering students; the emphasis on community involvement and civic engagement; and the involvement of faculty in undergraduate advising and mentoring. Each of these should be possible to implement at a larger institution, as long as the structural/physical separation of its engineering school from other parts of the university is not too great. Finally, any engineering school should be able to invest attention, energy, and resources into inclusive faculty hiring procedures. At larger schools, these procedures might need to take place at the departmental level, with oversight provided at the level of an associate dean.

The Tufts SOE is proud of the programs, infrastructural supports, culture, and climate that it has created, not only for women engineers but for *all* engineers. Men as well as women benefit, and the SOE is hopeful that the innovative engineering education being built at Tufts will lead not only to the continued recruitment and retention of women but to the creation of better engineers.

V

The Internationalization of Doctoral Education

15

Do Foreign Doctorate Recipients Displace U.S. Doctorate Recipients at U.S. Universities?

Liang Zhang

Many people believe that foreign students are crowding out U.S.-citizen students from graduate—especially doctoral—programs at U.S. universities. Borjas (2003) has documented that the share of nonresident aliens enrolled in graduate programs in the United States rose from 5.5 percent in 1976 to 12.4 percent in 1999. In science and engineering (SE) fields, the increase was even more pronounced. In the 1999–2000 academic year, nonresident aliens received 38.2 percent of the doctorates awarded in the physical sciences, 52.1 percent in engineering, 26.6 percent in the life sciences, and 22.8 percent in the social sciences. Data show that in 2002 about 26 percent of all doctorates awarded at U.S. universities went to temporary residents, and in the SE fields more than 32 percent of the degrees were conferred on temporary residents (Hoffer et al. 2003).[1]

The increase in PhDs awarded to foreign students has raised several concerns among U.S. researchers and policymakers. Doctoral education demands enormous intellectual and financial resources; thus, an increase in the number of doctorates earned by foreign students limits educational opportunities for U.S. students, unless additional financial resources can be gained by educating foreign students. This can be achieved only when the benefits (e.g., tuition revenue) outweigh the costs, a situation that is unlikely given the heavy subsidies at the doctoral level of study in both public and private institutions in the United States. For example, more than 90 percent of foreign doctorate recipients in 2002 received various forms of financial assistance from their universities during their graduate studies (Hoffer et al. 2003).

The influx of foreign doctoral recipients has a tremendous impact on the U.S. economy. Stephan and Levin (2001) have shown that individuals making exceptional contributions to science and engineering in the United States were disproportionately drawn from the foreign born. On the other hand, the influx of these highly educated workers could also have displaced U.S. doctoral degree holders from some professional positions and lowered wages. Borjas (2004) has found that a 10-percentage-point immigration-induced increase in the supply of doctorates lowers the wage of competing doctorates by about 3 to 4 percentage points.

One particular concern raised by the growing enrollment of foreign doctoral students is that they may contribute to the continued underrepresentation of U.S. minorities among the doctoral population in the United States, either by directly replacing minority students in the admissions process or by discouraging minority students from pursuing doctoral studies because of the lowered salaries the presence of foreign degree holders has induced. Although it is not clear that an increase in the number of doctorates awarded to foreign students hurts minorities more than it might hurt other U.S. groups, that increase is usually an easy scapegoat for the continued underrepresentation of minorities in the doctoral population.

The increase of foreign doctorate recipients is but one aspect of the changing pattern of doctorate production at U.S. universities; another is that graduate programs are becoming increasingly feminized. Between 1967 and 2002, the proportion of female doctorate recipients increased from 11.6 percent to 45.4 percent for all fields at U.S. universities. In non-SE fields, doctorates granted to women comprise the majority of degrees conferred. For example, in 2002, 67 percent of doctorate recipients in psychology, 61 percent in sociology, 60 percent in foreign languages, 66 percent in education, 58 percent in communication and librarianship, 58 percent in anthropology, and 59 percent in linguistics were women.

The gender shake-up among doctorate recipients has far-reaching social significance. On one hand, as women move into fields traditionally dominated by men, they elevate their positions in the labor market, thereby contributing to gender equality in general. On the other, as the proportion of women with doctorates in some fields goes up, male students may avoid these fields, anticipating that wages will go down when the fields become "too female." Furthermore, male students may find it socially stigmatizing to pursue fields of study that have a preponderance of women (England et al. 2004). If this trend continues, segregation among academic fields is likely to occur, and a stable, integrated gender equilibrium will be at stake.

Somewhat surprisingly, very few studies have addressed whether more doctorates granted to foreign students have led to fewer being granted to U.S. students, and why certain academic fields are becoming predominantly women's fields. Moreover, when examined at all, these two issues are often addressed separately. This study looks at these issues as interconnected by linking findings from both areas, thus enabling us to have a more complete picture of the changing pattern of doctorate production at U.S. universities. In particular, I examine two questions: (1) Is there a crowding-out effect of foreign doctoral degree holders on U.S. degree holders and if so, in what fields, and is there a difference by gender? (2) Do male students exhibit women-avoiding behaviors in pursuing doctoral studies, and if so, in what fields, and is there a difference according to citizenship?

Models of Doctorate Production

The *crowding-out effect* is a term used loosely by researchers to attribute the shrinkage of one group to the growth of others. For example, if foreign doctorate recipients crowd out U.S. doctorate recipients, it means that a decrease in the number of U.S. doctorate recipients is due to an increase in the number of foreign doctorate recipients. This crowding out may take several forms, but one form is clear: in the short run, the total number of doctoral students who can be educated is relatively fixed, and one additional doctorate awarded to a foreign student may translate directly into one fewer awarded to a U.S. student. Another form is less clear, in that in the long run the number of degrees earned by both foreign and U.S. students could be rising, but the proportion of degrees earned by U.S. students could be decreasing. In fact, a variety of crowding-out effects could be defined using different benchmarks. For example, the numbers of both foreign and U.S. doctorate recipients could be rising, yet the number of U.S. doctorate recipients might have increased more if the number of foreign students had not increased as greatly. In essence, all types of crowding-out effects depend on what is assumed to be neutral. To avoid ambiguity, the simplest form of crowding-out analysis is used in this chapter—that is, a crowding-out effect exists if the number of doctorates awarded to U.S. students actually falls as the number of doctorates awarded to foreign students rises.[2]

Doctoral degree recipients are often categorized according to demographic characteristics such as gender, race or ethnicity, and citizenship. Institutions have to make decisions regarding the number of students in each category to admit to their doctoral programs. Although preferences and missions may vary among institutions, a well-balanced and diversified cohort of graduates is generally a legitimate goal of doctorate production at U.S. universities. Quality is probably the primary reason. Presumably, the average quality of doctorates in a particular category declines when the number of doctorates in that category increases. For example, if the distribution of talent is about the same for male and female students, universities may wish to produce about the same number of doctorates in these two groups, assuming their goal is to maximize the aggregated talent for a fixed number of degrees.[3]

Furthermore, diversity itself may be a reasonable goal, so universities may give preference to underrepresented groups. Those fields with few doctoral degrees awarded to women may have as a priority an increase in the number of female students. With regard to both gender and ethnicity, a division occurs between the SE and non-SE fields. The former includes the physical sciences, life sciences, and engineering but not the social sciences.[4] Historically, the SE fields produced a small number of female doctoral degree holders while the non-SE fields usually produced a small number of foreign degree holders. For example, in the late 1960s, women with doctorates made up less than 6 percent of the population in the SE fields, but over 17 percent in non-SE fields. In contrast, foreign students earning doctorates made up about 15 percent of the population in the SE fields in the late 1960s, but less than 6 percent in non-SE fields.

Needless to say, institutional decisions about the representation of different categories of doctorates are influenced by other factors such as the pool of applicants in each category. One factor that may contribute to the increasing share of female doctoral recipients in some fields is male students' unwillingness to enter fields that have a high proportion of women. Sociologists and economists have studied similar avoidance behaviors in other areas. Schelling's (1978) model of residential segregation suggests that whites' unwillingness to live in neighborhoods with a high proportion of blacks could lead neighborhoods to become all black. Similar trends were observed in other social phenomena. For example, Lieberson, Dumais, and Baumann (2000) have examined the trends in unisex names, and found that as the proportion of girls with a particular unisex name increased, parents stopped giving that name to boys. Likewise, England et al. (2004) have invoked the tipping model (Schelling 1978) to study doctorate production at U.S. universities. Their results suggest that the higher the proportion of women receiving degrees in a

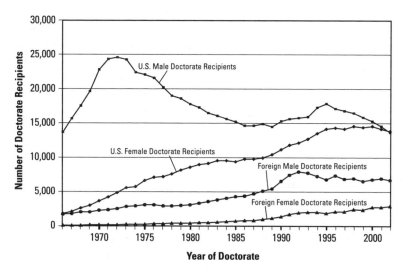

Figure 15.1. Number of doctorates granted in the United States, 1966–2002.

field in a given year, the smaller the number of men who enter the field four to seven years later.

However, U.S. and foreign male students could have quite different patterns of woman-avoiding behavior. For example, because U.S. male students have a better idea of the gender composition in a particular field in the United States through observing the gender of junior professors, teaching assistants, and graduate students, it may be easier for them to exhibit woman-avoiding behaviors than for foreign male students to do so. On the monetary front, the relatively lower wage in fields with a high proportion of women might dampen the enthusiasm of U.S. male students to pursue doctorates in those fields more than it might for foreign male students, because the relatively lower wage might still be attractive to the latter when compared to wages in their home countries. In fact, aggregate-level data suggest that the number of U.S. versus foreign male doctorate recipients produced at U.S. universities have exhibited quite different trends over the past forty years or so (see figure 15.1).

For example, a decrease in the total number of doctorates awarded occurred only for U.S. men but not for foreign men. It seems necessary to separate these two groups of male doctoral recipients if we are to understand the changing gender composition of doctorate production at U.S. universities.

Further, there are important differences among fields of study. In the SE fields, the number of doctorates awarded to women is about half that awarded to men, while in the non-SE fields female doctorate holders outnumber male doctorate holders, and in some fields female doctorate holders have reached a substantial majority of all doctoral degree holders. Thus it is reasonable to expect that the tipping effect is more pronounced in the non-SE fields than in the SE fields. Practically speaking, even if a negative correlation is observed between the proportion of women receiving doctoral degrees in a given year and the number of men receiving the degrees several years later in the SE fields, these fields are not tipping toward women; instead, they are moving toward gender equilibrium.

Data and Methods

The analyses in this chapter use data drawn from the Survey of Earned Doctorates (SED), which provides a population census of all doctorate recipients in U.S. universities each year. The National Science Foundation makes the data publicly available through its WebCASPAR database.[5] I have extracted data on the number of doctorates in all fields of study from 1966 to 2002, a span of thirty-seven years. The WebCASPAR database classifies doctorates into forty-nine fields. For each field, the SED reports the number of doctorates awarded by gender, citizenship, and race or ethnicity. I have treated U.S. citizens and permanent residents as one category (termed *U.S.* degree holders), and temporary residents as another category (termed *foreign* degree holders). After aggregating small categories appropriately, I have obtained the number of degree holders in various groups, such as total female, total male, U.S. male, and minority degree holders. Further, I have calculated the share of a particular subcategory within a larger category, such as the share of female degree holders, the share of U.S. female degree holders, and the share of foreign female degree holders.

The National Center for Education Statistics has data on the number of baccalaureate recipients from U.S. universities each year. The WebCASPAR database also reports these numbers in the same fields as does the SED. I have used the number of college graduates to control for the year-to-year fluctuation in the number of doctorates awarded due to the change in the flow of college graduates. Finally, the decision of foreign students to pursue doctoral degrees might be influenced by the prospect of remaining in the United States after graduation. Since 1967 the National Research Council has published a series of annual reports based on the SED that asks doctorate recipients about their postgraduation plans. Among those who have definite commitments after graduation, the proportion of foreign doctorates who will remain in the United States is reported. Although these statistics are available only since 1988 in the published annual report, the data are probably sufficient because the tipping effect is most likely to happen after 1990 when the proportion of female doctorates has reached a certain level.

To test the crowding-out effect of one group on another, the number of doctorates awarded to the two groups in the same year is used. For example, the crowding-out effect of foreign doctorate recipients on U.S. doctoral recipients is estimated by a fixed-effect model in which the number of U.S. degree holders is the left-hand side variable and the number of foreign degree holders is the right-hand side variable in a regression. The model also controls for field fixed effect, year fixed effect, and other covariates such as the number of college graduates for the doctoral cohort. Because the field classification is somewhat arbitrary and there are substantial variations in the size of the fields, it is necessary to weigh the analysis by the total number of doctorates in each field.

In estimating the tipping effect—that is, the impact of the proportion of female doctorates on the number of male doctorates—it is important to match up the proportion variables with the correct doctoral cohort. The rationale is that male students form their idea of the gender composition of a field from observing the gender of junior professors, teaching assistants, and graduate students. The Time to degree of a doctoral cohort would probably be a good choice of the length of time lags. The SED measures time to degree in two ways: (1) the total time elapsed from the completion of the baccalaureate to the completion of the doctorate, and (2) the total time spent in graduate school to complete the doctoral degree. Typically, the former is about two to three years longer than the latter. Both measures of time to degree vary over time and by fields of study. The length of time lags for the proportion of female doctoral degrees is determined by the median time to degree when enrolled in graduate school, because that is the actual time of doctoral study. Hoffer et al. (2003) have calculated that the median duration of graduate study has increased over the years, from 6.2 years in 1977 to about 7.5 years in 2002. Graduate-school time to degree is shortest in the physical sciences (6.8 years) and engineering (6.7 years) and longest in the humanities (9.0 years), as reported for the 2002 cohort of doctorate recipients (Hoffer et al. 2003). To account for the fact that male students observe the gender composition of several doctoral cohorts and also to avoid large year-to-year fluctuations in small fields, I have averaged the proportion of women in a field five to eight years before the year when the cohort in question receives its doctorates. Hoffer et al. (2003) have also calculated that the median time to degree since completion of the baccalaureate has increased from 8.9 years in 1977 to 10.6 years in 1997. As a result, the number of students earning baccalaureate degrees in a particular field nine years earlier is used to control for the available "pipeline" of students with an undergraduate major in the field. The last variable to be matched up is the proportion of foreign doctoral degree holders remaining in the United States after graduation. Because on average foreign students spend about half a year less in graduate school than U.S. students, this variable is matched up with the cohort that graduate six years later.

Primary Results

As a baseline specification, I have first estimated the crowding-out effect of foreign doctorates on U.S. doctorates. Because this effect may vary across fields, it is estimated for the SE fields, non-SE fields, non-SE fields except for nonscience education, and nonscience education. Nonscience education deserves special attention because the number of doctorates awarded in this field account for one-sixth of doctorates in all fields and about one-third of doctorates in the non-SE fields. As a result, it is possible that the regression results for the non-SE fields are driven mainly by nonscience education. Results indicate that an additional foreign doctorate recipient, at the margin, is associated with about one (1.03) additional U.S. doctorate recipient in the SE fields. Estimating the effect of foreign male and foreign female doctorate recipients separately gives similar results. For example, results show that an additional foreign male degree holder is associated with 0.65 additional U.S. degree holders. The estimated effect of foreign female degree holders is much larger at 1.54.

While the crowding-out effect of foreign degree holders on U.S. degree holders seems nonexistent in the SE fields, the picture is quite different in the non-SE fields. Regression estimates show that in the aggregate, an additional foreign doctorate recipient, at the margin, is associated with about 1.17 fewer U.S. doctorate recipients in the non-SE fields. Estimating the effect of foreign male and foreign female doctorate recipients separately indicates that they might have quite a different impact on the production of U.S. doctoral degrees. For example, an additional foreign male doctorate recipient is associated with about 1.11 more U.S. recipients, while an additional foreign female doctorate recipient is associated with 4.78 fewer U.S. recipients. Estimating the model separately for nonscience education and other non-SE fields shows that the field of nonscience education drives much of the negative correlation between the number of U.S. and foreign doctoral degree holders. Leaving out nonscience education greatly reduces the magnitude of the negative association between the number of U.S. and foreign doctoral degree holders in non-SE fields.

The aggregate results, however, may disguise a great deal of dispersion within the U.S. population. Indeed, much concern focuses on certain categories of the U.S. population, such as male (especially white male) and minority groups. Because in both the SE and non-SE fields the number of U.S. female degree holders has increased over the years, excluding female degree holders from the U.S. population would significantly decrease the estimated coefficient of foreign degree holders on U.S. degree holders. For example, in the SE fields, an additional foreign doctorate recipient, at the margin, is associated with about 0.1 additional U.S. male recipients. And in the non-SE fields, an additional foreign doctorate recipient is associated with almost two fewer U.S. male recipients.

Again, nonscience education is the main driver of the large negative correlation between foreign and U.S. doctorate recipients in the non-SE fields. In the field of nonscience education, each additional foreign doctorate recipient is associated with nine fewer U.S. male recipients. This seemingly large crowding-out effect certainly needs further explanation and interpretation. The number of doctorates awarded in nonscience education makes up about one-third of the total doctorates in the non-SE fields. Since the early 1970s, the number of female doctorate recipients (both foreign and U.S.) has increased while the number of U.S. male doctorate recipients has decreased. Despite its more than tenfold increase in number (from 26 in 1966 to 273 in 2002), foreign female doctorate recipients still represent a very small proportion (less than 5 percent) of the total number of doctorates awarded in nonscience education in 2002. Incidentally, the number of U.S. male doctorate recipients in this field decreased from over 4,000 in the early 1970s to about 1,700 in 2002. As a result, a large negative correlation between foreign doctorate recipients and U.S. recipients is observed. It would not be correct, however, to interpret this negative correlation as a crowding-out effect.

Concerns about the crowding-out effect are often targeted at specific U.S. groups, such as white men and minorities. Because white male doctoral degree holders make up the majority of the male U.S. academic population, the estimation of the crowding-out effect on white men is similar to that on all male U.S. doctoral degree holders. One particular concern about the growing number of foreign degree holders is that they might cause the continued underrepresentation of minorities among the doctoral population. To test whether foreign students replace minority students in doctorate production, I have examined the association between the numbers of foreign and minority doctorates. In the aggregate, there is a positive association between the number of foreign doctorates and the number of minority doctorates in both fields.

Several extensions of the above model are to be considered. First, it is possible that the year-to-year fluctuation in doctorate production might disguise the crowding-out effect of foreign degree holders on U.S. degree holders. A small crowding-out effect each year could accumulate into a large effect over time. To check the robustness of the above analysis, I have reestimated the model using the moving averages of the number of doctorates awarded in each field over a certain number of years. The results turn out to be quite similar. I have are also tested different lengths of moving averages, and the results are quite consistent.

Second, in all models estimated in this analysis, a series of binary variables for year are included to account for time-specific factors that affect doctorate production. However, it is possible that these time-specific effects contain some crowding-out effects. To check for this possibility, I have dropped year dummies from the fixed-effect model and reestimated it for different groups of U.S. degree holders. Results suggest that excluding time-specific effects does not change the results much, although most estimates decrease slightly.

The third extension of the model excludes observations after 1990. Because the number of doctorates in some categories (such as the U.S. male and foreign male categories) has stabilized since the early 1990s, it is probable that the crowding out occurred before then. Thus, the model is estimated using observations before 1990. In the SE fields, it seems that foreign doctorates crowded out both U.S. male and white U.S. male degree holders with coefficients of –0.54 and –0.50, respectively; however, when the number of U.S. female doctorates is included in the model, these negative coefficients reduce to –0.02 and –0.05, respectively, and both are insignificant. In the non-SE fields without non-science education, there is no evidence of a crowding-out effect either.

The final extension is the possibility of the existence of the crowding-out effect at certain institutions. For example, it is possible that foreign doctoral candidates do not crowd out U.S. doctoral candidates in general, but that a crowding-out effect may exist in high-ranking institutions. In other words, U.S. students could be pushed out of high-ranking institutions into lesser institutions because of increased competition at those high-ranking institutions. To examine the crowding-out effect at the institution level, however, is tricky. Assuming that the number of doctorates produced each year by an institution is fixed, it follows mechanically a –1 coefficient between the number of U.S. doctorates and the number of foreign doctorates. Another possibility is that students moving from one institution to another of similar ranking could also create a spurious crowding-out effect when institution-specific crowding-out effects are examined.

A straightforward approach is to examine the aggregate level of doctorate production at institutions of similar quality. If it is the case that U.S. doctoral students have been pushed out of high-ranking programs into lesser programs, we may find that the growth of foreign doctorate recipients is more pronounced at high-ranking institutions than at other institutions. To assign a quality ranking to an institution, I have used the data on total academic research and development expenditures in 2002 collected by the National Science Foundation, which are available through WebCASPAR.[6] In 2002, for example, the top twenty-five institutions produced approximately one-fourth of all doctorate recipients, and the top 60 produced near one-half of all doctorate recipients.

Comparing the growth of foreign degrees across institutions does not reveal a disproportional increase of foreign recipients in the top programs. For example, in the SE fields the proportion of foreign recipients increased from approximately 15 percent to 38 percent, while in the top twenty-five institutions this proportion increased from 18 percent to 34 percent, and in the top fifty institutions from 17 percent to 36 percent. The increase in the proportion of foreign recipients is driven by the increasing number of foreign recipients but not by the decreasing number of U.S. recipients. Clearly, the growth rate of foreign recipients at high-ranking institutions is not faster than at other institutions. If anything, the growth rate is slower at high-ranking institutions. In the non-SE fields the proportion of foreign doctorates increased from approximately 6 percent to 15 percent, while in the top twenty-five institutions this proportion increased from 8 percent to 23 percent, and in the top fifty institutions from 7 percent to 21 percent. The relatively faster growth of foreign doctorate recipients in high-ranking institutions is mainly driven by the disproportionate decrease of U.S. male recipients in certain non-SE fields such as education. For example, in the late 1960s and early 1970s, the top twenty-five institutions produced about one-fourth of all education doctoral recipients while since 2000, these institutions produced less than one-eighth of all education doctoral recipients.

The tipping-effect models answer the question whether men avoid fields when those fields get "too female." Regression estimates suggest a negative effect of a field's proportion of female doctoral recipients on the number of male recipients in that field five to eight years later. On average, a 1-percentage-point increase in the proportion of female recipients (i.e., an increase of about 25 female recipients) in a field leads to 17.76 fewer male doctorates awarded in that field five to eight years later. Pooling all fields together disguises a great deal of difference between the SE and non-SE fields, especially when the proportion of female recipients in these two fields generally falls into two different ranges. As expected, in the SE fields, an increase in the proportion of female recipients does not appear to deter men's entry into these fields. In contrast, in the non-SE fields, there is a large and significant negative effect of a field's proportion of female recipients on the number of male doctorates awarded in that field 5 to 8 years later. Meanwhile, if a higher proportion of female recipients in a field lowers the salary in that field, even women may also exhibit women-avoiding behavior. Indeed, results show that an increase in the proportion of female recipients in the SE fields does not appear to deter women's entry into those fields, while an increase in the non-SE fields does appear to lead to avoidance. Excluding the field of nonscience education yields similar results.

If both male and female doctoral students exhibit women-avoiding behaviors, then how does one explain the growing proportion of female doctorate recipients in most of the non-SE fields? One possibility is that male and female students might have different thresholds for engendering the avoidance response. Nonlinear functional forms seem appropriate for estimating the threshold of female candidates that brings on the tipping effect. When the square of the proportion of female doctorate recipients are added to the base model, the reflection points of the male and female equations are both around 50 percent (50.4 percent for the male equation, and 52.6 percent for the female equation). That is, both men and women start to avoid fields when female candidates and degree holders constitute the majority.

Another possible explanation for the increasing share of female doctoral degrees in the non-SE fields could be the growing number of women earning baccalaureate degrees in these same disciplines, coupled with an increasing general propensity on the part of these women to pursue doctoral degrees in these fields. For example, in the non-SE fields, the share of female college graduates was slightly less than 50 percent in the late 1960s and early 1970s. In 2002, the share of female college graduates in these fields has increased to more than 58 percent.[7] In some fields, such as nonscience education, women account for about three-fourths of college graduates. Consequently, the growing proportion of female college graduates in the non-SE fields could lead to a high proportion of female doctorate recipients. However, female students' women-avoiding behavior may keep these fields from tipping too far toward feminization. Indeed, when the number of college graduates is dropped from the female equation, the negative effect of the proportion of female doctoral recipients on the number of female recipients five to eight years later is eliminated. In contrast, when the number of college graduates is dropped from the male equation, the tipping effect is reduced to half in magnitude but is still marginally significant at the 0.1 level. These results suggest that although both male and female students exhibit women-avoiding behaviors in their pursuit of doctoral studies, the faster growth in numbers of female college graduates in the non-SE fields drives up the proportion of female doctoral recipients in these fields.

Finally, to test whether U.S. male and foreign male students have different behaviors, I have estimated the model for each category of doctorates. In the aggregate, U.S. male doctoral candidates avoid fields with a high proportion of both U.S. female and foreign female doctorates. In contrast, foreign male doctoral students seem to avoid fields with a high proportion of foreign female recipients, but not fields with a high proportion of U.S. female recipients.

Discussion and Implications

Do foreign doctoral degree holders crowd out U.S. degree holders? It is unlikely. In the SE fields, there is no evidence of a negative association between the number of foreign versus U.S. doctorate recipients. In fact, each additional foreign doctorate recipient, on average, is associated with an increase of one more U.S. recipient. Much of the growth in the U.S. population has been fueled by women. However, even after excluding female recipients from the U.S. population, no evidence of a negative association between the number of foreign versus U.S. male recipients can be observed. Moreover, there is no evidence of foreign recipients crowding out specific groups of the U.S. population, such as white men and minority students, who are often regarded as primary victims of the growing number of foreign doctoral recipients.

In the non-SE fields, the picture is different, however. In the aggregate, an additional foreign doctorate recipient, at the margin, is associated with about 1.17 fewer U.S. recipients. This negative association is mainly driven by the negative association between foreign female doctoral recipients and U.S. male recipients in nonscience education. Over the years, in the field of nonscience education, the number of U.S. male doctoral recipients has dropped sharply, and the number of doctorate recipients in other categories (U.S. female, foreign male, and foreign female) has risen modestly. As a result, a large negative correlation between foreign and U.S. recipients is observed.

When all fields are aggregated and the large negative association between foreign and U.S. recipients in the field of nonscience education is attenuated by other fields, it is tempting to interpret the mitigated negative association as a crowding-out effect. Nonetheless, the analyses in this chapter show no evidence of a crowding-out effect on U.S. recipients as a whole in the non-SE fields after excluding nonscience education. Although there is some evidence of a small negative association between foreign recipients and U.S. male recipients in the non-SE fields even after excluding nonscience education, the effect is rather small considering the relatively small increase in the number of foreign recipients in these fields.

Is there any tipping toward feminization in some fields? Again, it seems unlikely. In most SE fields, the proportion of female recipients is relatively low; specifically, it has not reached the 50 percent tipping point that engenders the women-avoiding behaviors apparent in the non-SE fields. As a result, the tipping effect is not observed in the SE fields for either the male or female groups. In non-SE fields, however, both male and female groups exhibit women-avoiding behaviors. In particular, when the proportion of female doctoral and recipients reaches 50 percent in a given field, both men and women avoid that field. Because of these two countervailing forces, the feminization of some non-SE fields has largely been driven by the growing number of female college graduates in these fields. Since the early 1990s, however, the share of female college graduates in "feminine fields" has started to stabilize.[8] When these cohorts earn doctoral degrees, it is unlikely that these fields will be tipping toward feminization. Further research should probably focus on the determinants of undergraduate-major choice decisions because in the final analysis it is the "pipeline" of students that matters.

The women-avoiding behavior of male students, especially U.S. male students, is very suggestive for the interpretation of the large negative association between U.S. male doctoral recipients and foreign female recipients in the field of nonscience education. If U.S. men indeed have avoided "feminine" fields, then it is not convincing to make the case that it is foreign women who have crowded out U.S. men. This women-avoiding behavior suggests that U.S. male students have *opted out* instead of having been crowded out of fields with a high proportion of female doctoral recipients.

One finding that has important policy implications is the impact of the proportion of foreign doctorate recipients staying in the United States after graduation on the number of U.S. doctorate recipients. Results suggest that in the SE fields the higher proportion of foreign doctorate recipients remaining in the United States after graduation does not seem to negatively affect the number of U.S. students pursuing doctoral studies in those fields, probably because most of the foreign degree holders continue their work research as postdoctorate researchers and do not compete in the same labor market with U.S. doctorate recipients. In contrast, because postdoctoral work is less common in the non-SE fields, foreign doctorate recipients' staying in the United States after graduation does seem to affect U.S. students' decisions to pursue doctoral studies, although the effect is small and not significant in most cases.

The prospect of remaining in the United States after graduation clearly affects the number of foreign students pursing doctoral degrees at U.S. universities. The effect is largest in the SE fields, where the majority of foreign doctorate recipients continue to work as postdoctorate researchers at relatively low wages. Although there is some evidence that an increasing supply of foreign recipients lowers the wages of competing workers, it is the foreign recipients themselves who bear the brunt of the wage reduction (Borjas 2004).

If the United States wants to attract more foreign talent, immigration policies should encourage foreign candidates to stay in the United States after completing their doctoral studies. Recent stringent visa and immigration policies have significantly reduced applications (though not necessarily enrollments) from foreign students. A recent survey by the Council of Graduate Schools (2004) indicates that more than 90 percent of U.S. institutions saw a drop in foreign applications for fall 2004. The drop in applications crossed all fields of study, with an 80 percent plunge in engineering and a 65 percent decrease in the physical sciences. Even worse, there was a significant drop in foreign applications to take the Graduate Record Examination. For example, applications from China and India were reduced by 50 and 37 percent, respectively. If this trend continues, the number of foreign doctoral recipients is bound to decrease in the years ahead. While this reduction will in the short run presumably have certain benefits for U.S. students, such as greater educational resources and higher wages, in the long run it will inevitably harm this nation's leadership in science.

16

Opening (and Closing) Doors

Country-Specific Shocks in U.S. Doctoral Education

Emily Blanchard, John Bound, and Sarah Turner

The representation of students from abroad among doctorate recipients—particularly in science and engineering—in U.S. universities has increased dramatically in recent decades, rising from 27 percent in 1973 to over 50 percent in 2005. This growth has not been uniform across source countries, and increases in doctorate attainment have been particularly large among those countries where the rate of growth in undergraduate degree attainment has exceeded that in the United States (Bound, Turner, and Walsh, forthcoming).

Although some of the changes in doctorate attainment by country of origin reflect relatively smooth adjustments in the choices of students from nations with long-standing diplomatic and trade ties with the United States, other adjustments reflect sharp changes in access to the U.S. education market. Perhaps the most dramatic examples of the latter type are the entry into the United States of PhD students from China in the early 1980s and from Eastern Europe and the former Soviet Union in the late 1980s and early 1990s.

Such sharp changes present both challenges and opportunity for economic analysis. In this chapter, we are interested in modeling the flow of students from abroad into U.S. doctoral programs. As a starting point, we show how changes in access to the U.S. education market correspond to changes in the granting of U.S. doctorates to students from particular countries. More generally, we suggest the potential for an important dynamic whereby the initial flow of students into the United States from countries with sufficiently strong growth trajectories eventually expands the capacity of the local higher education institutions and skill-intensive industries. To the extent that doctoral recipients return to their home countries, then, "brain drain" and attendant negative net flows are not inevitable consequences from the flow of students into the United States at the graduate level.

We will begin with a review of the overall rise in the participation of foreign students in U.S. doctoral programs and then focus on specific political transformations and the associated opening of doors to graduate education in the United States to additional foreign students. We will then sketch a model of transition in the pattern of PhD attainment before turning to empirical analysis of entry to U.S. programs among doctoral students by country of origin after political transitions open access to U.S. universities. Focusing on China, Eastern European countries, and the former Soviet states, we will note a clear pattern: opening markets to trade and reducing travel restrictions coincide with an immediate and sharp increase in the entry of foreign graduate students, leading to U.S. doctorates for students from other nations. Our analysis suggests that access to U.S. universities and their doctoral programs may be important for those nations with transitioning economies, which may have long-term demand for highly skilled labor but little short-term capacity within their own universities to produce these skills. Although changes have been more gradual in other countries with strong development trajectories, such as India and South Korea, there is good reason to suggest that access to higher education in the United States also has served to build the pool of highly trained labor and to facilitate the expansion of higher education in the students' home country.

FOREIGN PARTICIPATION OVER TIME IN U.S. DOCTORAL EDUCATION

As early as the first part of the twentieth century, universities in the United States attracted a substantial number of students from abroad, particularly in the sciences. For example, in the period from 1936 to 1956, nearly 20 percent of PhDs in engineering and about 12 percent of PhDs in the life sciences were awarded to students who had completed undergraduate studies in their countries of origin. Advances in air travel and global communication combined with the strengthening of U.S. universities in the 1950s and 1960s (stimulated by the growth of

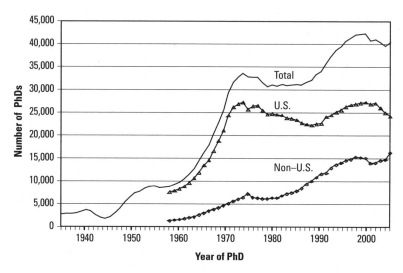

Figure 16.1. PhDs awarded by U.S. universities, by national origin, 1958–2003.

Source: NSF Survey of Earned Doctorates microdata and, before 1958, National Academy of Sciences 1958.

Note: National origin is defined by the country in which an individual went to high school.

federal research investments) made advanced study in the United States increasingly attractive to foreign students thereafter.

The Survey of Earned Doctorates provides a comprehensive picture of PhD recipients from U.S. universities by country of origin from the late 1950s to 2005; Figure 16.1 shows the overall trend in PhDs awarded by U.S. universities and the respective series for U.S. and non-U.S. degree recipients.[1]

The overall rise in PhDs awarded to students from abroad from the late 1950s to the mid-1990s is clear, with a considerable acceleration in growth beginning in the late 1970s. This pattern is accentuated in the sciences (see figures 16.2A–D).

In economics and engineering, degrees awarded to students from abroad have outnumbered those awarded to U.S. students for a number of years; in all but the life sciences, the foreign-born share has equaled or exceeded the share of U.S.-born PhD recipients.

Focusing on explaining the rise in the participation of students from abroad in U.S. doctoral programs, Bound, Turner, and Walsh (forthcoming) emphasize that much of the rise in foreign doctorate attainment can be explained by the growth in demand for U.S. degrees from abroad, with countries such as India and South Korea expanding undergraduate degree attainment at a rate greater than that observed in the United

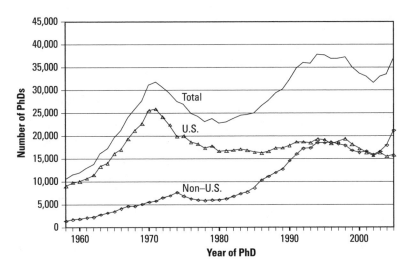

Figure 16.2A. Physical sciences PhDs awarded by U.S. universities, by national origin, 1958–2003.

Source for figures 16.2A–D: NSF Survey of Earned Doctorates microdata.

Note for figures 16.2A–D: National origin is defined by the country in which an individual went to high school. Fields defined using NSF classification, from SED annual reports.

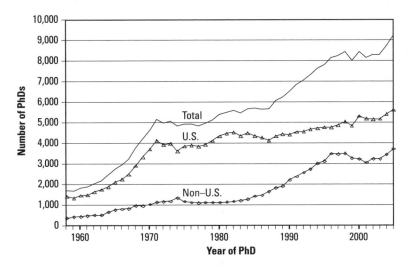

Figure 16.2B. Life sciences PhDs awarded by U.S. universities, by national origin, 1958–2003.

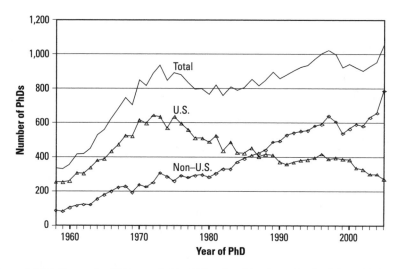

Figure 16.2C. Economics PhDs awarded by U.S. universities, by national origin, 1958–2003.

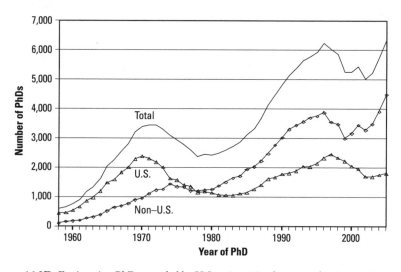

Figure 16.2D. Engineering PhDs awarded by U.S. universities, by national origin, 1958–2003.

States. In addition, political shocks in countries such as China have opened a new source of "realizable demand" for U.S. graduate education that had been largely closed in the 1960s and 1970s. A final explanation offered by Bound, Turner, and Walsh (forthcoming) is that substantial increases in public support for science and engineering research (and, in turn, for graduate education) may yield somewhat greater expansion in the demand for doctoral education among foreign students.[2]

A point of emphasis of the Bound, Turner, and Walsh (forthcoming) analysis is that there has been considerable heterogeneity across source countries, both in the overall representation of PhD students in the United States over time and in the quality of programs attended by foreign students. The returns of a U.S. doctoral degree relative to the best alternative in the home country determines the decision to pursue graduate education in the United Sates; thus, selection varies markedly across countries. The result is differences in the rate at which foreign students pursue U.S. PhDs and the extent to which these students are concentrated in the most highly ranked PhD programs. Necessarily, weaker options in the home country pull more students toward study in the United States, while stronger home country universities produce lower aggregate levels of foreign study in the United States, though often higher levels of skills among those students who do choose to study in the United States. The focus of this analysis is on what happens as other nations open (and close) opportunities for doctoral study in the United States. A particular advantage of the Survey of Earned Doctorates for this analysis is that it permits us to organize recipients of doctorates from U.S. universities by country of origin (distinguishing place of birth, place of high school, and bachelor's degree institution) and year of entry into graduate school. The year of entry into graduate school, as distinguished from the year of receipt of the PhD, is particularly helpful because time to degree varies appreciably, and it is thus difficult to discern sharp changes in access to U.S. higher education from year of receipt alone. We will discuss relevant economic theory before illustrating the link between political shifts and doctorate attainment in the data.

EXPECTED RESPONSES WITH THE OPENING OF THE U.S. MARKET

Beyond exchange in goods and services, one of the most visible demonstrations of the opening of trade relations with the United States is the development of education exchange. Some educational exchange is largely symbolic, wrapped in the rhetoric of improving cross-cultural understanding. Yet the visible flows of foreign students to U.S. institutions following political and economic transformations are grounded in basic economics of skill acquisition and comparative advantage.

As with the more general pattern of foreign study in the United States, it is the strong advantage of graduate education that leads to the immediate draw of students to universities in the United States.[3] Because few students from nations with economies in transition can negotiate the hurdles to enter education programs that require full payment of tuition (undergraduate and professional programs), students from these countries studying in the United States are found disproportionately in doctoral programs, as these programs are likely to offer financial support through fellowships, research assistantships, and teaching assistantships. Moreover, pursuing a PhD in the United States offers not only the direct advantage of skill acquisition but also the indirect benefit of greater access to the U.S. labor market.

Of theoretical and empirical importance in modeling the educational flows in transition economies is the extent to which transition countries hold (or actively seek through government initiatives) a long-term comparative advantage in the production of goods and services intensive in the type of highly skilled labor represented by PhD recipients. If this is the case, there is good reason to believe that the flow of students from abroad to receive doctorates in this country is an intermediate input in the production of these skill-intensive export goods. To the extent that the infrastructure of the home country improves over time, and as PhD recipients educated in the United States return to their home countries, we would expect that the steady-state demand for U.S. doctorates will decline in the (very) long run.[4] In this scenario, foreign students' attainment of U.S. PhDs can be viewed quite legitimately as an important component of future development and growth for both the private and public sectors in countries of origin.

If, on the other hand, the economy in the home country has few economic opportunities for highly skilled workers, or if educational institutions there do not improve, we would anticipate the continuation of the flow of foreign students into U.S. PhD programs.[5] Moreover, for those (primarily "least-developed") countries in which there is little or no production of skilled-labor intensive goods, the flow of students into U.S. PhD programs will likely be permanent, fulfilling developing country fears of "brain drain."[6]

Our hypothesis about the flow of students subsequent to political shocks is captured by the simple time path sketched in figure 16.3. Before the opening of educational exchange there is little (if any) doctorate attainment in the United States among students from the host country. The establishment of full trade and diplomatic relations yields a sharp increase in study in the United States. Yet, unlike trade in final products, which may continue indefinitely on an upward trajectory, doctorate attainment eventually declines from this peak. One mechanism behind the sharp peak is the presence of pent-up demand; had the market not been closed, one would have expected at least some previous flow into U.S. doctoral programs. Although many of those denied opportunities to pursue U.S. PhDs will have made other investments or will be of an age at which there are insufficient years left to accrue the benefits of

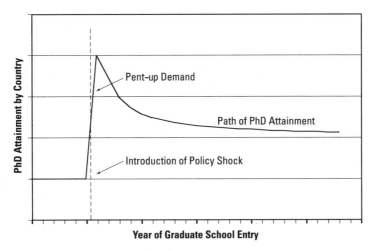

Figure 16.3. Dynamic effect of policy shock on U.S. PhD attainment for transitioning countries.

a PhD, there will be some marginal older students still likely to have a positive demand for U.S. doctoral study opportunities. If this is the case, the age distribution of students entering U.S. doctoral programs in the years immediately following a diplomatic shock may be somewhat wider, including more older students than those entering in later years—a hypothesis that may be checked easily within our data set.

After the initial peak has subsided, the longer-term trajectory of PhD attainment may increase or decrease in response to shifting economic and institutional conditions. If, holding higher education resources and infrastructure fixed, the economy in the home country expands in relatively skill-intensive sectors that demand engineering and science PhDs, the demand for U.S. degrees may reasonably be expected to continue to rise. If, on the other hand, the educational infrastructure in the home country improves with the rest of the economy, then "residual" demand for U.S. PhD degrees may level off or even decrease as the institutions in the home country become better substitutes for U.S. universities. The time path of U.S. degree attainment in this scenario would depend, predictably, on the relative rate of growth of the local high-tech sectors (demand for PhD holders) and local institutions (supply). Further, as local education institutions improve, we would expect to observe a greater concentration of students at the best U.S. institutions; we are also able to examine this proposition in our data.

Although we focus primarily on the opening of markets in this chapter, it is natural to discuss the closing of markets brought about by regime shifts that close off trade and diplomatic exchange with the United States. Such shifts include the Hungarian Revolution of 1956 or the Iranian

Revolution of 1979. The outcome of market closure leading to sustained decline in the flow of students into U.S. doctoral programs is, perhaps, tautological. What we predict (and observe) is somewhat more complex, with a short-term period resembling refugee emigration, as some very able potential students outside the current regime escape through U.S. graduate education, producing a short-term spike in doctorate attainment.

OPENING MARKETS AND FOREIGN DOCTORATE ATTAINMENT

The data show clearly that opening markets—both politically and economically—generally leads to a substantial and rapid flow of students into U.S. PhD programs. Perhaps not surprisingly, those students coming to U.S. institutions after political transitions disproportionately study in the sciences.[7] We present here the data on PhD recipients by country of origin organized by year of graduate school entry.[8] Because year of PhD receipt reflects variation in time to degree as well as year of program entry, the changes tied to market transitions are much more visible when we organize the data by year of entry into graduate school. One downside of organizing the data by year of entry to graduate school is that the most recent cohorts have somewhat fewer years to complete graduate study within the time frame of our data availability, as such total degree attainment for these cohorts is truncated. Moreover, as will be shown in the empirical work that follows, the data on year of entry appears to represent year of entry to master's degree programs in cases (such as China's) where it is common for students to finish a master's degree in their home country before studying in the United States. Assuming that students go directly from master's degree to PhD programs, we make some adjustment to project the year of entry to U.S. doctoral programs as the year of master's completion for those students with foreign master's degrees. We will proceed now with an overview of the specific of cases of China, Eastern European countries, and the former Soviet states, and then turn to a discussion of the general findings from these cases.

China

There has been a decisive increase in the number of U.S. degrees, largely in the sciences, awarded to students from China over the last twenty-five years. These numbers rise from tens in the 1970s to thousands of degrees awarded in the 1990s. Corresponding to the growth in degrees awarded in the 1990s in figure 16.4A, figure 16.4B shows degrees attained as arranged by year of graduate school entry, along with an adjustment

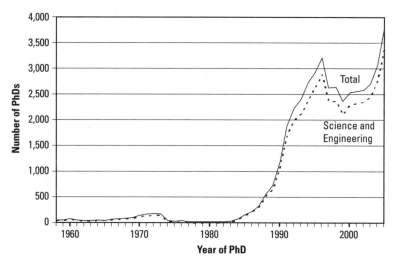

Figure 16.4A. PhDs awarded by U.S. universities to students from China, by year of PhD.

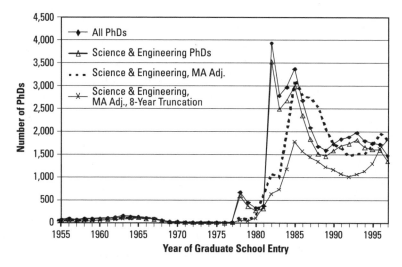

Figure 16.4B. PhDs awarded by U.S. universities to students from China, by year of graduate school entry.

for students receiving master's degrees in China before coming to the United States, which is particularly common in the initial cohorts.

To understand the dynamic in the evolution of student flows from China, it is important to consider the link between political and educational transitions. University activity during Mao Zedong's Cultural Revolution (1966–1976) was largely disrupted, and many facets of universities ceased operations. Immediately thereafter, China sought to jump start its development process through access to science and engineering technology via U.S. universities. The establishment of diplomatic relations with the United States in 1979 led to the (re)opening of educational exchange between the two countries. A disproportionate share of the first wave of exchange students coming to the United States were related to high-level Chinese officials, including the son of former Chinese Communist Part head Deng Xiaoping and the son of foreign minister Huang Hua (Wong 1981), though there was also considerable competition among U.S. universities to identify the most talented among the Chinese students.

The several age cohorts that went to college in 1976, immediately after the end of the Cultural Revolution, had a dramatic impact on doctoral degree attainment. Yet, with very few college graduates available in the 1970s, the surge in Chinese participation in U.S. graduate education was delayed until the mid-1980s; students had first to acquire the necessary undergraduate credentials before they could apply for graduate education.[9] Most notable is the group of students receiving bachelor's degrees in China in 1982, with many students from this cohort entering graduate school that same year.[10] Many in this cohort appear to have finished master's degrees in China before entering U.S. PhD programs in about 1984 (compare "S&E" and "S&E, MA adj" in figures 16.4A and B).[11] Note that after this initial large influx of doctoral students, we see some retrenchment with current levels of PhDs awarded well below the initial post-transition peak. From the early 1980s to the early 1990s, U.S. universities awarded more PhDs to students from China than did Chinese universities. In the last decade, doctoral-level instruction in China has continued its exponential growth, and degrees awarded to Chinese students by Chinese universities now exceed the number awarded by U.S. institutions.

Eastern European Countries and the Former Soviet States

For Eastern Europe, access to Western markets in general, and U.S. education in particular, came to different countries at different points in time. Some cases of political change, such as Romania's, were unambiguously revolutionary, while other countries, most notably Hungary and Poland, experienced more gradual political transitions. This differential rate of opening across Eastern European countries is clearly in stark contrast with China's experience. A further fundamental difference between the Eastern European countries and China is that higher education institutions continued to operate under Communist Party rule and a number of Eastern European countries had relatively uninterrupted collegiate traditions going back several centuries.

Figures 16.5A–F present the pattern of award of PhDs to students from Eastern European countries and the former Soviet states by year of graduate school entry. Bulgaria, Czechoslovakia (we combine both the

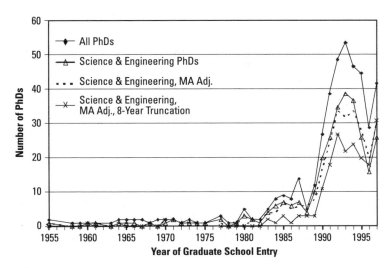

Figure 16.5A. PhDs awarded to students from Bulgaria.

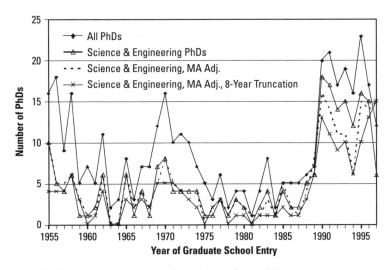

Figure 16.5B. PhDs awarded to students from the Czech Republic.

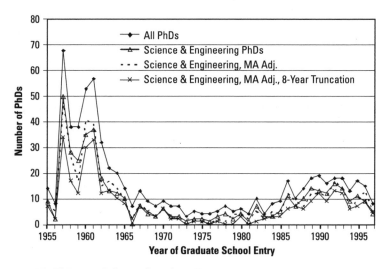

Figure 16.5C. PhDs awarded to students from Hungary.

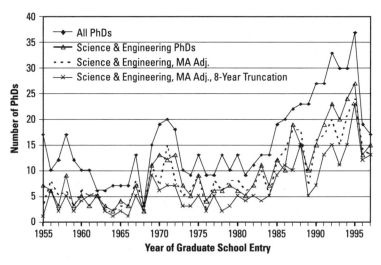

Figure 16.5D. PhDs awarded to students from Poland.

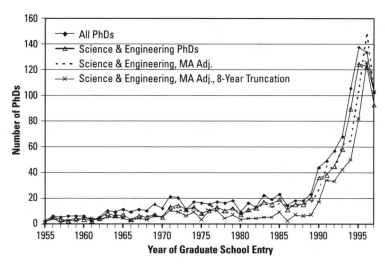

Figure 16.5E. PhDs awarded to students from Romania.

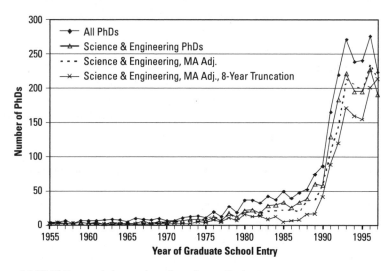

Figure 16.5F. PhDs awarded to students from former Soviet states.

Czech Republic and Slovakia in later years), Romania, and the former
Soviet states demonstrate sharp increases in entry into U.S. programs
among doctorate recipients. In the Czech Republic, student protests led
to the Velvet Revolution and the end of Communist rule in November of 1989. The transition from Communist rule was somewhat more
violent in Romania with the overthrow of the Communist regime of
Nicolae Ceaușescu in December 1989.

For Poland and Hungary, the transition is much more gradual, appearing to start in the early 1980s. At the frontier, labor turmoil and the Solidarność (Solidarity) movement in Poland during the early 1980s were quite visible to the West, generating considerable support from the United States throughout the decade; the end of Communist Party rule in 1989 could be viewed, therefore, as perhaps more evolutionary than revolutionary. One manifestation of this gradual opening of exchange with Poland is the incremental increase in Polish students pursuing PhDs at U.S. universities that began in the mid-1980s.

After the fall of the Berlin Wall in 1989, notable initiatives among the governments of Eastern Europe included efforts to reconstruct systems of higher education, moving away from the compartmentalized and specialized organizations adopted under Soviet influence. Moreover, other Western countries and U.S. philanthropic interests were eager to promote the development of university infrastructure (libraries and computing facilities) as well as advanced graduate capacity. To illustrate, Quandt (1992) notes, "One of the first projects [as an adviser to the Andrew W. Mellon Foundation] was the establishment of the Center for Economic Research and Graduate Education, a joint effort by Charles University (Prague) and the University of Pittsburgh to create a Western-style PhD program in economics." Similarly, other major U.S. institutions such as the Ford and Soros foundations have been active in attempting to strengthen higher education in Eastern Europe.

While a quite different type of change than the opening of access to U.S. universities that occurred in the early 1990s, the most visible episode in the graph for Hungary is the spike in students entering U.S. graduate programs in 1957, subsequent to the revolution. With the Soviet occupation and ensuing violence after student protests in October 1956, many students and citizens fled to the West. In the United States, nonprofit organizations and universities made considerable efforts to aid refugee students from Hungary, with one estimate suggesting that about 1,000 students received financial assistance to continue education (Ficklen 2006). This is a salient example of what in other contexts economists have described as "refugee sorting" (Borjas 1987), with the clear implication of a loss of talent for the home country as many of the best students left the country.

On the surface, the dissolution of the Soviet Union and the opening of U.S. education to these formerly Soviet students would appear very similar to the case of the Eastern European countries. In the years before 1989, barely a trickle of students from the Soviet Union completed doctoral degrees in the United States, with most of those students likely related to political émigrés. Then, during the Soviet presidency of Mikhail Gorbachev, perestroika initiated the modest exchange of graduate students and scholars (Raymond 1989) and much more significant numbers of graduate students came to the U.S. with the collapse of the Soviet Union in 1991. But the collapse of the former Soviet Union also led to significant declines among the traditional Soviet universities, which had long-standing strengths in the physical sciences and had been generously supported by the government during the Cold War.[12] By one estimate, funding for science in Russia declined 44.2 percent between 1989 and 1991 (Shkolnikov 1995). With the formal dissolution of the Soviet Union in 1991, students entered graduate programs in the United States in substantial numbers, with further increases through 1993. As former Soviet universities have continued to lose funding rather than increase in strength—as is the case in a number of the Eastern European countries—there has been less motivation for U.S.-educated students to return to their home countries as there are few prospects for employment and high-level scientific research funding.

GENERALIZATIONS FROM MULTIPLE MARKET OPENINGS

From this set of countries experiencing the opening of access to U.S. higher education as well as trade more generally, there are some common themes. Beyond the increases in PhD pursuit in the initial years following opening of study in the United States, there is not a continued increase in PhD receipt for students from these countries. Quite the contrary, doctorate receipt tends to decline among later cohorts of graduate school entrants. The case of China is, perhaps, the most dramatic in this regard. The cohort that entered college in 1978 and, in turn, started graduate study between 1981 and 1985, is extraordinary in representation among U.S. PhD recipients in the sciences. To illustrate the unusual impact of this single cohort, we note that of the PhD degrees awarded to students from China in the decade between 1985 and 1994, 46.6 percent of the 11,197 awardees had started college in 1978. The same pattern appears to some degree in the East European countries and former Soviet states.[13]

In considering the mechanism generating the transition, we have suggested that one element in this dynamic is that opening the option of doctoral study in the United States comes with high initial flows from pent-up demand. As such, we might expect PhD recipients from these initial cohorts to be somewhat older than those pursuing U.S. doctoral study in the subsequent years. Figures 16.6A–C start with age distribution at the time of entry into graduate study among PhD recipients in the case of China, in comparison with U.S. doctorates and doctorates from nontransitioning countries, in three-year intervals.

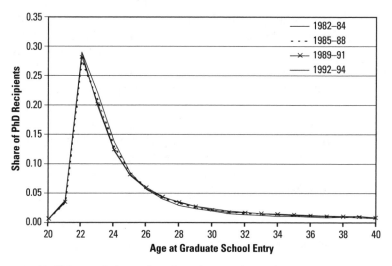

Figure 16.6A. PhDs awarded to students from the United States by age and year of graduate entry.

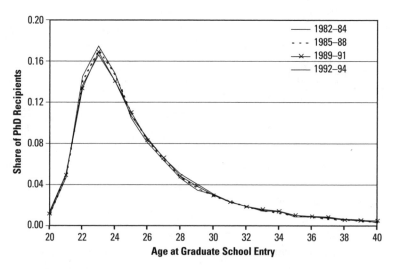

Figure 16.6B. PhDs awarded to students from other nontransitioning countries by age and year of graduate entry.

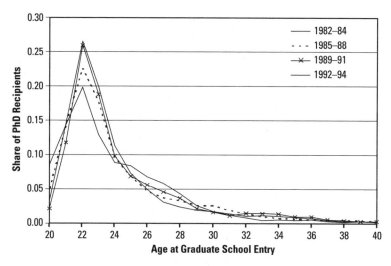

Figure 16.6C. PhDs awarded to students from China by age and year of graduate entry.

While there is little change over the twelve-year interval in the control groups, doctorate recipients from China are increasingly "younger" with ages at graduate school entry more tightly clustered near the ages 22–23. In turn, the mean age at entry among Chinese doctorate recipients fell from about 24.2 years in the early 1980s to 23.7 years for those entering graduate programs between 1992 and 1994. Turning to the Eastern European countries, we see a similar pattern in all but Poland and Romania in figures 16.7A–F.

While the exhaustion of the pent-up demand is potentially one of the factors that explains the stabilization in the rate of doctorate attainment among transitioning countries, it is also possible that growth in home country university sectors reduce the flow of students into the United States in subsequent cohorts.

A second suggested demonstration of the connection between U.S. doctorate attainment and economic transition is the potential for changing selection into doctorate-granting institutions in the United States. In the case of China, where we have observed PhD attainment for about two decades since the start of that country's transition, there have been substantial changes in the concentration of students by program quality (see table 16.1).

Particularly in the early 1980s, it is clear that students from China were concentrated in relatively low-ranked programs, with more than 50 percent of degree recipients starting their degrees between 1981 and 1984 in chemistry, physics, and life sciences receiving doctorates from institutions outside the top fifty programs. Yet, over the course of a decade

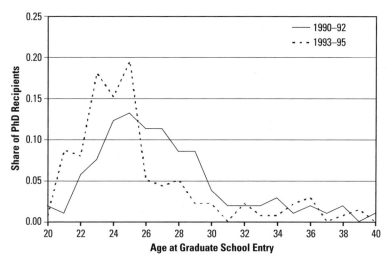

Figure 16.7A. PhDs awarded to students from Bulgaria by age and year of graduate entry.

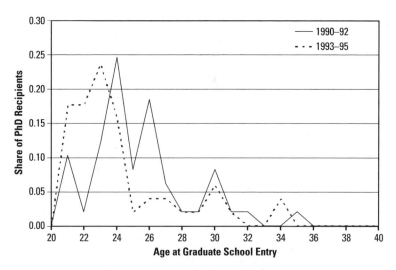

Figure 16.7B. PhDs awarded to students from the Czech Republic by age and year of graduate entry.

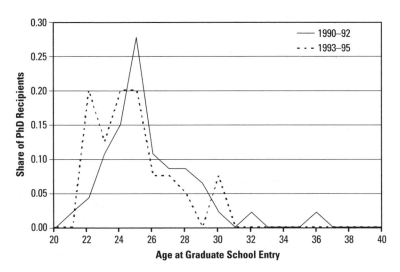

Figure 16.7C. PhDs awarded to students from Hungary by age and year of graduate entry.

Figure 16.7D. PhDs awarded to students from Poland by age and year of graduate entry.

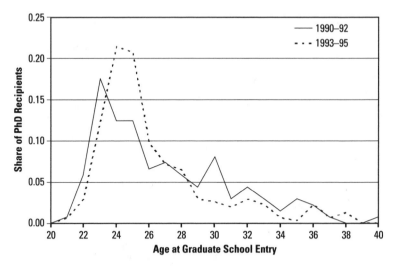

Figure 16.7E. PhDs awarded to students from Romania by age and year of graduate entry.

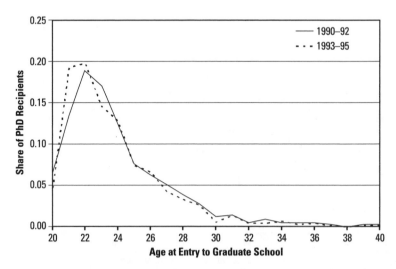

Figure 16.7F. PhDs awarded to students from former Soviet states by age and year of graduate entry.

TABLE 16.1
Share of Degrees Awarded to Students in Top-Fifteen U.S. Doctoral Programs, by Field and Place of Origin

Country of Origin	Year of Graduate Entry	Physics	Chemistry	Biochemistry	Economics	Engineering
China	1980–84	0.151	0.131	0.093	0.201	0.202
	1985–89	0.189	0.131	0.104	0.222	0.183
	1990–94	0.211	0.159	0.141	0.312	0.262
	1995–99	0.218	0.190	0.121	0.247	0.300
India	1980–84	0.121	0.094	0.047	0.167	0.257
	1985–89	0.190	0.092	0.035	0.208	0.284
	1990–94	0.163	0.094	0.076	0.178	0.267
	1995–99	0.256	0.125	0.083	0.246	0.348
South Korea	1980–84	0.202	0.198	0.114	0.269	0.328
	1985–89	0.191	0.218	0.155	0.269	0.309
	1990–94	0.241	0.227	0.147	0.250	0.395
	1995–99	0.338	0.215	0.257	0.317	0.471
Taiwan	1980–84	0.204	0.153	0.133	0.166	0.307
	1985–89	0.183	0.155	0.157	0.298	0.332
	1990–94	0.240	0.237	0.188	0.217	0.443
	1995–99	0.360	0.250	0.320	0.235	0.470
USSR	1990–94	0.218	0.184	0.133	0.226	0.338
	1995–99	0.319	0.163	0.077	0.358	0.387

Source: Authors' tabulations from the Survey of Earned Doctorates (restricted access file).

it appears that the representation has shifted toward higher-ranking programs and recent entry cohorts are appreciably more likely to receive degrees from the top fifteen programs than those entering in the early 1980s, presumably as educational options improve in China.

Thus, a clear point from this descriptive presentation is that political transitions that open education markets, such as those that occurred in China in the early 1980s and Eastern Europe in the early 1990s, have substantial effects on participation in U.S. doctoral education. To the extent that these countries have been on steep growth trajectories, what we expect is that the initial rise in PhD pursuit in the United States will plateau or decline, accompanied by greater selectivity among those choosing U.S. universities for study as educational options in their home countries increase. While this dynamic is most clearly demonstrated in the cases of countries with sharp policy changes, the basic intuition can be extended to countries like India and South Korea and the Chinese island of Taiwan (formerly an independent republic). In these places, economic policies that began in the mid-1970s and generated substantial expansion of trade were also accompanied by a growth in PhD attainment at U.S. institutions (see figures 16.8A–C).

What we see in these figures is that there was a period of quite rapid expansion in the number of students starting (and completing) PhD programs in the United States, followed by a substantial decline that began

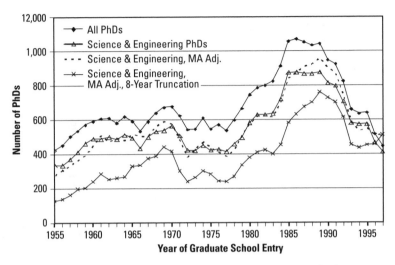

Figure 16.8A. PhDs awarded to students from India by year of graduate school entry.

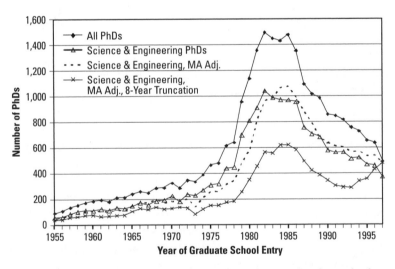

Figure 16.8B. PhDs awarded to students from South Korea by year of graduate school entry.

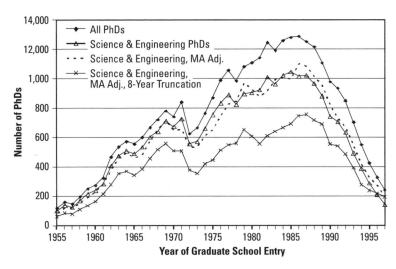

Figure 16.8C. PhDs awarded to students from Taiwan by year of graduate school entry.

in the late 1980s. We also find that recipients of U.S. PhDs from these countries are much more concentrated today in the top U.S. graduate programs than they were in the late 1970s, as table 16.1 shows clear increases in the share receiving degrees from the top fifteen U.S. programs.

Yet, as fewer students from these countries are pursuing PhDs in the United States, table 16.2 makes clear that the higher education sectors—and advanced degrees in the sciences, specifically—have grown at an extraordinary pace during the last 15 years. To illustrate, the number of science and engineering PhD holders produced in Taiwan increased from 109 in 1985 to 1,167 in 2003, while in South Korea the number grew from 281 in 1983 to 3,225 in 2002. Such evidence is suggestive of a process of transition whereby substantial doctorate attainment from U.S. universities among students from these countries was part of the development of robust universities producing advanced degrees in the home country, as well as more general expansion into industries dependent on scientific research and engineering skills.

The story that we have sketched, in which bright students from developing countries go abroad (perhaps even encouraged by their home governments) and eventually return to fuel economic growth is not inevitable, but depends on the persistence of positive prospects and the development of higher education institutions in the countries of origin. We suspect that the continued deterioration of universities in the former Soviet states has generated a circumstance in which few of the U.S.-educated PhD holders will return, thus more closely resembling traditional presentations of "brain drain."

TABLE 16.2
PhDs Awarded in Science and Engineering Fields in
Asian Growth Countries

	China	India	South Korea	Taiwan
1983	—	3,886	281	58
1985	125	4,007	548	109
1987	218	4,123	759	197
1989	1,024	4,209	984	257
1991	1,198	4,294	1,135	370
1993	1,895	4,320	1,421	513
1995	3,417	4,000	1,920	650
1997	5,328	4,764	2,189	839
1999	6,778	5,317	2,607	892
2000	7,304	5,395	2,865	931
2001	8,153	5,394	—	970
2002	—	5,527	3,225	—
2003	—	6,318	—	1,167

Source: National Science Board, 2006, appendix table 2–43.

The Next Steps

What we take away from this short analysis is that political shocks in other nations, represented by the opening of trade and educational exchange, have had demonstrable effects on the flow of students into U.S. doctoral education programs. With large increases in the flow of students from China during the 1980s and subsequent increases in the flow of students from Eastern European and the former Soviet countries in the early 1990s, there is a common theme present in the data characterized by a sharp increase in the entrance of new doctoral students followed by the establishment of a steady-state flow.

Much work remains to be done on the question of how exchange in postsecondary education affects economic outcomes in the sending and receiving countries. We suggest that the impact of educating foreign students from transitioning economies like those of China and Eastern Europe has important long and short term differences from the case for poor developing countries. For transitioning economies, doctorate attainment from U.S. institutions may well prove to be an "intermediate product" used in the development of education and industry in the home country. To this end, transitioning economies may generate return migration among U.S. PhD recipients if they have strong institutions and investment in universities. As such, "brain drain" is far from an inevitable consequence of the advanced training of students from transitioning countries at U.S. universities.

What the "War on Terror" Has Meant for U.S. Colleges and Universities

Michael A. Olivas

A number of the chapters in this volume have directly addressed the perceived decline in the attractiveness of graduate professional education in the United States, offering a multitude of observations and proposing a number of solutions. As is the case with so many complex problems, virtually all of the diagnoses and prescriptions are correct in their own ways, and completely wrongheaded in others. In the crowded Chinese city, a young girl only vaguely senses her possibilities as a chemist, medical researcher, or legal scholar; the young boy in the Mexican *milpa* (field) only understands the study of physics or the poetry of Pablo Neruda in the most ethereal sense. As social scientists like to study the "pathways" to degree completion, most of us remember our own paths as accidental, idiosyncratic, and unlikely. Take, for example, the tales of Ronald Ehrenberg's winding road to his own field of study and how it morphed over time (Ehrenberg 1999, 2000), or this author's false starts before finding niches in higher education law and immigration studies (Olivas 2000)—most people's studies and arcs of professional exploration often defy description or prediction.

Regardless of how scholars come to the United States, the real question is where they land and do their work, and what conditions drive the Paul Chus, Jill Kerr Conways, Albert Einsteins, Henry Kissingers, and Mario Molinas to devote their lives to research agendas in U.S. labs and higher education institutions. This chapter addresses these issues in three ways, in an attempt to triangulate how the United States regulates entry into college for international students, how antiterrorism laws have affected these practices, and how the changed ground rules since September 11, 2001, have affected the place of U.S. higher education in the world.

Foreign Study in the United States

Foreign students apply to U.S. institutions of higher education in the same manner that anyone else does—and then some. The "then some" is largely an overlay of international student requirements on top of the admissions process and additional paperwork—both of which involve the immigration process. Conceptually, the steps are quite simple and transparent, but they mask the complexities that underpin international student admissions (Berger and Borene 2005). The purpose of this chapter is not to parse these immigration requirements, which feed a large industry practice and support network. For example, NAFSA, the Association of International Educators (formerly the National Association for Foreign Student Advisers) represents these students' interests in the United States, organizes the process, and has professionalized the international student adviser network (Bollag 2006c).[1] A number of NAFSA studies have clearly documented the extent to which there are structural problems in student application processing, consular delays (including evidence in 2001 that over one-fourth of consular visa applications for students intending to study here were denied), and flaws in the immigration requirements, especially in the domiciliary requirements of those intending to study here (NAFSA 2003, 2006). Another network, the Institute of International Education, fosters exchange programs, evaluates transcripts, and provides technical assistance among world higher education systems (Institute of International Education 2006).[2] Other allied organizations, governmental agencies, and nongovernmental organizations also coordinate these functions. As a result, millions of students and scholars travel outside their countries and interact with colleges on a formal basis (Institute of International Education 2006). The truth is that the system works well, and not that it bogs down and fails its participants (although failures are more evident since 2001).

In the United States, international students travel for the most part on F-1 visas (traditional college attendance) or M-1 visas (short-term college attendance or language study), while exchange scholars and researchers travel on F-1 visas. Their families and dependents are allowed to follow in related visa categories. (There are a number of other immigration

categories that allow study, but those mentioned here are the major ve-
hicles.) Students must be admitted for study and submit timely paperwork that shows requisite financial support, insurance coverage, security clearances, and other eligibility for study (McMurtie 1999). These
required documents have grown more complex and time-consuming to
process, and it is not unusual that delays in processing will affect timing for admission and travel to the United States (Kapoor 2005). And,
while most international students will have permission to remain in the
United States for the duration of their studies (assuming satisfactory academic progress and no disqualifying behavior), this is not an easy task.
In my twenty-five years observing immigration and higher education,
I have seen students deported for failure to register properly in summer
transfer work, for "dropping" a class that was not offered, for working
required overtime in a permitted summer program, and for other minor
transgressions that were not properly documented or approved. I had to
seek senior political intervention (name omitted for political purposes, in
case I need another favor) for a student of mine who returned to his home
country during the semester break and who missed his flight, rendering
him technically ineligible for return. In the usual case, students can extend their studies for many years, can go on for additional studies, and
can "work" in limited circumstances. Once they complete their studies,
they can often apply for and be eligible for employment in the United
States. Many do so, especially in academic appointments for which they
are qualified (Berger and Borene 2005; Steiner-Long 2005).

This sketch covers many circumstances and does not refer to the many
horrible situations that can occur. But most of these horribles implicate
immigration status and its structural apparatus, and this overlay, with its
many technical details, is quite unforgiving and punitive—more so in the
post-9/11 world. There is still too much discretion accorded overseas
consular officials, whose judgments concerning intending sojourners is
virtually unreviewable (McMurtie 1999). Additionally, there has been
a surprising amount of litigation involving international students and
scholars, ranging from financial aid eligibility (in the case of *Nyquist v.
Mauclet*, 1977)[3]; employment issues; the ability to travel to the United
States—and its converse, the ability of U.S. citizens to travel on scholarly
exchanges to such places as Cuba (Bollag 2006b, 2006d, 2006e); insurance requirements (the legal case *Ahmed v. University of Toledo*, 1986)[4];
discrimination allegations (Gott 2005), retaliation for diplomatic reasons
(Bollag 2006b, 2006c; Bollag and Canevale 2006); and many other dimensions (Cooper and Shanker 2006; Guterman 2006; Jordan 2006).
Suffice it to say that this is a rich legal literature and substantial practice
area (see, e.g., *Toll v. Moreno*, 1982).[5] And the results reveal that international students prevail as well as lose in these cases, particularly when the

college actions are thinly veiled instances of prejudice, as in the example of the actions by New Mexico State University trustees to punish enrolled Iranian NMSU students for militants' takeover of the U.S. embassy in Tehran in the late 1970s (see *Tayyari v. NMSU*, 1980) (concerns punitive actions taken by trustees against enrolled students who were from a country whose residents have taken U.S. hostages).[6] Moreover, under shifting norms of national security, there is a long-standing practice in the United States of restricting the travel of controversial figures, including intellectuals and scholars. The 2006 American Academy of Religion v. Chertoff decision, which forced the U.S. government to either issue a visa to Tariq Ramadan, a Muslim scholar from Switzerland, or articulate reasons for not doing so (he had an offer to assume a tenured position at the University of Notre Dame; see Bollag 2006f), gives cause for cheer, only to be offset by the government's refusal to allow U.S. citizens to reenter the country from Pakistan (Bulwa 2006). After the initial good news about Ramadan's fate, the U.S. government refused him entry on different grounds (Shuppy 2006). Such accomplished people who want to work in this country, as well as many who simply wish to interact in scholarly forums, have many options and will find refuge elsewhere (Archibold 2006). Ramadan, after being refused entry to the United States, was appointed by then British prime minister Tony Blair to a working group to advise him on terrorism in Britain (Blair 2006; Labi 2006). We have forgotten the lessons of World War II, when the "brain drain" from Europe brought our country extraordinary academic, humanitarian, and political talents as they escaped Nazi persecution. Accomplished people will find regimes willing to allow them to ply their trade, and U.S. colleges and corporations will read about their achievements from abroad and see them recorded in patent offices elsewhere (Bollag and Neelakantan 2006).

U.S. HIGHER EDUCATION RESPONSES
AFTER SEPTEMBER 11, 2001

Of course, the events of September 11, 2001, changed everything— and, predictably, changed them for the worse.[7] Dozens of statutes have been enacted or amended by the U.S. Congress to address terrorism since the 9/11 attacks against the United States, and several of these either directly implicate higher education institutions or affect them in substantial fashion. In addition, new legislative proposals have arisen in areas that will affect colleges and universities should they become law. Regulations to implement this legislation have cascaded, and many more are in process. Like an elaborate billiard game, these new statutes cross-reference, compound, and alter existing statutes, including well-established laws.

The primary statutes enacted by Congress to combat terrorism since the 9/11 attacks include the October 26, 2001, Uniting and Strengthening America by Providing Appropriate Tools Required to Intercept and Obstruct Terrorism Act (USA-PATRIOT Act, P.L. 107–56), major omnibus antiterrorism legislation that amends many statutes; the November 19, 2001, Aviation and Transportation Security Act (P.L. 107–71), which affects flight training schools; the May 13, 2002, Enhanced Border Security and Visa Entry Reform Act (Border Security Act, P.L. 107–173), which mandates data collection on international students and scholars; and the June 12, 2002, Public Health Security and Bioterrorism Preparedness and Response Act (P.L. 107–188), which controls the use and distribution of toxins and other biological agents used in scientific research and instruction.

Other relevant legal initiatives include the Student and Exchange Visitor Information System (SEVIS), a comprehensive computerized system designed to track international students and exchange scholars; the U.S. Department of State's Technology Alert List, an enhanced consular official review process for detecting terrorists who seek to study sensitive technologies; the Visas Mantis, a program intended to reduce security clearances for certain students and scholars in the science and engineering fields; the Interagency Panel on Advanced Science Security, designed to screen foreign scholars in security-sensitive scientific areas; the Consumer Lookout and Support System, a file-sharing program that incorporates crime data into immigration-screening records; the Interim Student and Exchange Authentication System, a transitional program in effect until the SEVIS is fully operational, and replacing the Illegal Immigration Reform and Immigrant Responsibility Act of 1996 (IIRIRA), which was itself the major overhaul of the core Immigration and Nationality Act of 1952. In addition, there are many presidential directives and other federal statutory and regulatory matters that govern the intersection of immigration, national security, and higher education ("U.S. Citizens" 2006).

As one careful immigration scholar has commented in this area,

Let us be clear: Immigration law does not revolve around national security or terrorism. As you will see, national security is merely one of many policy ingredients in the mix. Moreover, only the most minute proportion of actual immigration cases present any national security issues at all. Conversely, while many of the policy responses to September 11 have been immigration-specific, most have been generic national security strategies. A full chapter devoted solely to national security runs the risk, therefore, of lending that subject undue prominence. This must be acknowledged. For two reasons, separate treatment of this

material is useful nonetheless. First, in the aftermath of September 11, the inevitable preoccupation with terrorism and war has utterly dominated the public
discourse on immigration. Welcome or not, that reality cannot be ignored. Second, Congress and the executive branch have responded with a wave of coun-
terterrorism initiatives. Many of them specifically target either noncitizens or
particular classes of noncitizens. Synthesizing these measures makes it easier to
describe, digest, and evaluate them in context. (Legomsky 2005, 843)

After the planes crashed on 9/11, some of these changes would have
been enacted, even if some of the hijackers had never been students
enrolled in U.S. flight schools (Kobach 2005). The resultant revisions
have been accelerated, and have breathed life into dormant statutes.
For example, the SEVIS initiative had been mandated by the IIRIRA
in 1996 but had never been implemented. Concerned generally about
foreigners overstaying their visas, Congress had ordered that an auto-
mated entry-exit system be developed, and when it was not developed,
enacted two additional statutes in 1998 and 2000 to deal with this issue.
Following 9/11, the USA-PATRIOT Act was signed into law, including Section 414, which lent additional urgency. In 2002, Congress once
again acted on this subject, enacting the Enhanced Border Security and
Visa Entry Reform Act of 2002. In June 2002 the Department of Justice
announced the creation of the National Security Entry-Exit Registration System (NSEERS). The postsecondary corollary is the SEVIS, a
web-based student tracking system that has been delayed and is vexing
for colleges required to use it. Both the NSEERS and the SEVIS will
be rolled into a more comprehensive database called the U.S. Visitor
and Immigration Status Indication Technology System once technical,
legal, and system problems have been resolved. In the meantime, campus officials have had to spend countless hours tracking and identifying
international students and scholars through an immigration regime that
is extraordinarily complex and detailed (Berger and Borene 2005). The
delays have been responsible for disrupting the flow of international
students and researchers into U.S. institutions, and lags in processing
the paperwork and technical requirements can require a year's time in
advance of enrollment.

One area that mixes domestic and international issues has been the
rise of residency statutes and regulations for undocumented college students, or those whose parents brought them into the country by evad-
ing. With regard to residency, the most important development has been
the introduction and consideration of federal legislation to deal with
the confusion of Section 505 of the IIRIRA—the Development, Relief,
and Education for Alien Minors (DREAM) Act. Senators Orrin Hatch
(R-UT) and Richard Durbin (D-IL) reintroduced the DREAM Act,
Section 1545, on July 31, 2003. By the autumn of 2003, it had thirty-five

U.S. Senate cosponsors, including a majority of the membership of the Senate Judiciary Committee, and in November 2003, was passed out of committee. In the House of Representatives, Chris Cannon (R-UT), Lucille Roybal-Allard (D-CA), and Howard Berman (D-CA) reintroduced the Student Adjustment Act (H.R. 1684) on April 9, 2003, which mirrors the DREAM Act but has different provisions (National Immigration Law Center 2006). In early 2006, an essentially-similar bill was reintroduced into Congress, where it died in fall 2007. If the DREAM Act were passed in its present form, it would have the following effects: (1) it would repeal Section 505 of the IIRIRA, which has come to discourage some states from offering in-state, resident tuition to all students who graduate from their high schools (the repeal would be retroactive, as if Section 505 never existed); and (2) it would allow eligible undocumented students to begin the path toward legalization through a two-step process. In addition, there are special protections inherent in the DREAM Act, including protection from deportation and work authorization for certain young students (over the age of twelve) who have not yet graduated from high school. Once the students complete high school, the first step of the process would give them conditional status lasting between six and eight years. In the second step, upon completion of college, military service, or community service, immigrants would apply to remove the conditional status and receive permanent resident status. They could immediately begin the process of naturalization, because the time under conditional status and permanent status would be credited toward the five-year wait for citizenship. However, this legislation has stalled, and while state legislation has been enacted in a number of key states, only federal relief can comprehensively address this immigration/higher-education issue (Olivas 2004).

Developments in Other Countries

While terrorism is by definition a worldwide phenomenon, other countries have benefited from the excessive legalization that has resulted in the U.S. response to terrorism. While higher education remains a U.S. success story, a number of other countries and regions have capitalized upon the U.S. responses and have moved aggressively to attract international students and scholars (Hebel 2006). Britain's former prime minister Tony Blair made increasing the number of foreign students a centerpiece of his administration, targeting 100,000 more in five years. (This was a reasonable target, as the number increased by almost 125,00 from 1999 to 2005, beating his estimates of 75,000; see Blair 2006; Ramsden 2006.) The European Union (EU) has eased mobility restrictions and created mechanisms to improve the ability of member-nation residents to attend colleges within the union and transfer social benefits; there will be winners and losers in this scheme, and there have been several European Court of Justice decisions addressing benefits issues, including those of college students and scholars (Davies 2005; Dougan 2005; Kochenov 2003; Lambert and Butler 2006; Landler 2006; Van der Mei 2003a, 2003b). Australia has been a major beneficiary of increased U.S. restrictions, and has targeted Southeast Asian students in particular (Cohen 2006). Singapore and Hong Kong have actively recruited biomedical and stem cell researchers from all over the world—especially the United States, where federal restrictions on (and religious reservations about) developing stem cell lines have slowed the progress of such basic research—and have developed deep infrastructural mechanisms to develop these fields of study and their resulting commercial applications. Promising subnational state efforts in the U.S. to fund these efforts have not been entirely successful in countering competing countries' initiatives, although Korean and Taiwanese progress has been stalled by national humiliation over fraud and deception in highly publicized scientific results. To be sure, all these efforts will ebb and flow, and the advantage held by the United States and Western Europe will not be conceded, even in the face of terrorism. Of course, the interaction of science and terrorism is most evident in the issues surrounding Pakistani nuclear science and Iranian nuclear initiatives, which also reveal the interplay of European industry and import laws (Coll 2006; Cooper and Shanker 2006; Langewiesche 2005). Fraud killed a Philippine prepaid college tuition program, showing the extent to which corporate perfidy exists (Overland 2006).

U.S. and other countries' institutions—collegiate and corporate alike—have also sought to increase their enrollments and influence by migrating to other countries. Texas A&M University has a major development in Qatar, as does Cornell University and three other major U.S. universities; the World Bank has tracked more than seven hundred foreign colleges operating programs in China (the late Kermit L. Hall characterized this development as "'clearly the Klondike of higher education'"; Mooney 2006b, A46); and companies and colleges have bought existing colleges (Laureate Education, Inc. purchased Anhembi Morumbi University in Sao Paulo) and built new ones (Rochester Institute of Technology's new American University in Kosovo). Given these developments, and the fragility of some countries (various programs in China, Israel, Lebanon, and elsewhere have closed due to political instability), one cannot be certain of what to make of this phenomenon (McClure 2006). It is surprising how many of these enterprises have been undertaken by public institutions, which are traditionally either bound by legislatures or by local and/or state politics to serve more narrow state interests. For example, one cannot help but wonder how much (or even if) state legislators know about the Texas A&M campus in Qatar, given enrollment pressures at home in College Station, Texas. (If one were a cynic it would be tempting to say that as long as the Texas A&M football team goes to a college bowl game in the United States, and they can procure tickets to local games at Kyle Field, alumni and legislators will be satisfied and will not concern themselves with Qatar.) One can understand the presence of Troy University, a public Alabama college that has a dozen foreign branch campuses, as it has a longstanding mission of serving U.S. military personnel overseas, but exactly why is Oklahoma City University operating a campus in Canada, and why is the University of Texas–Arlington operating a program in China? State institutions in particular should have very clear justifications for operating outside of the country, especially when there are underserved populations—notably, low-income and minority communities—in the United States. For example, an underenrolled public college in Kansas has found virtual students in rural China, and offers extensive distance-learning in conjunction with a private college in Xinzheng (Bollag 2006a; Mooney 2006a).

This author directed and taught for seven years in the University of Houston Law Center's Mexican Legal Studies Program, a summer program in Guadalajara and then Mexico City; this program was the first American Bar Association–approved study abroad program, and it lasted over thirty years until it simply ran out of steam. I did not want to spend four to six weeks in Mexico every summer, and four or five others on my faculty who also were involved eventually felt the same way, so we closed it. But what will the staying power of these programs be, and what infrastructure will be built in the host countries when the inevitable enrollment fluctuations occur or local conditions change? For-profit, proprietary institutions have stockholders and balance sheets, unlike public and private colleges. What will their endurance be? Even law schools in the United States now include proprietary members, and I have seen their leadership and corporate ownership controls change rapidly, implicating accreditation standards and threatening stability (see, e.g, the legal case *Western State University v. ABA*, 2004).[8]

FINAL REFLECTIONS

There is no doubt that the United States was the prime beneficiary of worldwide scientific and academic mobility in the twentieth century, and that it remains so. But just as the United States—which developed basketball and presided over its worldwide popularity (and benefits from the National Basketball Association's prominence and its attractiveness to superb athletes from all over the world)—can lose at the Olympic Games, so too can the country lose in international academic competition. Other countries have not only organized themselves to attract worldwide enrollments, but a number have strategically targeted higher education and scientific research as important diplomatic, nation-building initiatives. To be sure, any reasonable assessment of this industry will reveal that the United States still retains the natural advantages it has developed over many years—including the preeminence of English as the language of academic discourse. But these are not carved in stone and certainly not permanent, especially as China and other Asian countries hit their stride and find their own places in the sun. The confederated EU could become greater than the sum of its parts, especially in those fields where European scholars have historically left their home countries to come to the United States. If this country continues its most recent trends of isolating critical ideas, enacting geographic restrictions, and erecting ideological barriers, impressionable students and scholars will seek their places of study elsewhere.

This country has both cultivated its advantages and built upon those that exist, such as the clear advantage that speaking English provides in academic discourse. But these investments will not renew themselves if the world views the United States as an undesirable place to engage in discourse and study, and if we continue to restrict fields of study on the basis of residence and make it more difficult and time-consuming for international students to navigate the admissions and immigration processes. In a "flattened" world, the more international students who interact with our institutions, students, and faculty, the more likely they are to appreciate the academic and civic virtues of U.S. society. The Jesuits understood this, and the Soviets did so as well, however imperfectly. As the Spanish-born George Santayana (educated at Harvard University and employed there for many years) once suggested, "the American Will inhabits the sky-scraper; the American Intellect inhabits the colonial mansion" (Santayana 1937, 129). Both the American will and the American intellect thrive because of the many Santayanas who take root in this soil and bloom here. As with any other garden, left to their own they will wither, not bloom.

LOOKING TO THE FUTURE

RONALD G. EHRENBERG AND CHARLOTTE V. KUH

The chapters in *Doctoral Education* have provided a road map for improving the functioning of doctoral education programs in the United States. Money matters, but it is not the only thing that matters; even well-funded doctoral programs have dropout rates that are higher than desirable. Efforts to improve doctoral education should focus on the characteristics of the curriculum, the advising provided to students, clearly articulating objectives and requirements, and integrating faculty and students into a community of scholars. Because the success of a doctoral program often depends heavily on the leadership of a few concerned faculty members, faculty leadership must be rewarded and programs must be periodically assessed to make sure that they remain on the correct track.

To assess program performance, data must be regularly collected on program characteristics and on student finances and progress through the system. A key role for graduate schools and their deans is to insist on the collection of such data, to monitor what is going on in the programs, and to share information across programs on the characteristics of programs that are doing well in an effort to encourage improvements in performance in programs faring poorly. Moreover, another key role of graduate deans is to disseminate to both the programs and the administration the information that has been learned about best practices from analyses conducted by the Council of Graduate Schools and the various foundations and organizations concerned with improving doctoral education.

Doctoral education is changing and, although the more traditional doctoral programs are congruent with disciplinary departments, progress on solving important problems increasingly requires interdisciplinary or multidisciplinary approaches. Now, more than in the past, it is likely that the careers of new PhD holders will differ from those of their advisers, as the share of tenure-track faculty positions in American colleges and universities decline and as a growing share of new doctorate holders seeks employment in the nonacademic sector. The skills required to work in interdisciplinary environments in the nonacademic sector are often quite different than those developed in traditional doctoral programs. Doctoral programs need to be aware of the changing nature of the skills that their graduates will need and the jobs that those graduates will likely attain.

Efforts to develop interdisciplinary doctoral programs in the sciences, engineering, technology, and mathematics have been stimulated by the National Science Foundation's Integrative Graduate Education and Research Training (IGERT) program. The program "seeks to train PhD scientists and engineers with the interdisciplinary background and the technical, professional and personal skills needed to address the global questions of the future."[1] Initial evaluations of the IGERT program have found that it has altered the educational experiences of participating students, engaged faculty in interdisciplinary teaching and research, and advanced interdisciplinary education at institutions that have hosted it.[2]

Ultimately the success of such programs will be judged by graduates' employment outcomes after receipt of their PhDs, and their contributions to new knowledge. While many graduates of such programs will seek nonacademic employment, those seeking academic employment may find that the vast majority of academic appointments are still in disciplinary-based departments. Faculty in such departments may view the graduates' interdisciplinary training as a dilution, rather than an extension, of their disciplinary training. There is a great variety of these doctoral programs, ranging from umbrella programs in the biological sciences to emerging disciplines such as nanotechnology. The goals and objectives of these programs should be clearly stated, and their success, both in the short and long runs, should be rigorously evaluated.

The chapters in this volume are also concerned with the students that U.S. doctoral programs will be educating in the future. Given the great uncertainty about our nation's ability to count on a continuation of the current flow of talented foreign residents to enroll in and complete PhDs at American universities and then undertake employment here, increasing the number of American citizens going on to PhDs is essential. Although we are beginning to understand the factors that cause some undergraduate institutions to send a larger proportion of their students on to PhD study than other institutions do, more analyses of this subject are required. Similarly, although we know that providing undergraduates with research experiences appears to enhance their probabilities of going on to PhD study, we do not yet fully understand what the most effective structure of such programs should be.

Increasingly, U.S.-citizen PhD holders are women, but these women remain underrepresented among faculty in America's research universities, especially in science and engineering fields. Recent research suggests that if female PhD holders apply for positions at research universities they are more likely than male applicants to be interviewed and, if they are interviewed, they are more likely to be offered positions than are male applicants.[3] Similarly, if they accept offers of employment, their probabilities of achieving tenure are comparable to those of male counterparts. Hence, the underrepresentation of female PhD holders at America's research universities is largely due to a lower probability than that of their male counterparts of applying for positions at such universities.

Although there are numerous reasons that may explain the underrepresentation of women in faculty positions, there is growing agreement that it reflects the difficulty female doctorate holders face in combining family and career at research universities, as well as their perceptions that these universities have inhospitable environments for female faculty. Several of the chapters in this volume have discussed the steps that universities have been taking to mitigate these concerns. Recently, efforts to make research universities more "family friendly" have filtered down from the faculty level to the doctoral student level as a number of universities have announced programs that provide paid parental leave, subsidized on-campus child care, and child-care-related travel funds for doctoral students.[4]

Although the number of female PhD students has increased substantially in recent decades, progress in improving the numbers of U.S.-citizen PhD holders of color has been much slower. To the extent that role models matter, increasing the numbers of doctoral degree holders of color and the number of these people in faculty positions is likely to have positive effects on the educational outcomes of undergraduate students of color. The chapters on this topic in this volume suggest some strategies for doing so, but also suggest that much more effort and evaluation of efforts will be required.

Finally, although the chapters in *Doctoral Education* agree that a continual flow of talented foreign students into U.S. PhD programs is somewhat uncertain, they also note that the presence of these students does not appear to discourage American citizens from pursuing PhD study. Hence, efforts to structure immigration policies that encourage international PhD students are desirable. In doing so, universities must remain aware that one important role of doctoral students is to serve as teaching assistants. Although American universities require all foreign students to achieve minimal competency in written and spoken English (through grades on the Test of English as a Foreign Language), foreign students' ability to serve effectively as teaching assistants is sometimes limited by their command of the English language and their lack of knowledge of American culture. For example, relations between teachers and students are sometimes more hierarchical in foreign countries than in the United States, and attitudes about the appropriateness of including women in higher education may also differ. Some studies suggest that American students learn less when taught by foreign teaching assistants; others suggest that this gap disappears with appropriate types of teaching assistant training.[5] Although our focus in this book has been on improving the quality of doctoral education and increasing the flow of students into American doctoral programs, one should not ignore the role of doctoral students in educating American undergraduates. Thus, more research on effective teaching-assistant training programs, especially those aimed at foreign doctoral students, is clearly needed.

Notes

Introduction

1. One chapter included in this volume was scheduled to be presented at the conference but not delivered due to an illness of its author at that time.

Chapter 1. Changing the Education of Scholars

1. See Bowen and Rudenstine 1992.

2. Ibid.

3. The recipients of the portable Mellon fellowships were thought to be among the most promising new humanities PhD students, and their decisions to enroll in these PhD programs thus provided a market test of the programs' perceived quality.

4. Detailed discussions of the analyses that a number of the departments undertook and the plans they developed are presented in our book, *Educating Scholars: Examining Doctoral Education in the Humanities* (see Ehrenberg, Zuckerman, Groen, and Brucker, forthcoming).

5. At the end of five years, it became clear that two departments did not really care to participate in the GEI or were judged to have made too little progress to continue. These departments ceased participating in the GEI and were replaced by three new departments and programs in 1996 and 1997. One additional program had previously been added in 1993.

6. Although there were fifty-four participating departments and programs, some departments ended their participation before ten years and some started after 1991–92. In total there were 515 department/years of support provided under the GEI.

7. Included in this total were funds provided in the form of planning grants and funds expended for data collection and data management.

8. Seven institutions had data going back a full eleven years, but those available for 1980–82 were not used in order to achieve comparability for all ten institutions.

9. That half of these institutions were unable to do so says a great deal about the low priority they placed on collecting information about their PhD students' progress prior to the development of the GEI. One major benefit of the GEI is that some universities began to regularly collect data to monitor the progress of their students.

10. This had the effect of giving greater weight to flagship public institutions in the comparison group than they had in the treatment group, a less than ideal outcome. However, the data these institutions had collected was of high quality, and the standing of their graduate programs was within the bounds of those in the treatment group.

11. Two of the universities at which there were no treatment departments (the University of North Carolina at Chapel Hill and the University of California, Los Angeles) received small amounts of funding to help them collect and provide student-level data to the Foundation.

12. Some analyses use a smaller number of departments; for example, the Graduate Education Survey, which we describe in this chapter, collected information for students from only forty-four treatment departments.

13. Some analyses use a smaller number of departments; for example, the Graduate Education Survey (GES), which we describe in this chapter, only collected information for students from forty-four treatment departments.

14. Summary tables were provided annually to the universities and departments for their own use.

15. Later, in 2002, when the Graduate Education Survey was undertaken, each university agreed to provide a file with student names and addresses matched to the identification numbers for the purpose of locating their current and former students so that they might participate in the GES. This file, by agreement with each institution's human subjects review board, was accessible only to one Mellon Foundation staff member, her assistant, and the staff at Mathematica Policy Research (which undertook the survey), all of whom had completed human subjects protocol training. At no time were these names associated with the data that the institutions provided to the Foundation.

16. Each year, institutions reported whether the student received the PhD, continued to study in the program, or terminated graduate study during the year. If a student advanced to candidacy or graduated during that year, the date of that event was reported.

17. However, these amounts were not reported for the early years by some departments. Treatment departments were more likely than comparison departments to provide dollar amounts.

18. Treatment departments were also asked to provide placement information for the students six months after they had received their PhDs. For the years prior to the start of the GEI, their responses were uneven; some institutions provided such information for over 90 percent of their graduates, while others slipped to 65 to 70 percent in some years. Once the GEI was under way, response rates tended to be even lower and the comparison departments were never asked to provide this information. We have not used these data in our research, but have focused instead on the placement information that students reported when they participated in the Graduate Education Survey.

19. To ensure the comparability of the data that were reported by the institutions, in 1993 a two-day meeting was held for all of the institutional representatives and Mellon Foundation staff to set standards for data reporting.

20. For example, if a student had been reported as graduating or leaving the program in year t-1, no new data should have been reported for the student in year t. If a new record were reported in year t, Mellon Foundation staff contacted the data representative at the university and requested a check be made as to which year's data accurately reflected the facts. Often this resulted in a revision of a prior year's record; a student who had been reported as having left the program may actually have been "on leave" and was retrospectively

"enrolled" in the program for the current year. Sometimes students who had been reported as continuing in the program in a prior year would retrospectively be reported as having left the program that year, based upon the report from the current year.

21. These individuals often spent long hours with staff at the individual departments to identify a student's status when the graduate school database did not capture the student's status accurately. The efforts of the institutional representatives were essential in maintaining the quality of the database and, as a by-product of their efforts, there have been many improvements in data collection and maintenance at the graduate schools of participating institutions.

22. Departments also prepared financial reports each year that showed how they spent the money they received from the foundation as well as all other funds that were spent supporting graduate education. These data were required because the foundation did not want their dollars to "crowd out" funds that the departments would otherwise be spending on graduate education. The foundation thus used these reports to check that the departments and universities were maintaining their own efforts in support of graduate education in these fields.

23. Since the departments listed were selected to illustrate changes that were made, no assumptions should be made about the relative frequency of adoption of each innovation.

24. Per agreement with the participating departments and universities, university names have been suppressed in table 1.2. In this table, *y* indicates that the department adopted that innovation, *n* indicates that it did not, and *y(plan)* indicates that the department planned to adopt the innovation but Foundation staff could find no mention in the department's annual narrative reports that it had done so.

25. In *Educating Scholars* we present vignettes gleaned from the same department reports, discussions with departmental representatives, and the individual student records that describe why this occurred. See Ehrenberg, Zuckerman, Groen, and Brucker, forthcoming.

26. A more complete description of the GES, including how it was administered and how Mathematica achieved such a high response rate, can be found in Kalb and Dwoyer, 2004.

27. The journal articles include Ehrenberg et al., 2007, and Groen et al., 2008, while the working papers include J. Price, 2005.

28. Our survey of findings here is necessarily selective and in our forthcoming book we discuss a much wider range of findings, including the role of gender, marital status, family status, race/ethnicity, and citizenship status on graduate school and early-career publications outcomes. See Ehrenberg, Zuckerman, Groen, and Brucker, forthcoming.

29. More precisely, it is not advantageous for students to increase their time to degree completion beyond seven years.

30. Reducing attrition did not evoke the same strong reaction that reducing time to degree completion received. It was given far less attention by the departments, and a number of faculty members believed attrition was the result of personal decisions by students rather than being connected to institutional or departmental policies.

31. Departmental or university-level studies of completion rates of PhD programs will understate systemwide completion rates, just as institutional-level studies of undergraduate completion rates understate the number of first-time freshmen who ultimately receive undergraduate degrees from any institution.

32. We have already suggested, at a National Research Council workshop conducted in June 2005, that this be done.

33. Clotfelter 2007 discusses this issue in much more detail.

Chapter 2. The Council of Graduate Schools' PhD Completion Project

1. Completion data will, for the first time, be included in the National Research Council's forthcoming Assessment of Research Doctorates, for example. See http://www7.national academies.org/resdoc/.

2. Important recent research on attrition and completion from PhD programs, generally, includes Golde 2000; Lovitts 2001; and Nettles and Millet 2006. For a more comprehensive bibliography, including field-specific studies, see http://www.phdcompletion.org.

3. Examples of such studies include the Mellon Graduate Education Initiative (Ehrenberg, R. G., Zuckerman, Z., Groen, J., and Brucker, S. M. 2006) and the Association of American Universities/Association of Graduate Schools Project for Research on Doctoral Education (http://www.aau.edu/education/ags/agsindex.html).

4. Bowen and Rudenstine (1992, 111) have calculated an overall completion rate of approximately 60 percent for students who entered doctoral programs between 1962 and 1966, but projected a completion rate of 50 percent for students entering between 1972 and 1976.

5. The request for proposals sought to ensure broad field coverage of research doctorates, even within a relatively small number of pilot programs per university. Participating universities were each required to submit data for a minimum of eight programs, with at least five drawn from STEM fields (including life sciences, engineering, physical sciences, and mathematics) and at least three from the social sciences and humanities. Many universities submitted data on more than the minimum number of programs, and an additional eight universities among the twenty-five project partners or affiliates submitted data even though they had not been selected to receive funding for the project's first phase. Project partners that submitted data include Florida State University, Fordham University, the University of Iowa, Marquette University, New York University, Pennsylvania State University, the University of Rhode Island, Rutgers University, Southern Illinois University, Carbondale, and Western Michigan University. A full list of project partners is available at http://www.phdcompletion.org/participants/institution.asp. Award announcements to universities for participation in the project's second phase are available at http://www. phdcompletion.org/participants/institution_PhaseII.asp.

6. The tools and templates developed by CGS to collect data for PhD Completion Project are available at http://www.phdcompletion.org.

7. This data set represents students in 313 programs at twenty-nine universities.

8. These preliminary demographic data have been updated and revised since the preparation of this article. Analysis of the finalized demographic data set is included in the Council of Graduate Schools 2008.

9. The preliminary baseline demographic data set in the PhD Completion Project contains completion rate data for 55,249 students (domestic and international) from 36 institutions, including 36,236 domestic students (U.S. citizens and permanent residents). For comparison of these percentages to national percentages of students enrolled and doctorates awarded, see Council of Graduate Schools 2006a and Hoffer et al. 2006.

10. Due to low sample sizes, completion rates for Native American students could not be calculated.

11. Race and ethnicity category definitions follow the guidelines in Hoffer, Hess, Welch, and Williams 2007.

12. Program profiles, with interventions listed for each participating institution, are available at http://www.phdcompletion.org.

Chapter 3. Advocating Apprenticeship and Intellectual Community

1. The ideas discussed in this chapter, and others, are explored in greater detail in Walker, Golde, et al. (2008), which also includes a detailed description of the CID. Detailed electronic depictions of departments' work can be found at http://gallery.carnegiefoundation .org/cid.

2. *Signature pedagogy* is a term coined by the Carnegie Foundation for the Advancement of Teaching's president Lee S. Shulman to describe "characteristic forms of teaching and learning . . . that organize the fundamental ways in which future practitioners are educated for their new professions" (Shulman 2005, 52). Examples of signature pedagogies include the case dialogue method of teaching in law schools, and bedside teaching on daily clinical rounds in medical education. Signature pedagogies share three features: they are pervasive and routine; they entail public student performance; and "uncertainty, visibility, and accountability inevitably raise the emotional stakes of the pedagogical encounters" (Shulman 2005, 56–57).

3. "Elbow learning" is how the first president of Clark University, noted psychologist G. Stanley Hall, has described students and faculty working side by side in research labs (Ryan 1939). At the time this was an educational innovation.

4. Our conceptual framing draws heavily on the work of John Seely Brown and his colleagues on cognitive apprenticeship. The term *cognitive apprenticeship* draws attention to this as a strategy for learning to solve problems and carrying out complex cognitive tasks and developing expertise in formal schooling settings (Collins, Brown, and Holum 1991, 457). Their work has focused on the elementary grades, for teaching reading, writing, and mathematics (Brown, Collins, and Duguid 1989; Collins, Brown, and Newman 1989; Collins, Brown, and Holum 1991). Our colleagues at the Carnegie Foundation have found it useful for analyzing professional education. We believe it is also applicable in doctoral education, and are extending it into that arena.

5. For this chapter we have elected to use the term *mentor* rather than *adviser* or *teacher*. The role of adviser is a formal one, and most doctoral students have an adviser. Mentors play an advocacy role, and the term mentorship conveys sponsorship and support that extends beyond the years of graduate school. We are also drawn to the term *mentor* because popular usage assumes that anyone can, and perhaps should, have multiple mentors. *Mentorship* connotes the goal of the development of a person's complete professional identity, and is not limited to particular skills or tasks. The term implies affection and care, but we associate it with high standards. It is not about being nice or friendly, but rather about setting the conditions that elicit high-quality work.

6. The idea that the purpose of doctoral education is the preparation of "stewards of the discipline" was central to the CID. A longer discussion of this can be found in Golde 2006, 9–14.

7. Unfortunately, this seems altogether too rare. Hartnett's survey of nine leading departments found that a minority of students (ranging from 6 to 35 percent, depending on the department) agreed strongly with the statement that said "this department has a humane environment characterized by mutual respect and concern between students and professors" (Hartnett 1976, 75).

Chapter 4. Three Ways of Winning Doctoral Education

This paper is based upon work supported in part by the Lilly Endowment, Inc., under Grant No. 950437; the Spencer Foundation under Grant No. 9980004; the National Center for Postsecondary Improvement under Grant No. R309A60001; and the National Science Foundation under Grant No. REC 9903080. Any opinions, findings, and conclusions or recommendations expressed in this material are those of the authors and do not necessarily reflect the views of either the Lilly Endowment, Inc., the National Center for Postsecondary Improvement, the Spencer Foundation, or the National Science Foundation.

Chapter 6. Generating Doctoral Degree Candidates at Liberal Arts Colleges

1. Boyer (1990) has argued that the traditional definition of scholarship is too limiting, especially in a liberal arts setting, and should be thought of as any activity that strengthens and contributes to one's teaching.

2. Ehrenberg (2005) suggests such interaction as a means to encourage undergraduates at research universities to consider pursuing a PhD.

3. While generating PhD candidates has changed modestly for American universities and colleges, foreign institutions have witnessed a huge increase in generating PhD candidates since 1980 (Blanchard, Bound, and Turner, this volume; Ehrenberg 1991).

4. The data for both surveys can be found at http://www.webcaspar.org.

5. The results are qualitatively unchanged if a seven-year rolling window is used. Fuller (1986) also allows for a five-year window.

6. With particular emphasis on the role that expectation forming plays in the decision, Ehrenberg (1991) discusses factors that likely influence one's decision to pursue a PhD, including the pecuniary and nonpecuniary benefits, time to complete the degree, and cost of graduate school. Given the close relationship between students and professors at liberal arts colleges, these students arguably can form fairly good expectations of the nonpecuniary benefits of being a professor at such an institution.

7. To what extent the issues regarding one's choice of undergraduate institution, reasons for going to graduate school, and the decision to work at a liberal arts college affect the results are unclear.

8. Boylan (this volume) finds there is general empirical support that research experiences for undergraduates positively influence students to pursue a graduate degree.

9. When American College Test (ACT) scores were reported, they were converted to the SAT scale using the College Board's conversion table. To limit missing observations, data for some colleges was obtained from other sources.

10. For information on the Web of Science database, see http://scientific.thomson.com/products/wos/.

11. The sample was separated according to tiers to partially account for student quality differences across colleges. Each college's 75th percentile SAT score is also included in the analysis to further account for these quality differences. While *U.S. News* classified Reed College as a tier 4 school in 1994 because Reed refused to complete its survey, Reed is classified as a tier 2 college here to better reflect its reputation.

12. To be considered as offering a business degree, the college must have awarded at least 100 degrees in the area of business between 1989 and 1998 according to the IPEDS/HEGIS data. Colleges located in Connecticut, Massachusetts, Maine, New Hampshire, New Jersey, New York, Rhode Island, or Vermont are considered to be in the Northeast.

13. Siegfried and Stock (2007) and Townsend (2005) study the undergraduate origins of future PhD students in economics and history, respectively. Kaufman and Woglom (2005) and Lemke et al. (2005) conduct econometric analyses concerning, respectively, PhD generation rates at liberal arts colleges in general and in economics in particular.

14. A dummy variable for tier 2 colleges is insignificant in the first model; a dummy variable for tier 4 colleges is statistically significant at the 10 percent level in the second model. The coefficient estimates, however, are insensitive to the inclusion of these dummy variables. The results are also qualitatively unchanged if one includes per-student expenditures (as is done here) or the log of per-student expenditures (as Kaufman and Woglom, 2005, do).

15. Although there is a measurable difference in average student ability between the colleges in the top two tiers and the bottom two tiers, there is also likely to be a difference in the research abilities of the professors across the colleges. To what extent these findings on

faculty scholarship are due to the students or are due to the faculty remains unknown, and would be a worthwhile subject for future research.

16. The division-specific PhD generation rates were calculated as a percentage of all college graduates. They are not measured as a percentage of college graduates from within the division, as the Completions Survey does not allow for accurate calculation of this sort. Division-specific PhD generation rates averaged 1.0 percent in the humanities, 1.3 percent in the social sciences, and 1.9 percent in the natural sciences. The humanities include art, art history, communications/librarianship, English, foreign and modern languages, history, philosophy, and religion; the social sciences include anthropology, economics, government, political science, psychology, and sociology; the natural sciences include biology, biochemistry, chemistry, mathematics, physics, and all engineering programs. Omitted from the analysis are doctoral programs in education, social service professions, vocation studies, and home economics.

17. A full set of empirical results is available from the author upon request.

18. For more information about the K-Plan, see www.kzoo.edu/about_kplan.htm.

19. For more I formation on the Scripps College Core Program, see http://www.scripps college.edu/dept/cor/about/index.html.

Chapter 8. Minority Students in Science and Math: What Universities Still Do Not Understand about Race in America

Material for this paper is excerpted from Richard Tapia's forthcoming book on the education of American underrepresented minority students, *Precious Few*.

1. Source: Commission on Professionals in Science and Technology, data derived from U.S. Department of Education, National Center for Education Statistics; unpublished data.

2. For an interesting look at the problem of attrition, see Alexander et al. 1998.

3. One of those trials for graduate students can be the adviser-student relationship. Over the years many students have suffered under a demanding professor whose goal seems to be to drive off as many students as possible. The old model required students to say "How high?" when the professor commanded "Jump." Many of today's faculty members can give examples of these tough masters and the paces they themselves were put through as graduate students. Unfortunately, academic hazing to weed out the weak still exists, and for minority students this kind of behavior can be unbearable. Hazing is no picnic even without the element of race, and many students have been made miserable or chosen to drop out because of it. Add to this the element of racial difference (for most STEM faculty are, to this day, white) and we have a recipe for disaster.

4. To be fair, the caliber of students who come to the United States may not be typical for their countries of origin. These students are competing with *our* best, however, and performing very well. They do not need developmental work.

5. One solution offered is to direct minority students into minority-serving institutions, those that offer a nurturing environment. Many minority families have a long and happy relationship with historically black colleges and universities (HBCUs) in particular. However, for students who anticipate joining the faculty of a major university in one of the STEM fields, the HBCU or Hispanic-serving institution is not the best choice. The limited access to good research laboratories, among other things, hampers candidates from these institutions in the highly competitive STEM fields. There are many good reasons to choose a minority-serving institution, but students and parents need to be realistic about the likely long-term effect of this decision on an academic career.

6. This observation is based on interviews conducted with students at Rice University in 2006.

7. See Chubin and Malcom 2006.

8. For an example of how quickly the atmosphere becomes "unfriendly" in the face of change in spite of what we have learned about the unreliability of standardized tests in predicting the academic success of women and minorities, teaching faculty strongly uphold the use of standardized tests—a prime example of the irresistible force of changing demographics meeting the immovable university. When standards are invoked, albeit tactfully and indirectly, as a reason for the small numbers of minorities in STEM education, we soon alienate the minority community.

9. See Lewis 2006, 50.

10. A highly effective program has been developed at the University of Iowa under the direction of David Manderscheid; Freeman Hrabowski has had good results with the Meyerhoff Scholars Program at the University of Maryland–Baltimore County; and Richard Tapia's programs at Rice University have achieved notable success, producing half of the nation's Hispanic female PhD holders in mathematics. See also Castillo-Chavez and Castillo-Garsow, this volume.

Chapter 9. The Mathematical and Theoretical Biology Institute

The research and mentorship activities in this project have been partially supported by grants from the National Science Foundation (NSF—Grant DMS—0502349), the National Security Agency (NSA—Grant H98230–06–1–0097), the Alfred P. Sloan Foundation (ASU-Sloan National Pipeline Program in the Mathematical and Statistical Sciences) and the Office of the Provost of Arizona State University. Maintaining a research program closely tied in to an intense summer program for eleven years is tough. This project has been carried out with the support of a large number of graduate students over the past decade. It would be impossible to list them all, but we thank each and every one.

We have had several outstanding individuals involved over the past eleven summers. Although we can't list them all, our mentors include the following professors: Abdul Aziz-Yakubu, Howard University, who has mentored students for six summers; Carlos Hernandez Suarez, Universidad de Colima in Mexico (six summers); Christopher Kribs-Zaleta, University of Texas–Arlington (six summers); Baojun Song, Montclair State University, (ten summers); Steve Tennenbaum, Innovative Emergency Management, Inc. (seven summers); and Steve Wirkus, California State Polytechnic University, Pomona (eight summers).

At Cornell University, our thanks go to David Call, W. Kent Fuchs, Biddy Martin, Malden Nesheim, Don Randel, Hunter R. Rawlings III, and Frank Rhodes.

At Arizona State University, we are grateful to Maria Allison, Elizabeth Capaldi, Peter Crouch, Michael Crow, Jon Fink, Milton Glick, Andrew Webber, David Young, and Marjorie Zatz, who have done everything possible to help the goals and the vision of the MTBI/SUMS. At the ASU Hispanic Research Center thanks are due to Antonio Garcia, Gary Keller, Albert McHenry, and Michael Sullivan; they are the kind of public minded individuals that every university dreams of having.

The encouragement and confidence given to the MTBI by Barbara Deuink, James Schatz, Michelle Wagner at NSA, Lloyd Douglas at NSF, and Ted Greenwood at the Alfred P. Sloan Foundation, have played a critical role.

Many thanks go to David Sanchez and Melissa Castillo-Garsow for their comments and suggestions. Carlos Castillo-Chavez's family, particularly his children, have given up their summers to keep this project alive; we can't thank them enough.

1. Rice University professor Richard Tapia, the foremost U.S. minority mentor of applied mathematicians, has expressed similar views.

2. In 1995 UT–El Paso was awarded a National Science Foundation grant that would allow it to become a Minority Institution of Excellence in the science, technology, engineering, and mathematics fields.

3. Herbert Medina collaborated on this project in 1996 and spent 1997 cobuilding a similar program, the Summer Institute in Mathematics for Undergraduates, but with an emphasis in pure mathematics. Medina and Ivelisse Rubio's program made tremendous contributions to the training of minority students in the mathematical sciences from 1998 to 2002 from its base at the University of Puerto Rico–Humacao.

4. In 2000 Randel would leave his position at Cornell to become the twelfth president of the University of Chicago, a position he would leave six years later to become president of the Andrew W. Mellon Foundation.

5. Although the MTBI is proud to have provided a large pool of U.S. minority applicants to the Department of Mathematics at the University of Iowa, most if not all of the credit should go to the university's mathematics faculty and departmental leadership, who have welcomed, mentored, supported, and graduated these students. The mathematics department at the University of Iowa was recognized with a Presidential Award for Excellence in Science, Mathematics and Engineering Mentoring in 2004.

6. These groups are Latinos, African Americans, and Native Americans who are permanent U.S. residents or citizens.

7. Oberwolfach, located in southern Germany, is a famous retreat where mathematicians get together to exchange ideas in an environment that, by design, facilitates interactions between established and young scientists.

8. SUMS and the MTBI merged in 2004 under the direction of Carlos Castillo-Chavez. The SUMS Institute is a winner of a 2003 White House President's Award for Excellence in Science, Mathematics and Engineering Mentoring.

9. The data for national PhD graduates were obtained from the AMS's 2005 Annual Survey of the Mathematical Sciences at http://www.ams.org/notices/200602/05first report.pdf.

10. Two students enrolled in master's of science programs and had no plans to complete a PhD; one enrolled in the PhD program but did not complete it because of personal reasons.

11. The University of Iowa Department of Mathematics is a winner of a 2005 White House President's Award for Excellence in Science, Mathematics and Engineering Mentoring.

12. See http://www.ams.org/employment/citation2007.html.

13. See http://www.amssi.org/.

14. On the "new American university," see http://www.asu.edu/president/newamerica nuniversity/arizona/. Here we are paraphrasing ASU's mission, but in the context of the work that is being carried out at the MTBI.

15. See http://www.asu.edu/president/newamericanuniversity/arizona/.

16. See http://www.amssi.org/.

Chapter 10. Curriculum Intensity in Graduate Preparatory Programs

1. Our approach to examining the determinants of performance approximates that of Grove, Dutkowsky, and Grodner (2005), Grove and Wu (2007), and Krueger and Wu (2000) in their analyses of graduate students of economics.

2. For examples of using bivariate probit models for estimating treatment effects, see Evans and Schwab (1995) and Fairlie (2005).

3. Asian American groups regarded as underrepresented in the profession and historically disadvantaged in the American context (and hence that receive priority in consideration for the AEASP Minority Scholarship) include Native Americans and Americans of Filipino, Hmong, Lao, Pacific Islander, and Vietnamese descent. Americans of Bangladeshi, Chinese, Japanese, Indian, Korean, Pakistani, or Thai descent are not included in this group.

4. A student's mother's and father's education are binary variables equal to 1 if the mother and father have levels of education that exceed the median reportable category of having a baccalaureate degree—which is the same basis for the two parents' education binary variable.

5. These regressions are not shown here, but are available from the authors upon request.

Chapter 11. Assessing Programs to Improve Minority Participation in the STEM Fields

1. This notion of institutionalization is the basis for intervention programs that focus on institutional transformation, such as the National Science Foundation's ADVANCE Program.

2. Bridglall and Gordon (2004, 75) define a "connoisseurial" evaluation as one in which a connoisseur's judgment is used to amplify and explain more traditional evaluation research.

3. See http://www.instituteonteachingandmentoring.org/Compact.

4. See http://preparing-faculty.org.

Chapter 13. Increasing Women's Representation in the Life Sciences

1. The nine universities were California Institute of Technology; Harvard University; Massachusetts Institute of Technology; Princeton University; Stanford University; University of California, Berkeley; University of Michigan, Ann Arbor; University of Pennsylvania; and Yale University.

2. These universities participated with the assurance of anonymity.

3. For information about the NSF ADVANCE program see http://www.nsf.gov/fund ing/pgm_summ.jsp?pims_id=5383 and http://research.cs.vt.edu/advance/index.htm.

4. For a list of NSF ADVANCE Institutional Transformation awardee institutions and their websites see http://www.nsf.gov/crssprgm/advance/itwebsites.jsp. ADVANCE program institutions have devised numerous programs to deal with the challenges in recruiting women faculty:

- The Columbia University Earth Institute provides information to aid in the recruiting process, including institutional programs, child care service options, and the tenure and promotion process at http://www.earthinstitute.columbia. edu/advance/index.html.
- The Georgia Institute of Technology offers a modified duties program for faculty at http://www.advance.gatech.edu/asmdp.html.
- New Mexico State University offers a program to train department heads at http://www.nmsu.edu/%7Eadvprog/faculty-dev.htm.
- The University of California, Irvine, offers a wealth of information on the recruiting process at http://advance.uci.edu/.
- The University of Michigan, Ann Arbor, ADVANCE project provides guidance to departmental search committees on conducting diverse searches. Information

from its Committee on Strategies and Tactics for Recruiting to Improve Diversity and Excellence (STRIDE) is available at http://sitemaker.umich.edu/advance/STRIDE.

- The University of Washington offers a faculty recruiting tool kit for recruiting diverse faculty at http://www.washington.edu/admin/eoo/forms/ftk_01.html.
- The University of Wisconsin, Madison, offers information on avoiding bias in the search process at http://wiseli.engr.wisc.edu/initiatives/hiring/Bias.pdf.

ADVANCE program institutions have developed a number of programs and initiatives to address retention and advancement for women faculty:

- Institutions can examine the ADVANCE institutional data collection kit for pointers on the methods and types of data to be collected at http://www.nmsu.edu/~advprog/data%20&%20toolkit.htm.
- Case Western Reserve University offers a faculty executive coaching program for women faculty, department chairs, and deans at http://www.case.edu/admin/aces/coaching.htm.
- Cornell University offers faculty recruitment, faculty development, climate assessment, and evaluation initiatives on its ADVANCE site: http://advance.cornell.edu/#CUADV.
- New Mexico State University offers a faculty mentoring program, a leadership development program, and a workshop on promotion and tenure, respectively, at http://www.nmsu.edu/%7Eadvprog/mentoring.htm; http://www.nmsu.edu/%7Eadvprog/Leaders.htm; and http://www.nmsu.edu/%7Eadvprog/promotion.htm.
- The University of Colorado, Boulder, has designated its entire ADVANCE program as being dedicated to growing leadership; see http://advance.colorado.edu/.
- The University of Washington offers a faculty retention tool kit at http://www.engr.washington.edu/advance/resources/Retention/index.html.

Chapter 14. Attracting and Retaining Women in Engineering

1. These statistics come from 2006, and were gathered using the American Society for Engineering Education's data mining tool.

2. See http://www.nerdgirls.org.

Chapter 15. Do Foreign Doctorate Recipients Displace U.S. Doctorate Recipients at U.S. Universities?

1. Hoffer et al. (2003) include the social sciences in the science and engineering fields. Excluding the social sciences would increase the proportion of doctorates awarded to foreign students in these fields to 38 percent. For simplicity, in this study I refer to temporary resident students as *foreign students*, and to U.S. citizens and permanent resident students as *U.S. students*.

2. A similar definition of the crowding-out effect has been used in Borjas 2003. It is noteworthy that the term *crowding-out* in this study does not necessarily suggest a causal relation. In particular, I use the term to refer to a negative correlation between the number of U.S. doctoral candidates and recipients versus the number of foreign candidates and recipients. A negative correlation might be consistent with mechanisms other than the casual crowding out. However, the nonexistence of a negative correlation between the numbers

of foreign versus U.S. candidates and recipients is evidence of no causal crowding out. between the two groups.

3. A similar argument has been made by Ehrenberg and Sherman (1984) in establishing a model of optimal financial aid and admissions policies for a selective university.

4. This classification is slightly different from that used in the Survey of Earned Doctorates, where the social sciences are classified in the broad category of the SE fields. For the present analyses, the social sciences are deemed similar to the non-SE fields in terms of the proportion of female and foreign doctorates.

5. See http://caspar.nsf.gov/index.jsp.

6. WebCASPAR is available at http://webcaspar.nsf.gov/includes/checkJavascriptAbility2. jsp?submitted=1

7. Data source: The National Center for Education Statistics' Integrated Postsecondary Education Data System (IPEDS); see http://www.nces.ed.gov/. The numbers of college graduates in non-SE fields was around 200,000 for both men and women in the late 1960s and early 1970s, and in 2002 these numbers have risen to 360,000 and 530,000, respectively. These non-SE fields include the social sciences.

8. Data source: The National Center for Education Statistics' Integrated Postsecondary Education Data System (IPEDS); see http://www.nces.ed.gov/. The share of female college graduates in the non-SE fields overall increased slowly during the 1990s. And in fields with a high proportion of female college graduates, their share has started to stabilize. In fact, in fields such as education and sociology there has been a slight decrease in the share of female college graduates since 2000.

Chapter 16. Opening (and Closing) Doors

1. The Survey of Earned Doctorates is an individual-level census of recipients of doctorates at U.S. institutions. Because survey participation is often coupled with the formal process of degree receipt, response rates have been quite high.

2. The argument is that the elasticity of demand among foreign students may be somewhat larger than among U.S. students if foreign students are simply choosing where to attend graduate school rather than weighing the choice between a graduate program and an alternative profession.

3. Although it is difficult to rank universities in an international context, the top U.S. universities are often considered leaders at an international level. One effort has been made to compare universities on an index scale including measures such as Nobel Prize laureates, articles published in major scientific publications, and citations finds that fifteen of the top twenty, as well as thirty-five of the top fifty, universities are in the United States (Shanghai Jiao Tong University Institute of Higher Education 2003). While the strength of U.S. universities at the top of the international rankings is widely recognized, it should also be noted that there is considerable variance in the quality of U.S. doctoral programs. One British observer, comparing the United States and the United Kingdom, has noted that "the U.S., with 4,000 institutions of higher education, probably has 50 of the best universities in the world and undoubtedly has 500 of the worst" (Stevens 2004, cited in Bowen, Kurzweil, and Tobin 2005, 314).

4. For the transitioning countries at the center of this study, there is considerable variation in the initial quality and functioning of the university systems in the home country. China bounds one end of the distribution with a university system largely in disarray in the late 1970s following the Cultural Revolution; indeed, the lack of options in the home country was a primary motivation for sending students to the United States and Canada. To varying degrees, Eastern European Communist rule did not dismantle university

infrastructures with long historical roots, though social science subjects such as economics were not offered at levels that met international standards. For the Soviet Union, the end of the Cold War did not bode well for the university system, which had been quite strong in the sciences, as state support was largely eliminated.

5. In the very long run, as other countries' educational infrastructure improves, we might expect systematic sorting among PhD students across the globe; indeed, one might argue that strong institutions in the United States captured foreign demand that a century earlier necessarily would have belonged to Oxford and Cambridge Universities in England, or the Sorbonne in France. There is no reason not to expect competition for top students from now-emerging educational powerhouses in future decades.

6. To this end, models of "brain drain"—where leaving the country to study abroad often ends up being a permanent emigration—apply most directly to very poor countries.

7. It is likely that a primary explanation for these trends is that they are a reflection of the undergraduate training received in the home countries, reflecting the emphasis of the Chinese institutions on developing engineering strengths in the late 1970s and the emphasis on math and physical sciences under the Soviet Cold War regime. Moreover, we expect that this pattern of concentration is consistent with subject matter that would bring a relatively high return in the home countries.

8. Rather than using country of birth, which may include some students coming to the United States at young ages, we organize the data by country of high school attendance.

9. For example, in 1981, the United States granted 2,678 F-1 (student) visas and 3,121 J (exchange) visas to students from China. By 1991, the corresponding numbers were 14,594 F-1 and 7,431 J visas. A concern that began to play out in the 1990s was that some Chinese students saw student visas from U.S. institutions in fields such as physics and mathematics as points of entry to either the U.S. labor market and lucrative fields such as electrical engineering. An article in *Physics Today* (Hargreaves 2001) discusses concerns about the unusually high dropout rate among students from China.

10. To illustrate this concentration, of the 32,127 students from China receiving U.S. PhDs between 1985 and 2003, 25 percent received bachelor's degrees in 1982, and 40.3 percent entered graduate school between 1982 and 1985, with 12 percent entering in 1982 alone.

11. The establishment of networks early on was particularly important in opening doctoral education. One important example was the China–United States Physics Examination and Application (CUSPEA) program initiated in the fall of 1979 by the Chinese American Nobel Laureate physicist T. D. Lee of Columbia University. The intent of the initiative was to identify gifted graduate students through examination in China and to place these students at U.S. universities. During the course of the program, CUSPEA placed more than nine hundred students in physics programs at U.S. universities. To put these numbers in perspective, the total number of PhD degree recipients from China receiving degrees in physics between 1980 and 1992 was 1,062. Of course, there were other channels through which Chinese students could study physics in the United States, but the CUSPEA program clearly had a substantial impact in generating a network or link between leading U.S. and Chinese universities.

12. With the dissolution of the Soviet Union in 1991, the now separately identified former Soviet republics are Armenia, Azerbaijan, Belarus, Georgia, Kazakhstan, Kyrgyzstan, Moldova, Russia, Tajikistan, Turkmenistan, Ukraine, and Uzbekistan.

13. One might argue that the same pattern is hard to identify in the data for Eastern European countries and former Soviet states because students in the most recent graduate cohorts entering from these countries may still be in graduate school with continuing likelihood of receiving PhDs. To address this concern, we also plot the pattern of degree receipt within eight years of graduate school entry, with common truncation across cohorts. Clearly the patterns persist.

Chapter 17. What the "War on Terror" Has Meant for U.S. Colleges and Universities

1. For more on NAFSA, see http://www.nafsa.org.

2. For more on the Institute of International Education, see http://www.IIE.org.

3. *Nyquist v. Mauclet*, 432 U.S. 1 (1977) notes that states may not limit financial aid programs to citizens and preclude permanent residents.

4. *Ahmed v. University of Toledo*, 664 F. Supp. 282 (N.D. Ohio 1986) states that colleges may require international students to obtain insurance coverage.

5. *Toll v. Moreno*, 458 U.S. 1 (1982) states that nonresident visa holders are entitled to establish residency for tuition purposes.

6. *Tayyari v. New Mexico State University*, 495 F. Supp. 1365 (D. N.M. 1980) cites additional requirements for enrolled students who are from a country whose residents have taken U.S. hostages.

7. This section is drawn from Olivas 2004, and due to length considerations I have not reproduced all of the notes that appeared in the original version. Other treatments of this intersection of higher education and terrorism include Couter and Giroux 2006 and Gott 2005.

8. *Western State University of Southern California v. American Bar Association*, 301 F.Supp.2d 1129 (C.D. Cal. 2004) addresses proprietary law school and accreditation.

Looking to the Future

1. See the National Science Foundation's Integrative Graduate Education and Research Training website, http://www.igert.org.

2. See Abt Associates 2006; Panofsky and Rhoten 2005.

3. See National Research Council 2008.

4. See Millman 2007.

5. See, for example, Borjas 2000, which presents evidence that foreign-born teaching assistants adversely affect students' academic performance in introductory economics classes; and Fleisher, Hashimoto, and Weinberg 2002, which finds that when foreign teaching assistants are properly screened and trained in spoken English and in teaching skills, they are at least as effective in undergraduate economics classes as American teaching assistants.

REFERENCES

Aanerud, R., L. Homer, M. Nerad, and C. Cerny. 2006. "Using Ph.D. Career Path Analysis and Ph.D.s' Perceptions of Their Education as a Means to Assess Doctoral Program." In *Assessing Learning at the Doctoral Level*, edited by Peggy L. Maki and Nancy Borkowsk, 109–144. Sterling, Va.: Stylus.

Aanerud, R., L. Homer, E. Rudd, E. Morrison, M. Nerad, and J. Cerny. 2007. "Widening the Lens on Gender and Tenure: Looking beyond the Academic Labor Market." *NWSA Journal* 19:3.

Abedi, Jamal, and Ellen M. Benkin. 1987. "The Effects of Students' Academic, Financial, and Demographic Variables on Time to the Doctorate." *Research in Higher Education* 27, no. 1: 3–14.

Abriola, Linda M. 2007. *Annual Report [2006–2007]*. Medford, Mass.: School of Engineering, Tufts University. http://engineering.tufts.edu/docs/SOE_2007_Annual_Report.pdf

Abt Associates. 2006. *Evaluation of the Initial Impacts of the National Science Foundation's Integrative Graduate Education and Research Training Program: Final Report*. Bethesda, Md., February.

Alexander, Benjamin, Julie Foertsch, Dianne Bowcock, and Steve Kosciuk. 1998. *Minority Undergraduate Retention at UW–Madison: A Report on the Factors Influencing the Persistence of Today's Minority Undergraduates*. LEAD Center, University of Wisconsin–Madison.

American Society for Engineering Education. 2006. ASEE Engineering Data Mining System. http://www.asee.org/datamining.

Archibold, Randal C. 2006. "Wait Ends for Father and Son Exiled by F.B.I. Terror Inquiry." *New York Times*, October 2.

Arts & Sciences and Engineering (AS&E) Office of Diversity Education and Development. 2006. *Faculty Retention Cohort Study*. Medford, Mass.: Tufts University, February.

Astin, A. W. 1999. "How the Liberal Arts College Affects Students." *Daedalus* 128: 77–100.

Banks, James, ed. 2004. *Diversity and Citizenship Education: Global Perspectives*. San Francisco: Jossey-Bass.

Barlow, A. E. L., and M. Villarejo. 2004. "Making a Difference for Minorities: Evaluation of an Educational Enrichment Program." *Journal of Research in Science Teaching* 41, no. 9: 861–81.

Barron's. 1994. *Profiles of American Colleges*. 20th ed. New York: Barron's Educational Series.

Bauer, Karen, and Joan Bennett. 2003. "Alumni Perceptions Used to Assess Undergraduate Research Experience." *Journal of Higher Education* 74, no. 2 (March–April): 210–30.

Becker, Charles, and Gregory Price. 2006. "Curriculum Intensity in Graduate Preparatory Programs: Impact on Performance and Progression to Graduate Study among Minority Students in Economics." Paper presented at the 2006 Cornell Higher Education Research Institute Policy Research Conference "Doctoral Education and the Faculty of the Future," Cornell University, Ithaca, N.Y., October 8–10.

Bellas, M. L. 1992. "Comparable Worth in Academia: The Effects on Faculty Salaries of the Sex Composition and Labor Market Conditions of Academic Disciplines." *American Sociological Review* 59, no. 6: 807–21.

Bender, T. 2006. "Expanding the Domain of History." In *Envisioning the Future of Doctoral Education: Preparing Stewards of the Discipline. Carnegie Essays on the Doctorate*, edited by C. M. Golde and G. E. Walker, 295–310. San Francisco: Jossey-Bass.

Berger, Dan H., and Scott M. Borene, eds. 2005. *Immigration Options for Academics and Researchers*. Washington, D.C.: American Immigration Lawyers Association.

Bhattacharjee, Y. 2004. "Family Matters: Stopping Tenure Clock May Not Be Enough." *Science* 306: 2031–33.

———. 2005. "Princeton Resets Family-Friendly Tenure Clock." *Science* 309: 1308.

Blair, Tony. 2006. "Why We Must Attract More Students from Overseas." *Guardian*, April 2006.

Blythe, Stephen E. 2006. "The Tiger of the Peninsula Is Digitized: Korean E-Commerce Law as a Driving Force in the World's Most Computer-Savvy Nation." *Houston Journal of International Law* 28: 573–661.

Bollag, Burton. 2006a. "America's Hot New Export: Higher Education." *Chronicle of Higher Education*, February 17.

———. 2006b. "College Fined for Cuban Program." *Chronicle of Higher Education*, July 21.

———. 2006c. "Education Group Calls for National Foreign-Student Recruitment Strategy." *Chronicle of Higher Education*, June 23.

———. 2006d. "Greek Professor Barred from U.S." *Chronicle of Higher Education*, July 7.

———. 2006e. "U.S. Again Bars Cuban Scholars." *Chronicle of Higher Education*, March 17.

———. 2006f. "U.S. Won't Appeal Tariq Ramadan Ruling." *Chronicle of Higher Education*, September 8.

Bollag, Burton, and Dan Canevale. 2006. "Iranian Academics Are Denied Visas." *Chronicle of Higher Education*, September 1.

Bollag, Burton, and Shailaja Neelakantan. 2006. "After Visa Delay, Prominent Indian Scientist Spurns U.S. Invitation." *Chronicle of Higher Education*, March 10.

Borjas, George. 1987. "Self-Selection and the Earnings of Immigrants." *American Economic Review* 77, no. 4 (September): 531–53.

——. 2000. "Foreign-Born Teaching Assistants and the Academic Performance of Undergraduates." *American Economic Association Papers and Proceedings* 90 (May): 355–59.

——. 2003. "Immigration in High-Skill Labor Markets: The Impact of Foreign Students on the Earnings of Doctorates." Paper presented at the conference of the Science and Engineering Workforce Project at the National Bureau of Economic Research, New York, N.Y.: Columbia University, May 15.

——. 2004. *Do Foreign Students Crowd Out Native Students from Graduate Programs?* NBER Working Paper 10349. Cambridge, Mass.: National Bureau of Economic Research.

——. 2007. "Do Foreign Students Crowd Out Native Students from Graduate Programs?" In *Science and the University*, edited by P. Stephan and R. Ehrenberg). Madison: University of Wisconsin Press.

Bound, J., and S. Turner. 2004. "Cohort Crowding: How Resources Affect Collegiate Attainment." *Journal of Public Economics* 91, issues 5-6 (June), 877–99.

——. 2006. "Cohort Crowding: How Resources Affect Collegiate Attainment." The National Bureau of Economics Research Working Paper Number 12424. Cambridge, Mass.: National Bureau for Economic Research.

Bound, J., S. Turner, and P. Walsh. Forthcoming. "Internationalization of U.S. Doctorate Education." In *Brainpower, Science and Engineering Careers in the United States*, edited by R. Freeman and D. Goroff. Chicago: University of Chicago Press.

Bourque, S. C. 1999. "Reassessing Research: Liberal Arts Colleges and the Social Sciences." *Daedalus* 128: 265–72.

Bowen, W., M. Kurzweil, and E. Tobin. 2005. *Equity and Excellence in American Higher Education.* Charlottesville: University of Virginia Press.

Bowen, William G., and Derek Curtis Bok. 1998. *The Shape of the River: Long-Term Consequences of Considering Race in College and University Admissions.* Princeton, N.J.: Princeton University Press.

Bowen, William G., and Neil L. Rudenstine. 1992. *In Pursuit of the PhD.* Princeton, N.J.: Princeton University Press.

Boyer, E. L. 1990. *Scholarship Reconsidered: Priorities of the Professoriate.* Princeton, N.J.: Carnegie Foundation for the Advancement of Teaching.

Bransford, J. D., A. L. Brown, and R. R. Cocking, eds. 2000. *How People Learn: Brain, Mind, Experience, and School.* Washington, D.C.: National Research Council.

Bridglall, B. L., and E. W. Gordon. 2004. *Creating Excellence and Increasing Ethnic Minority Leadership in Science, Engineering, Mathematics, and Other Technical Disciplines: A Study of the Meyerhoff Scholars Program at the University of Maryland, Baltimore County.* New York: Institute for Urban and Minority Education, Teachers College, Columbia University.

Brown, J. S., A. Collins, and P. Duguid. 1989. "Situated Cognition and the Culture of Learning." *Educational Researcher* 18, no. 1: 35–42.

Brown, J. S., and P. Duguid. 2000. *The Social Life of Information.* Boston: Harvard Business School Press.

Building Engineering and Science Talent. 2004. *A Bridge for All: Higher Education Design Principles to Broaden Participation in Science, Technology, Engineering, and Mathematics.* San Diego: Building Engineering and Science Talent.

Bulwa, Demian. 2006. "Man OKd to Return to U.S. from Pakistan." San Francisco *Chronicle*, September 13.

Castillo-Chavez, C., and C. W. Castillo-Garsow. Forthcoming. "The New American University: Mentorship in the Mathematical Sciences," In *Models That Work: Building Diversity in Advanced Mathematics*, edited by Abbe H. Herzig and Patricia Hale.

Chowell, G., A. Cintron-Arias, S. Del Valle, F. Sanchez, B. Song, J. M. Hyman, H. W. Hethcote, and C. Castillo-Chavez. 2006. "Mathematical Applications Associated with the Deliberate Release of Infectious Agents." In *Modeling the Dynamics of Human Diseases: Emerging Paradigms and Challenges*, edited by A. Gumel, C. Castillo-Chavez, D. P. Clemence, and R. E. Mickens, vol. 410 of *Contemporary Mathematics*, 51–72. Providence, R.I.: American Mathematical Society.

Chowell, G. P., W. Fenimore, M. A. Castillo-Garsow, and C. Castillo-Chavez. 2003. "SARS Outbreaks in Ontario, Hong Kong, and Singapore: The Role of Diagnosis and Isolation as a Control Mechanism." *Journal of Theoretical Biology* 224: 1–8.

Chubin, Daryl E., and Shirley M. Malcom. 2006. "The New Backlash on Campus." *College and University Journal* 81, no. 4: 65–68.

Clotfelter, Charles. 2007. "Patron or Bully? The Role of Foundations in Higher Education." In *Reconnecting Education and Foundations: Turning Good Intentions into Educational Capital*, edited by Ray Bacchetti and Thomas Ehrlich, 211–48. San Francisco: Jossey-Bass.

Cohen, David. 2006. "Growth of Foreign-Student Enrollments Slows in Australia." *Chronicle of Higher Education*, March 24.

Coll, Steve. 2006. "A Reporter at Large: The Atomic Emporium, Abdul Qadeer Khan, and Iran's Race to Build the Bomb." *New Yorker*, August 7–14, 50–63.

Collins, A., J. S. Brown, and A. Holum. 1991. "Cognitive Apprenticeship: Making Thinking Visible." *American Educator* (Winter): 6–24.

Collins, A., J. S. Brown, and S. Newman. 1989. "Cognitive Apprenticeship: Teaching the Crafts of Reading, Writing, and Mathematics." In *Knowing, Learning, and Instruction: Essays in Honor of Robert Glaser*, edited by. L. B. Resnick, 453–94. Hillsdale, N.J.: Lawrence Erlbaum.

Committee on Equal Opportunity in Science and Engineering. 2004. *Broadening Participation in America's Science and Engineering Workforce: The 1994–2003 Decennial and 2004 Biennial Reports to Congress*. Arlington, Va.: National Science Foundation.

Committee on Policy Implications of International Graduate Students and Postdoctoral Scholars in the United States. 2005. *Policy Implications of International Graduate Students and Postdoctoral Scholars in the United States*. Washington, D.C.: National Academies Press.

Committee on Science, Engineering, and Public Policy. 1997. *Adviser, Teacher, Role Model, Friend: On Being a Mentor to Students in Science and Engineering*. Washington, D.C.: National Academies Press.

Congressional Commission on the Advancement of Women and Minorities in Science, Engineering and Technology Development. 2000. *Land of Plenty: Diversity as America's Competitive Edge in Science, Engineering and Technology*. www.nsf.gov/pubs/2000/cawmset0409/cawmset_0409.pdf.

Considine, Mark, Simon Marginson, and Peter Sheehan. 2001. *Comparative Performance of Australia as Knowledge Nation*. Melbourne, Australia: Chifley Research Centre.

Cooper, Helene, and Thom Shanker. 2006. "Draft Iran Resolution Would Restrict Students." *New York Times*, October 26.

Council of Graduate Schools. 1990. *A Policy Statement: The Doctor of Philosophy Degree*. Washington, D.C.: Council of Graduate Schools.

——. 2004. *Ph.D. Completion and Attrition: Policy, Numbers, Leadership, and Next Steps*. Washington, D.C.: Council of Graduate Schools.

——. 2006a. *Enrollment and Degrees: 1986–2005.* Washington, D.C.: Council of Graduate Schools.

——. 2006b. *Ph.D. Completion and Attrition: Analysis of Baseline Program Data from the Ph.D. Completion Project.* Washington, DC: Council of Graduate Schools.

Couter, Michel, and Marie-Helen Giroux. 2006. "The Aftermath of 11 September 2001: Liberty vs. Security before the Supreme Court of Canada." *International Journal of Refugee Law* 18: 313–32.

Cox, A., and R. Wilson. 2001. "Leaders of 9 Universities Pledge to Improve Conditions for Female Scientists." *Chronicle of Higher Education* 47, no. 22 (February).

Damrosch, D. 2006. "Vectors of Change." In *Envisioning the Future of Doctoral Education: Preparing Stewards of the Discipline,* edited by C. M. Golde and G. E. Walker, 34–45. San Francisco: Jossey-Bass.

Davies, Gareth. 2005. "Higher Education, Equal Access, and Residence Conditions: Does EU Law Allow Member States to Charge Higher Fees to Students Not Previously Resident?" *Maastricht Journal of European and Comparative Law* 12: 227–40.

Del Valle, S., A. Morales Evangelista, M. C. Velasco, C. M. Kribs-Zaleta, and S. F. Hsu Schmitz. 2004. "Effects of Education, Vaccination, and Treatment on HIV Transmission in Homosexuals with Genetic Heterogeneity." *Mathematical Biosciences* 187: 111–33.

DeNeef, A. L. 2002. *The Preparing Future Faculty Program: What Difference Does It Make?* Washington, D.C.: Association of American Colleges and Universities.

Dougan, Michael. 2005. "Fees, Grants, Loans and Dole Checks: Who Covers the Costs of Migrant Education within the EU?" *Common Market Law Review* 42: 943–86.

Educational Testing Service. 2006. Educational Testing Service News.

Ehrenberg, Ronald G. 1991. "Academic Labor Supply." In *Economic Challenges in Higher Education,* edited by. C. Clotfelter, R. Ehrenberg, M. Getz, and J. Siegfried, 143–260. Chicago: University of Chicago Press.

——. 1999. "My Life and Economics." *American Economist* 43: 9–18.

——. 2000. *Tuition Rising: Why College Costs So Much.* Cambridge, Mass.: Harvard University Press.

——. 2005. "Involving Undergraduates in Research to Encourage Them to Undertake Ph.D. Study in Economics." *American Economic Review Papers and Proceedings* 95: 184–88.

Ehrenberg, Ronald G., George H. Jakubson, Jeffrey A. Groen, Eric So, and Joseph Price. 2007. "Inside the Black Box of Doctoral Education: What Program Characteristics Influence Doctoral Students' Attrition and Graduation Probabilities?" *Educational Evaluation and Policy Analysis* 29, no. 2 (June): 134–50.

Ehrenberg, Ronald G., and Panagiotis G. Mavros. 1995. "Do Doctoral Students' Financial Support Patterns Affect Their Times-to-Degree and Completion Probabilities?" *Journal of Human Resources* 30, no. 3: 581–609.

Ehrenberg, Ronald G., and Daniel R. Sherman. 1984. "Optimal Financial Aid Policies for a Selective University." *Journal of Human Resources* 19, no. 2: 202–30.

Ehrenberg, Ronald G., Harriet Zuckerman, Jeffrey A. Groen, and Sharon M. Brucker. Forthcoming. *Educating Scholars: Examining Doctoral Education in the Humanities.* Princeton N.J.: Princeton University Press.

Eley, A. R., and R. Jennings. 2005. *Effective Postgraduate Supervision: Improving the Student/Supervisor Relationship.* Berkshire, England: Open University Press.

England, P., P. Allison, S. Li, N. Mark, J. Thompson, M. Budig, and H. Sun. 2004. "Why Are Some Academic Fields Tipping toward Female? The Sex Composition of U.S. Fields of Doctoral Degree Receipt, 1971–1998." Northwestern University Institute for Policy Research Working Paper WP-03-12. Evanston, Ill.: Northwestern University.

Evans, William N., and Robert M. Schwab. 1995. "Finishing High School and Starting College: Do Catholic Schools Make a Difference?" *Quarterly Journal of Economics* 110: 941–74.

Fairlie, Robert. 2005. "The Effects of Home Computers on School Enrollment." *Economics of Education Review* 24: 533–47.

Ficklen, E. 2006. "50 Years Later, the Hungarian Revolution's Legacy to the West Lives On." *Chronicle of Higher Education*, November 3.

Finn, M. 2003. *Stay Rates of Foreign Doctorate Recipients from U.S. Universities.* Oak Ridge, Tenn.: Oak Ridge Institute for Science and Engineering. http://www.orau.gov/orise/pubs/stayrate03.pdf.

Fitzsimmons, Stephen, Kenneth Carlson, Larry Kerpelman, and Diane Stoner. 1990. *A Preliminary Evaluation of the Research Experiences for Undergraduate (REU) Program.* Washington, D.C: National Science Foundation, 1990.

Fleisher, Belton, Masanori Hashimoto, and Bruce A. Weinberg. 2002. "Foreign GTAs Can Be Effective Teachers of Economics." *Journal of Economic Education* 33 (Fall): 299–325.

Flora, Joseph R., and Adrienne T. Cooper. 2005. "Incorporating Inquiry-Based Laboratory Experiments in the Undergraduate Environmental Engineering Laboratory." *Journal of Professional Issues in Engineering Education and Practice* 131, no. 1: 19.

Friedman, Thomas L. 2005. *The World Is Flat: A Brief History of the Twenty-First Century.* New York: Farrar, Straus and Giroux.

Fuller, C. 1986. "Ph.D. Recipients: Where Did They Go to College?" *Change* 18: 42–52.

Geiger, R. 1993. *Research and Relevant Knowledge: American Research Universities since World War II.* New York: Oxford University Press.

Gillingham, Lisa, Joseph J. Seneca, and Michael K. Taussig. 1991. "The Determinants of Progress to the Doctoral Degree." *Research in Higher Education* 32, no. 4: 449–68.

Gjorgjieva, J., K. Smith, G. Chowell, F. Sanchez, J. Snyder, and C. Castillo-Chavez. 2005. "The Role of Vaccination in the Control of SARS." *Journal of Mathematical Biosciences and Engineering* 2, no. 4 (October): 753–69.

Golde, Chris. M. 2000. "Should I Stay or Should I Go? Student Descriptions of the Doctoral Attrition Process." *Review of Higher Education* 23, no. 2: 119–227.

———. 2006. "Preparing Stewards of the Discipline." In *Envisioning the Future of Doctoral Education: Preparing Stewards of the Discipline*, edited by Chris M. Golde and George E. Walker, 3–20. San Francisco: Jossey-Bass.

Golde, Chris M., and Timothy M. Dore. 2001. "At Cross Purposes: What the Experiences of Doctoral Students Reveal about Doctoral Education." Report prepared for The Pew Charitable Trusts, Philadelphia, Pa. http://www.phd-survey.org/.

Golde, Chris M., and George E. Walker, eds. 2006. *Envisioning the Future of Doctoral Education: Preparing Stewards of the Discipline.* Carnegie Essays on the Doctorate. San Francisco: Jossey-Bass.

Gonzalez, B., E. Huerta-Sanchez, A. Ortiz-Nieves, T. Vazquez-Alvarez, and C. Kribs-Zaleta. 2003. "Am I Too Fat? Bulimia as an Epidemic." *Journal of Mathematical Psychology* 1, no. 47: 515–26.

Gonzalez-Espada, Wilson, and Daphne Zaras. 2006. "Evaluation of the Impact of the National Weather Center REU Program Compared with Other Undergraduate Research Experiences." Paper presented to the Fifteenth Symposium on Education, American Meteorological Society, Atlanta, January 30, 2006–February 3, 2006.

Good, J., G. Halpin, and G. Halpin. 2002. "Retaining Black Students in Engineering: Do Minority Programs Have a Longitudinal Impact?" *Journal of College Student Retention: Research, Theory and Practice* 3, no. 4: 2001–2001: 351–64.

Gott, Gil. 2005. "The Devil We Know: Racial Subordination and National Security Law." *Villanova Law Review* 50: 1073–1133.

Gould, Douglas, and Brian MacPherson. 2003. "Evaluation of an Undergraduate Neuroscience Research Program at the University of Kentucky." *Journal of Undergraduate Neuroscience Education* 2, no. 1 (Fall): A23–A27.

Greenwood, M. R. C. 2007. Personal communication.

Groen, Jeffrey A., George H. Jakubson, Ronald G. Ehrenberg, Scott Condie, and Albert Y. Liu. 2008. "Program Design and Student Outcomes in Graduate Education." *Economics of Education Review* 27, no. 2 (April): 111–24.

Groen, Jeffrey A., and Michael J. Rizzo. 2007. "The Changing Composition of U.S.-Citizen PhDs." In *Science and the University*, edited by Ronald G. Ehrenberg and Paula E. Stephan, 177–96. Madison: University of Wisconsin Press.

Grossman, Pam, Christa Compton, et al. 2005. "Unpacking Practice: The Teaching of Practice in the Preparation of Clergy, Teachers, and Clinical Psychologists." Paper presented at the American Educational Research Association, Montreal, April 11–16.

Grove, Wayne, Donald Dutkowsky, and Andrew Grodner. 2005. "Survive Then Thrive: Determinants of Success in the Economics Ph.D. Program." Working Paper no. edu0504. Greenville, N.C.: East Carolina University Department of Economics. http://www.ecu.edu/econ/wp/05/SurviveThenThrive.pdf.

Grove, Wayne, and Stephen Wu. 2007. "The Search for Talent: Doctoral Completion and Research Productivity of Economists." *American Economic Review* 97: 506–11.

Guterman, Lila. 2006. "The Taint of 'Misbehavior.'" *Chronicle of Higher Education*, February 24.

Hackett, Edward, Jennifer Croissant, and Blair Schneider. 1992. "Industry, Academe, and the Values of Undergraduate Engineers." *Research in Higher Education* 33: 275–95.

Handelsman, Jo, Nancy Cantor, Molly Carnes, Denice Denton, Eve Fine, Barbara Grosz, Virginia Hinshaw, Cora Marrett, Sue Rosser, Donna Shalala, and Jennifer Sheridan. 2005. "More Women in Science." *Science* 309 (August 19): 1190–91.

Hardy, K. 1974. "Social Origins of American Scientists and Scholars." *Science* 185 (August): 497–506.

Hargreaves, Lynley. 2001. "Dropout Rate among Chinese Physics PhD Students Seems High; Community Considers Why." *Physics Today* 54, 24–25. http://www.physicstoday.org/pt/vol-54/iss-5/p24.html.

Harman, Grant. 2002. "Producing PhD Graduates in Australia for the Knowledge Economy." *Higher Education Research and Development* 21, no. 2 (July): 179–90.

Harmon, L. 1978. *A Century of Doctorates: Data Analysis of Growth and Change*. Washington, D.C.: National Academy of Sciences.

Hartnett, Rodney T. 1976. "Environments for Advanced Learning." In *Scholars in the Making: The Development of Graduate and Professional Students*, edited by J. Katz and R. T. Hartnett, 49–84. Cambridge, Mass.: Ballinger.

Hartnett, Rodney T., and Warren W. Willingham. 1979. *The Criterion Problem: What Measure of Success in Graduate Education?* Research Report GREB-77-4R. Princeton, N.J.: Educational Testing Service.

Harvard University. 2005. *Report of the Task Force on Women Faculty*. http://www.hno.harvard.edu/gazette/daily/2005/05/women-faculty.pdf.

Hauptman, Arthur M. 1986. *Students in Graduate and Professional Education: What We Know and Need to Know.* Washington, D.C.: Association of American Universities.

Hebel, Sara. 2006. "Report Card on Colleges Finds U.S. Is Slipping." *Chronicle of Higher Education,* September 15.

Hechinger, F. 1979. "Iranian Plight Puts a Spotlight on U.S. Colleges." *New York Times,* February 20.

Hoffer, T. B., M. Hess, V. Welch, and K. Williams. 2007. *Doctoral Recipients from United States Universities Summary Report 2006: Survey of Earned Doctorates.* Chicago: National Opinion Research Center.

Hoffer, T. B., S. Sederstrom, L. Selfa, V. Welch, M. Hess, S. Brown, S. Reyes, K. Webber, and I. Guzman-Barron. 2003. *Doctorate Recipients from United States Universities: Summary Report 2002.* Chicago: National Opinion Research Center.

Hoffer, T. B., V. Welch Jr., K. Webber, K. Williams, B. Lisek, M. Hess, D. Loew, and I. Guzman-Barron. 2006. *Doctorate Recipients from United States Universities: Summary Report 2005.* Chicago, Ill.: National Opinion Research Center.

Hopkins, N. 2006. "Diversification of a University Faculty: Observations on Hiring Women Faculty in the Schools of Science and Engineering at MIT." *MIT Faculty Newsletter* 18, no. 4: 1, 16–23.

Hrabowski, F. A., and W. Pearson Jr. 1993. "Recruiting and Retaining Talented African American Males in College Science and Engineering." *Journal of College Science Teaching* 22: 234–38.

Hunter, Anne-Barrie, Sandra Laursen, and Elaine Seymour. 2006. "Becoming a Scientist: The Role of Undergraduate Research in Students' Cognitive, Personal, and Professional Development." Working Paper, Center to Advance Research and Teaching in the Social Sciences, Ethnography and Evaluation Research. Boulder: University of Colorado.

Ibarra, Robert A. 1996. "Latino Experiences in Graduate Education: Implications for Change. A Preliminary Report." In *Enhancing the Minority Presence in Graduate Education* 7, edited by Nancy Gaffney Washington, D.C.: Council of Graduate Schools.

Institute of International Education. 2006. *Open Doors Report on International Educational Exchange, 2004–05.* New York: Institute of International Education.

Isaac, Paul D., Roy A. Koenigsknecht, Gary D. Malaney, and John E. Karras. 1989. "Factors Related to Doctoral Dissertation Topic Selection." *Research in Higher Education* 30, no. 4: 357–73.

Jackson, S. A. 2003. *The Quiet Crisis: Falling Short in Producing American Scientific and Technical Talent.* San Diego: Building Engineering and Science Talent.

Jordan, Mirian. 2006. "New Backlash in Immigrant Fight, Grass-Root Groups Boost Their Clout." *Wall Street Journal,* September 26.

Kalb, Laura, and Emily Dwoyer. 2004. *Evaluation of the Graduate Education Initiative: Final Report.* Princeton, N.J.: Mathematica Policy Research, February.

Kanpol, Barry. 1997. *Issues and Trends in Critical Pedagogy.* Cresskill, N.J.: Hampton Press, 1997.

Kapoor, Romy, 2005. "F-1 Students." In *Immigration Options for Academics and Researchers,* edited by Dan Berger and Scott Borene, 57–76. Washington, D.C.: American Immigration Lawyers Association.

Kaufman, R. T., and G. Woglom. 2005. "Financial Changes and Measures of Success among the Second Tier of Top Liberal Arts Colleges, 1996–2001." *Journal of Education Finance* 32, no. 3: 285–303.

Keqi, S., and Z. Kaihua. 2001. "Early History of CUSPEA." Paper presented to the "CUSPEA and Beyond" symposium, Columbia University, November 24.

Kerdeman, Deborah. 2003. "Pulled Up Short: Challenging Self-Understanding as a Focus of Teaching and Learning." *Journal of the Philosophy of Education Society of Great Britain* 37, no. 2 (May): 294–308.

Kerr, Clark. 1994. *Higher Education Cannot Escape History.* Albany: State University of New York Press.

Knapp, R. H., and H. B. Goodrich. 1952. *Origins of American Scientists.* Chicago: University of Chicago Press.

Kobach, Kris W. 2005. "The Quintessential Force Multiplier: The Inherent Authority of Local Police to Make Immigration Arrests." *Albany Law Review* 69: 179–235.

Kochenov, Dimitry. 2003. "Pre-Accession, Naturalisation, and 'Due Regard to Community Law.'" *Romanian Journal of Political Science* 4, no. 2: 71–88.

Kribs-Zaleta, C., M. Lee, C. Román, S. Wiley, and C. M. Hernández-Suárez. 2005. "The Effect of the HIV/AIDS Epidemic on Africa's Truck Drivers." *Journal of Mathematical Biosciences and Engineering* 2, no. 4: 771–88.

Krueger, Alan, and Stephen Wu. 2000. "Forecasting Successful Economics Graduate Students." *Journal of Economics Education* 31: 81–94.

Kunstler, B. 2004. *Hothouse Effect: Intensify Creativity in Your Organization Using Secrets from History's Most Innovative Communities.* Saranac Lake, N.Y.: American Management Association.

Labi, Aisha. 2006. "Britain Expands Foreign-Student Recruitment." *Chronicle of Higher Education,* April 28.

Lambert, Richard, and Nick Butler. 2006. *The Future of European Universities: Renaissance or Decay?* London: Centre for European Reform.

Landler, Mark. 2006. "Seeking Quality, German Universities Scrap Equality." *New York Times,* October 20.

Langewiesche, William. 2005. "The Wrath of Khan: How A. Q. Khan Made Pakistan a Nuclear Power—and Showed That the Spread of Atomic Weapons Can't Be Stopped." *Atlantic Monthly* (November): 62–85.

Lave, J., and E. Wenger. 1991. *Situated Learning: Legitimate Peripheral Participation.* Cambridge: Cambridge University Press.

Law School Admission Council. 2008. *ABA-LSAC Official Guide to ABA-Approved Law Schools.* http://officialguide.lsac.org/.

Leeds, Michael. 1992. "Who Benefits from Affirmative Action? The Case of the AEA Summer Minority Program 1986–1990." *Journal of Economic Perspectives* 6: 149–56.

Leggon, C. B. 2006. "Women in Science: Racial and Ethnic Differences and the Differences They Make." *Journal of Technology Transfer* 31: 325–33.

Leggon, C. B., and S. M. Malcom. 1994. "Human Resources in Science and Engineering: Policy Implications." In *Who Will Do Science? Educating the Next Generation,* edited by W. Pearson Jr. and A. Fechter, 141–152. Baltimore: Johns Hopkins University Press.

Legomsky, Stephen. 2005. *Immigration and Refugee Law and Policy.* 4th ed. New York: Foundation Press.

Lemke, M., A. Sen, E. Pahlke, L. Partelow, D. Miller, T. Williams, D. Kastberg, and L. Jocelyn. 2004. "PISA 2003 Highlights." *International Outcomes of Learning in Mathematics Literacy and Problem Solving: PISA 2003 Results From the U.S. Perspective.* (NCES 2005–003). Washington, D.C.: U.S. Department of Education, National Center for Education Statistics.

Lemke, R. J., T. L. Barzev, D. N. Filipova, and V. I. Suleva. 2005. *Economics B.A.s and Ph.D.s from Liberal Arts Colleges: Do Degree Requirements or Faculty Scholarship Matter?* ERN Educator Working Paper Series. Social Science Research Network. http://ssrn.com/abstract=654241.

Lewis, Harry R. 2006. *Excellence without a Soul: How a Great University Forgot Education*. New York: PublicAffairs.

Lieberson, S., S. Dumais, and S. Baumann. 2000. "The Instability of Androgynous Names: The Symbolic Maintenance of Gender Boundaries." *American Journal of Sociology* 105, no. 5: 1249–87.

Lively, Kit. 2000. "Women in Charge." *The Chronicle of Higher Education*. June 16.

Long, J. Scott, ed. 2001. *From Scarcity to Visibility: Gender Differences in the Careers of Doctoral Scientists and Engineers*. Washington, D.C.: National Academy Press.

Lopatto, David. 2004. "Survey of Undergraduate Research Experiences (SURE): First Findings." *Cell Biology Education* 3 (Winter): 270–77.

Lovitts, Barbara. 2001. *Leaving the Ivory Tower: The Causes and Consequences of Departure from Doctoral Study*. Lanham, Md.: Rowman and Littlefield.

———. 2007. *Making the Implicit Explicit: Creating Performance Expectations for the Dissertation*. Sterling, Va.: Stylus.

Marginson, Simon. 2004. "Dynamics of National and Global Competition in Higher Education." *Higher Education: The International Journal of Higher Education and Educational Planning* 52: 1–39.

Massachusetts Institute of Technology. 1999. *A Study on the Status of Women Faculty in Science at MIT*. http://web.mit.edu/fnl/women/women.html.

Massy, William, Andrea Wilger, and Carol Colbeck. 1994. "Overcoming 'Hollowed' Collegiality." *Change* 26, no. 4: 11–21.

Maton, K., F. Hrabowski, and C. L. Schmidt. 2000. "African American College Students Excelling in the Sciences: College and Postcollege Outcomes in the Meyerhoff Scholars Program." *Journal of Research in Science Teaching* 37: 629–54.

McCaughey, R. A. 1994. *Scholars and Teachers: The Faculties of Select Liberal Arts Colleges and Their Place in American Higher Learning*. New York: Conceptual Litho Reproductions.

McClure, Ann. 2006. "Made in America." *University Business* (October): 50–54.

McMurtie, Beth. 1999. "Words from a Veteran U.S. Diplomat on How the Visa Process Works." *Chronicle of Higher Education*, September 24.

McWilliam, Erica, and Richard James. 2002. "Doctoral Education in a Knowledge Economy." *Higher Education Research and Development* 21, no. 2 (July): 131–41.

Miller, David, and Michael Hersen. 1992. *Research Fraud in the Behavioral and Biomedical Sciences*. New York: John Wiley.

Millman, Sierra. 2007. "Princeton Expands Family-Friendly Benefits for Graduate Students with Children." *Chronicle of Higher Education* 53, April 13.

Mooney, Paul. 2006a. "In a Rural Chinese Province, an American Educational Outpost." *Chronicle of Higher Education*, February 17.

———. 2006b. "The Wild, Wild East." *Chronicle of Higher Education*, February 17.

National Academy of Sciences. 2005. *Rising above the Gathering Storm: Energizing and Employing America for a Brighter Economic Future*. Washington, D.C.: National Academies Press.

National Academy of Sciences, National Academy of Engineering, and Institute of Medicine. 2006a. *Beyond Bias and Barriers: Fulfilling the Potential of Women in Academic Science and Engineering*. Washington, D.C.: National Academies Press.

———. 2006b. *Rising above the Gathering Storm: Energizing and Employing America for a Brighter Economic Future*. Washington, D.C.: National Academies Press.

National Academy of Sciences—National Research Council. 1958. *Doctorate Production in United States Universities, 1936–1956, with Baccalaureate Origins of Doctorates in Sciences, Arts, and Humanities*. Publication 582. Washington, D.C.: National Academies Press.

National Association of Foreign Student Advisors [Association of International Educators]. 2003. In *America's Interest: Welcoming International Students: Report of NAFSA's Strategic Task Force on International Student Access*. Washington, D.C.: NAFSA.

——. 2006. *Restoring U.S. Competitiveness for International Students and Scholars*. Washington, D.C.: NAFSA.

National Center for Education Statistics. 1997. *The Third International Mathematics and Science Study*. Washington, D.C.: U.S. Department of Education.

National Immigration Law Center. 2006. "DREAM Act." http://www.nilc.org/imm lawpolicy/DREAM/index.htm.

National Institute of General Medical Sciences. 2005. *Final Report of the NIGMS Council MORE Division Working Group*. Bethesda, Md.: National Institute of General Medical Sciences.

National Research Council (NRC). 1996. *The Path to the PhD: Measuring Graduate Attrition in the Sciences and Humanities*. Washington, D.C.: National Academies Press.

——. 1998. *Trends in the Early Careers of Life Scientists*. Committee on Dimensions, Causes, and Implications of Recent Trends in the Careers of Life Scientists. Washington, D.C.: National Academies Press.

——. 2001. *From Scarcity to Visibility: Gender Differences in the Careers of Doctoral Scientists and Engineers*. Edited by J. S. Long. Washington, D.C.: National Academies Press.

——. 2005a. *Advancing the Nation's Health Needs*. Committee for Monitoring the Nation's Changing Needs for Biomedical, Behavioral, and Clinical Personnel. Washington, D.C.: National Academies Press.

——. 2005b. *Assessment of NIH Minority Research and Training Programs: Phase 3*. Washington, D.C.: National Academies Press.

——. 2006. *To Recruit and Advance: Women Students and Faculty in Science and Engineering*. Washington, D.C.: National Academies Press.

——. 2008. *Assessing Gender Differences in the Careers of Science, Engineering, and Mathematics Faculty*. Committee on Gender Differences in the Careers of Science, Engineering, and Mathematics Faculty, Committee on Women in Science and Engineering. Washington, D.C.: National Academies Press.

National Science Board. 2004. *Science and Engineering Indicators 2004*. vol. 1, NSB 04–1; vol. 2, NSB 04–1A. Arlington, Va.: National Science Foundation.

——. 2006. *Science and Engineering Indicators 2006*. Vol. 1, NSB 06-01; vol. 2, NSB 06-01A. Arlington, Va.: National Science Foundation.

National Science Foundation. 1986. *Foreign Citizens in U.S. Science and Engineering: History, Status, and Outlook*. NSF 86-305. Washington D.C.: National Science Foundation.

——. 2005. *Broadening Participation through a Comprehensive, Integrated System*. Final Workshop Report. Arlington, Va.: National Science Foundation.

National Science Foundation, Division of Science Resources Statistics. 2004a. *Gender Differences in the Careers of Academic Scientists and Engineers*. NSF 04-323. Arlington, Va.: National Science Foundation.

——. 2004b. *Women, Minorities, and Persons with Disabilities in Science and Engineering: 2004*. NSF 04-317. Arlington, Va.: National Science Foundation.

——. 2006. *Women, Minorities, and Persons with Disabilities in Science and Engineering: 2004*. NSF 04-317. Arlington, Va.: National Science Foundation.

Nelson, D. J. 2004. *Nelson Diversity Surveys*. Norman, Okla.: Diversity in Science Association. http://cheminfo.chem.ou.edu/~djn/diversity/top50.html.

Nerad, M. 1994. *Untersuchung ausgewählter Graduiertenkollegs in Hessen im Vergleich mit dem Doktorandenstudium in den USA* [A comparison of selected doctoral programs at German universities with U.S. Ph.D. programs]. Kassel, Germany: Center for Higher Education and Work, University of Kassel.

Nerad, M. 2004. "The PhD in the US: Criticisms, Facts and Remedies." *Higher Education Policy* 17, no. 2: 183–99.

Nerad, M., R. Aanerud, and J. Cerny. 2004. "So You Want to Be a Professor! Lessons from the PhDs—Ten Years Later Study." In *Paths to the Professoriate: Strategies for Enriching the Preparation of Future Faculty*, edited by Donald H. Wulff, Ann Austin, and Associates, 137–158. San Francisco: Jossey-Bass.

Nerad, M., and J. Cerny. 1997. *PhDs–Ten Years Later*. Survey funded by the Mellon Foundation and National Science Foundation. Retrieved from www.cirge.washington.edu.

———. 1999a. "From Rumors to Facts: Career Outcomes of English Ph.D.s; Results from the PhDs—Ten Years Later Study." *Communicator* 32, no. 7, special ed. (Fall): 1–11.

———. 1999b. "Postdoctoral Patterns, Career Advancement, and Problems." *Science* 285: 1533–35.

———. 2000. "Improving Doctoral Education: Recommendations from the PhDs—Ten Years Later Study." *The Communicator* 33, no. 2 (March): 6.

———. 2002. "Postdoctoral Appointments and Employment Patterns of Science and Engineering Doctoral Recipients Ten-plus Years after Ph.D. Completion: Selected Results from the 'Ph.D.s—Ten Years Later Study.'" *The Communicator* 35, no. 7 (August–September): 1–2, 10–11.

Nerad, M., and M. Heggelund, eds. 2008. *Towards a Global Doctorate? Forces and Forms of Change in Doctoral Education Worldwide*. Seattle, Wash.: University of Washington Press.

Nerad, M., with R. June and D. Miller, eds. 1997. *Graduate Education in the United States*. New York: Garland Press.

Nerad, M., E. Rudd, E. Morrison, and J. Picciano. 2007. *Social Science PhDs–Five+ Years Out: A National Survey of PhDs in Six Fields*. CIRGE Report 2007-01. Seattle, Wash.: CIRGE.

Nettles, Michael T., and Catherine M. Millett. 2006. *Three Magic Letters: Getting to Ph.D.* Baltimore, Md.: Johns Hopkins University Press.

Nonnemaker, L. 2000. "Women Physicians in Academic Medicine: New Insights from Cohort Studies." *New England Journal of Medicine* 342, no. 6: 399–405.

Olivas, Michael A. 2000. "Immigration Law Teaching and Scholarship in the Ivory Tower: A Response to 'Race Matters.'" *University of Illinois Law Review* 2: 101–26.

———. 2004. "IIRIRA, the Dream Act, and Undocumented College Student Residency." *Journal of College and University Law* 30: 435–64.

———. 2006. "Reflections on Academic Merit Badges and Becoming an Eagle Scout." *Houston Law Review* 43: 81–124.

Overland, Martha Ann. 2006. "Shattered Dreams in the Philippines." *Chronicle of Higher Education*, March 3.

Panofsky, Aaron, and Diana Rhoten. 2005. "Innovative, Integrative Graduate Education and Training: New Concepts for Assessment; Second Interim Report to IGERT Program Directors." October. http://programs.ssrc.org/ki/fis/pubs/.

Parker, Walter. 1996. "'Advanced' Ideas about Democracy: Toward a Pluralist Conception of Citizen Education." *Teachers College Record* 98 (Fall): 104–25.

Pearson, W. Jr. 2005. *Beyond Small Numbers: Voices of African American Ph.D. Chemists*. New York: Elsevier.

Pearson, W. Jr., H. Etzkowitz, C. Leggon, J. Mullis, T. Russell, J. Brown, and C. Colhoun. 2004. *The Leadership Alliance Summer Research—Early Identification*

Program. Survey and Field Evaluation Report, 2003. Ann Arbor, Mich.: University of Michigan. March.

Price, Gregory. 2005. "The Causal Effects of Participation in the American Economic Association Summer Minority Program." *Southern Economic Journal* 72, no. 1: 78–97.

Price, Joseph. 2005. *Marriage and Graduate Student Outcomes.* Cornell Higher Education Research Institute Working Paper WP75. Ithaca, N.Y.: Cornell Higher Education Research Institute, July. http://www.ilr.cornell.edu/cheri.

Princeton University. 2003. *Report of the Task Force on the Status of Women Faculty in the Natural Sciences and Engineering at Princeton.* http://www.princeton.edu/pr/reports/sciencetf/sciencetf-9-19-03.pdf.

Quandt, R. 1992. *The Foundation's Program in Eastern Europe.* 1992 Annual Report of the Andrew W. Mellon Foundation. http://www.mellon.org/news_publications/annual-reports-essays/presidents-essays/the-foundation-s-program-in-eastern-europe/?searchterm=eastern%20europe.

Ramsden, Brian. 2006. *Patterns of Higher Education Institutions in the UK: Sixth Report.* London: Standing Conference of Principals.

Raymond, C. 1989. "17 Soviets Start Graduate Work at U.S. Institutions." *Chronicle of Higher Education,* October 11.

Rios-Soto, K. R., C. Castillo-Chavez, M. Neubert, E. S. Titi, and A. A. Yakubu. 2006. "Epidemic Spread in Populations at Demographic Equilibrium." In *Modeling the Dynamics of Human Diseases: Emerging Paradigms and Challenges,* edited by A. Gumel, C. Castillo-Chavez, D. P. Clemence, and R. E. Mickens, 297–310. Providence, R.I.: American Mathematical Society.

Rudd, Elizabeth, Emory Morrison, Renate Sadrozinski, Maresi Nerad, and Joseph Cerny. 2008. "Equality and Illusion: Gender and Tenure in Art History Careers." *Journal of Marriage and Family* 70.

Rudd, Ernest. 1986. "The Drop-outs and the Dilatory on the Road to the Doctorate." *Higher Education in Europe* 11, no. 4: 31–36.

Russell, Susan, Catherine P. Ailes, Mary P. Hancock, James McCullough, J. David Roessner, Charles Storey. 2005. *Evaluation of NSF Support for Undergraduate Research Opportunities; 2003 NSF–Program Participant Survey: Final Report.* Menlo Park, Calif.: SRI International, June.

Russell, Susan, Mary P. Hancock, and James McCullough, 2006. *Evaluation of NSF Support for Undergraduate Research Opportunities: Follow-up Survey of Undergraduate NSF Program Participants.* Menlo Park, Calif.: SRI International, June.

——. 2007. "Benefits of Undergraduate Research Experiences." *Science* 316: 548–49.

Ryan, W. C. 1939. *Studies in Early Graduate Education.* New York: Carnegie Foundation for the Advancement of Teaching.

Sadrozinski, R., M. Nerad, and J. Cerny. 2003. *PhDs in Art History—Over a Decade Later: A National Career Path Study of Art Historians.* http://depts.washington.edu/cirgeweb/c/publications/157/.

Sanchez, F., M. Engman, L. Harrington, and C. Castillo-Chavez. 2006. "Models for Dengue Transmission and Control." In *Modeling the Dynamics of Human Diseases: Emerging Paradigms and Challenges,* edited by A. Gumel, C. Castillo-Chavez, D. P. Clemence, and R. E. Mickens, 311–326. Providence, R.I.: American Mathematical Society.

Santayana, George. 2006. "The Genteel Tradition in American Philosophy." In *Winds of Doctrine: Studies in Contemporary Opinion,* 186–224. Whitefish, Mont.: Kessinger Publishing.

Schelling, T. C. 1978. *Micromotives and Macrobehavior.* New York: W. W. Norton.

Schiebinger, Londa. 1999. *Has Feminism Changed Science?* Cambridge, Mass.: Harvard University Press.

Schleicher, Andreas. 2006. *The Economics of Knowledge: Why Education Is Key for Europe's Success.* Brussels: Lisbon Council Policy Brief.

Schowen, K. B. 1998. "Research as a Critical Component of the Undergraduate Educational Experience." In *Assessing the Value of Research in the Chemical Sciences*, 73–81. Washington, D.C.: National Academies Press.

Shanghai Jiao Tong University Institute of Higher Education. 2003. *Academic Ranking of World Universities.* http://ed.sjtu.edu.cn/ranking.htm.

Shkolnikov, V. 1995. *Potential Energy: Emergent Emigration of Highly Qualified Manpower from the Former Soviet Union.* Santa Monica, Calif.: RAND.

Shoben, Elaine W. 1997. "From Antinepotism Rules to Programs for Partners: Legal Issues." In *Academic Couples: Problems and Promises*, edited by M. A. Ferber and J. W. Loeb, 266–247. Chicago: University of Illinois Press.

Shulman, L. S. 2005. "Signature Pedagogies in the Professions." *Daedalus* 134, no. 3: 52–59.

Shuppy, Annie. 2006. "Muslim Scholar Denied a U.S. Visa Again." *Chronicle of Higher Education*, October 6.

Siegfried, J. J., and W. A. Stock. 2007. "The Undergraduate Origins of Ph.D. Economists." *Journal of Economics Education* 38, no. 4: 461–482.

Singer, Jill, Michael Mayhew, Elizabeth Rom, Karolyn Eisenstein, Robert Kuczkowski, and Lloyd Douglas. 2003. "The Research Experiences for Undergraduates (REU) Sites Program: Overview and Suggestions for Faculty Members." *Council on Undergraduate Research Quarterly* (June): 158–61.

Song, B., M. Castillo-Garsow, K. Rios-Soto, M. Mejran, L. Henso, and C. Castillo-Chavez. 2006. "Raves, Clubs, and Ecstasy: The Impact of Peer Pressure." *Journal of Mathematical Biosciences and Engineering* 3, no. 1 (January): 1–18.

Spurr, Stephen Hopkins. 1970. *Academic Degree Structures: Innovative Approaches; Principles of Reform in Degree Structures in the United States.* New York: McGraw-Hill.

Steiner-Long, Kathy. 2005. "J-1 Exchange Visitors for Academic and Research Activities." In *Immigration Options for Academics and Researchers*, edited by Dan Berger and Scott Borene, 77–88. Washington, D.C.: American Immigration Lawyers Association.

Stephan, P., and M. M. Kassis. 1997. "The History of Women and Couples in Academia." In *Academic Couples: Problems and Promises*, edited by M. A. Ferber and J. W. Loeb, 44–79. Chicago: University of Illinois Press.

Stephan, P. E., and S. G. Levin. 2001. "Exceptional Contributions to U.S. Science by the Foreign-Born and Foreign-Educated." *Population Research and Policy Review* 20, nos. 1–2: 59–79.

———. 2003. "Foreign Scholars in U.S. Science: Contributions and Costs." Paper presented to the "Science and the University" conference at Cornell University, Ithaca, N.Y., May 20–21.

Stevens, Robert. 2004. *University to Uni: The Politics of Higher Education in England since 1944.* London: Politico's.

Stimpson, C. R. 2002. "General Education for Graduate Education." *The Chronicle of Higher Education*, November 1.

Tapia, Richard A. *Precious Few*, in progress.

Teller, Patricia, and Ann Gates. 2001. "Using the Affinity Research Group Model to Involve Undergraduate Students in Computer Science Research." *Journal of Engineering Education* 90: 549–55.

Thurgood, Lori, Mary J. Golladay, and Susan T. Hill. 2006. *U.S. Doctorates in the 20th Century.* NSF 06-319. Arlington, Va.: National Science Foundation, Division of Science Resources Statistics.

Townsend, R. B. 2005. "Privileging History: Trends in the Undergraduate Origins of History Ph.D.s." *Perspectives* (September): 14–20.

U.S. Census Bureau. 2004. "U.S. Interim Projections by Age, Sex, Race, and Hispanic Origin." Washington, D.C.: Bureau of the Census.

"U.S. Citizens Denied Entry into U.S." 2006. *Interpreter Releases* (September 11): 1944–45.

U.S. News and World Report. 1995. *Best National Liberal Arts Colleges. U.S. News and World Report* special issue, September 18.

Valian, V. 1999. *Why So Slow? The Advancement of Women.* Cambridge, Mass.: MIT Press.

Van der Mei, Anne Pieter. 2003a. *Free Movement of Persons within the European Community: Cross-Border Access to Public Benefits.* Oxford: Hart.

——. 2003b. "Residence and the Evolving Notion of European Union Citizenship." *European Journal of Migration and Law* 5: 419–33.

Walker, George E., Chris M. Golde, Laura Jones, Andrea Conklin Bueschel, and Pat Hutchings. 2008. *The Formation of Scholars: Rethinking Doctoral Education for the Twenty-First Century.* San Francisco: Jossey-Bass.

Warch, R. 2001. "Liberal Arts Colleges Lead the Way in Changing How We Teach and Learn Science." *Chicago Sun-Times,* April 21.

Wenger, E. 1996. "Communities of Practice: The Social Fabric of a Learning Organization." *Healthcare Forum Journal* 3, no. 3: 149–64.

——. 1998. *Communities of Practice: Learning, Meaning, and Identity.* Cambridge: Cambridge University Press.

Wilder, G. Z. 2003. "The Road to Law School and Beyond: Examining Challenges to Racial and Ethnic Diversity in the Legal Profession." Law School Admission Council Research Report 02-01, August. http://www.lsacnet.org/Research/Challenges-to-Racial-and-Ethnic-Diversity-in-Legal-Profession.pdf.

Wilson, K. M. 1965. *Of Time and the Doctorate: Report of an Inquiry into the Duration of Doctoral Study.* Atlanta: Southern Regional Education Board.

Wong, J. 1981. "China's Leap to American Campuses." *New York Times,* November 15.

Wright, B. F. 1957. "The PhD Stretch-Out." In *Vital issues in Education: A Report of the Twenty-first Educational Conference Held under the Auspices of the Educational Records Bureau and the American Council on Education, New York City,* edited by Arthur E. Traxler, 140–51. Washington, D.C.: American Council on Education.

Xie, Y., and K. A. Shauman. 2003. *Women in Science: Career Processes and Outcomes.* Cambridge, Mass.: Harvard University Press.

Yakubu, A.-A., R. Saenz, J. Stein, and L. E. Jones. 2004. "Monarch Butterfly Spatially Discrete Advection Model." *Mathematical Biosciences* 190: 183–202.

Zydney, A., J. Bennett, A. Shahid, and K. Bauer. 2002. "Impact of Undergraduate Research Experience in Engineering." *Journal of Engineering Education* 91: 151–57.

Contributors

Linda Abriola is the dean of the Tufts School of Engineering and a professor of civil and environmental engineering. She is a member of the National Academy of Engineering and a fellow of the American Geophysical Union.

Charles Becker is a research professor of economics at Duke University and from 2001 to 2007 served as director of the American Economic Association's Summer Program and Minority Scholarship Program.

Emily Blanchard is an assistant professor of economics at the University of Virginia.

John Bound is a professor of economics at the University of Michigan, a research associate at the National Bureau of Economic Research and a fellow of the Econometric Society.

Myles Boylan is a program director in the National Science Foundation's Division of Undergraduate Education and a program director in the NSF's Division of Undergraduate and Graduate Education. He received a PhD in industrial economics from Case Western University.

Sharon M. Brucker is the coordinator of the Andrew W. Mellon Foundation's Graduate Education Initiative database.

Andrea Conklin Bueschel is a senior program officer with the Spencer Foundation and served as a research scholar at The Carnegie Foundation for the Advancement of Teaching. She received her PhD in education from Stanford University.

Carlos Castillo-Chavez is a university regents professor and the Joaquin Bustoz Jr. Professor of Mathematical Biology at Arizona State University, where he directs the Mathematical and Theoretical Biology Institute. He is a recipient of the Presidential Award for Excellence in Science, Mathematics and Engineering Mentoring from the National Science Foundation and the Office of the President of the United States.

Carlos Castillo-Garsow is a mathematics education graduate student at the Mathematical and Theoretical Biology Institute at Arizona State University, and a former student of the Mathematical and Theoretical Biology Institute.

Margery Davies is the director of the Office of Diversity Education and Development and the affirmative action officer for the School of Arts and Sciences and School of Engineering at Tufts University. She received a PhD in sociology from Brandeis University.

Daniel Denecke is director of best practices at the Council of Graduate Schools. He received a PhD in British literature from the Johns Hopkins University.

Ronald G. Ehrenberg is the Irving M. Ives Professor of Industrial and Labor Relations and Economics at Cornell University, director of the Cornell Higher Education Research Institute, and a research associate at the National Bureau of Economic Research. He currently chairs the National Research Council's Board on Higher Education and the Workforce and is a member of the National Academy of Education, a fellow of the Society of Labor Economists, and a national associate of the National Academies.

Helen S. Frasier is the program manager of best practices at the Council of Graduate Schools.

Chris M. Golde is associate vice provost for graduate education at Stanford University and served as senior scholar at The Carnegie Foundation for the Advancement of Teaching. She received her PhD in education from Stanford University.

M.R.C. Greenwood is the chancellor emerita of the University of California, Santa Cruz, a fellow of the American Academy of Arts and Sciences, and a member of the Institute of Medicine. She is currently a professor of biology and internal medicine at the University of California, Davis.

Jeffrey Groen is a research economist at the Bureau of Labor Statistics and a faculty associate at the Cornell Higher Education Research Institute. He received his PhD in economics from the University of Michigan.

Jong-on Hahm is a research professor in the Elizabeth Somers Center for Women's Leadership at George Washington University and a distinguished senior fellow in the George Mason University School of Public Policy. She received her PhD in neuroscience from MIT.

Cynthia Johnson was executive director of the Center for Excellence and Equity in Education at Rice University from 2006 to 2008.

Laura Jones is director of heritage services and special projects at Stanford University. She was a senior scholar at The Carnegie Foundation for the Advancement of Teaching. Jones received her PhD in anthropology from Stanford University.

Charlotte V. Kuh is the deputy executive director of the Policy and Global Affairs Division of the National Research Council and is the staff officer for the NRC's Assessment of Research Doctorate Programs. A fellow of the Association for Women in Science, she earned a PhD in economics from Yale University.

Cheryl Leggon is an associate professor in the School of Public Policy at the Georgia Institute of Technology. A fellow of the American Association for the Advancement of Science and Sigma Xi, she earned her PhD in sociology from the University of Chicago.

Robert J. Lemke is an associate professor of economics at Lake Forest College. He received his PhD in economics from the University of Wisconsin-Madison.

Catherine M. Millett is a senior research scientist in the Policy Evaluation and Research Center at the Educational Testing Service. She received her PhD in public policy in higher education from the University of Michigan.

Maresi Nerad is the director of the National Center for Innovation and Research in Graduate Education, associate graduate dean, and associate professor in educational leadership and policy studies in the College of Education at the University of Washington. She received her PhD from the University of California, Berkeley.

Michael T. Nettles is the senior vice president for policy evaluation and research and the Edmund W. Gordon Chair for Policy Evaluation and Research at the Educational Testing Service. Prior to his ETS appointment, he was a professor at the University of Michigan and a member of the Board of Trustees of the College Board.

Michael A. Olivas is the William B. Bates Distinguished Chair of Law and director of the Institute of Higher Education Law and Governance at the University of Houston Law Center. He is a member of the American Law Institute and the National Academy of Education, the only person to hold membership in both academies.

Willie Pearson Jr. is a professor in the School of History, Technology and Society at the Georgia Institute of Technology. He is a national associate of the National Academies and a member of the American Association for the Advancement of Science.

Gregory Price is the Charles E. Merrill Professor of Economics and chair of the Economics Department at Morehouse College.

Kenneth Redd is the director of research and policy analysis at the Council of Graduate Schools. In 2005, the *Chronicle of Higher Education* named him as one of the ten up-and-coming "New Thinkers in Higher Education."

Richard Tapia is university professor, Maxfield-Oshman Chair in Engineering, and professor of computational and applied mathematics at Rice University. He is a member of the National Academy of Engineering and was a presidential appointee to the National Science Board.

Sarah Turner is a university professor of economics and education at the University of Virginia and a research associate at the National Bureau of Economic Research.

George E. Walker is the vice president for research and dean of the University Graduate School at Florida International University. He is former graduate dean at the University of Indiana and was director of The Carnegie Foundation's Initiative on the Doctorate. A theoretical nuclear physicist, he is a fellow of the American Physical Society.

Harriet Zuckerman is senior vice president of the Andrew W. Mellon Foundation and a professor emeritus of sociology at Columbia University, where she received her PhD degree. She is a member of the American Philosophical Society and the American Academy of Arts and Sciences.

Liang Zhang is an assistant professor of public policy and higher education at Vanderbilt University and a faculty associate of the Cornell Higher Education Research Institute. He received a PhD in higher education from the University of Arizona and a PhD in economics from Cornell University.

AUTHOR INDEX

Subject Index